Beyond Time-Out

—| FROM CHAOS TO CALM |—

Beth A. Grosshans, Ph.D.

with Janet H. Burton, L.C.S.W.

STERLING

New York / London
www.sterlingpublishing.com

To our children

and

for all the children who have pointed the way.

All the anecdotes in the book, while based on real-life stories, are composites of common experiences that help clarify relevant issues. The scenarios are adapted from stories told to me and to Jan Burton in our clinical practices, at lectures, during workshops, or observed first hand in day to day life. Any similarities between anecdotes used and any actual person are entirely coincidental. All of the names used in this text are fictitious in order to protect the confidentiality essential for all clients.

Library of Congress Cataloging-in-Publication Data

Grosshans, Beth A.
  Beyond time-out : from chaos to calm / Beth A. Grosshans, with Janet H. Burton.
      p. cm.
  Includes bibliographical references and index.
  ISBN-13: 978-1-4027-5297-1
  ISBN-10: 1-4027-5297-0
  1. Parenting. 2. Child rearing. 3. Parent and child. I. Burton, Janet H. II. Title.

HQ755.8.G757 2008
649'.64—dc22

                                        2007052565

10   9   8   7   6   5   4   3   2   1

Published by Sterling Publishing Co., Inc.
387 Park Avenue South, New York, NY 10016
© 2008 by Beth A. Grosshans and Janet H. Burton
Distributed in Canada by Sterling Publishing
c/o Canadian Manda Group, 165 Dufferin Street,
Toronto, Ontario, Canada M6K 3H6
Distributed in the United Kingdom by GMC Distribution Services
Castle Place, 166 High Street, Lewes, East Sussex, England BN7 1XU
Distributed in Australia by Capricorn Link (Australia) Pty. Ltd.
P.O. Box 704, Windsor, NSW 2756, Australia

Manufactured in the United States of America
All rights reserved

Sterling ISBN-13: 978-1-4027-5297-1
      ISBN-10: 1-4027-5297-0

For information about custom editions, special sales, premium and corporate purchases, please contact Sterling Special Sales Department at 800-805-5489 or specialsales@sterlingpublishing.com.

Contents

Introduction

As a child psychologist who has worked with over four hundred families in the past fifteen years, I have listened to the plaintive cries of parents who are struggling to understand and help their children, and I've also heard their deep frustration at having "tried everything," but to no avail. They have told me countless times about children who can't control their tempers, who are impossible to reason with, or who are disrespectful and demanding. Parents have told me about their children who are struggling with so much anxiety that even leaving their mothers to go to school or a birthday party becomes an ordeal. Issues pertaining to sleeping, eating, and toileting abound; children avoid, refuse, or make demands of their parents, all with extreme intensity. Far too many parents find themselves at a loss when trying to help their children master the basic life skills of self-control, respect, cooperation, sleeping alone, and eating.

It is my job to help these parents and their children, to give them answers, to help them understand what has gone wrong, and to provide strategies to correct the troublesome behaviors. Fifteen years ago when I first opened my private practice, I was ready to go. In fact, being a psychologist had been what I planned to do since the sixth grade. The only problem was that, despite all my formal training and knowledge, I quickly realized that I didn't have any clear answers or protocols to follow in actually treating the myriad difficulties that came into my office. I knew a lot about child development, psychodynamics, and how to make formal diagnoses but not much about what to actually do to help kids stop acting out, to temper their fears, and to create harmony in their discordant families—and to do so in a timely and direct fashion. I knew I wasn't alone in my uncertainty. Many of the families who came to me told me they had sought professional help in the past, read parenting books, and consulted with pediatricians, friends, and families, but nothing had worked. It is a part of my temperament, I suppose, that I have always been impatient when it comes to getting a job done. I am eager for results. More to the point, I couldn't bear the suffering and distress of the children: all the children who sat in the chair by my desk and told me how sad they were and how bad they felt to be having so much trouble.

Children can ill afford prolonged preoccupation with emotional investments that don't lead towards growing up healthy, confident, and strong.

I found myself struggling to figure out why so many children and families were in so much trouble, and why their efforts to improve matters weren't paying off. They needed efficient, practical solutions that really worked. It was from this position of urgency that I came to focus on and appreciate the role of power in the parent-child relationship. I began to see that many of the emotional and behavioral challenges that parents were confronting had their roots in an imbalance of family power, or IFP.

In my opinion, the parenting advice of the last forty years is largely responsible for this imbalance. An emphasis on talking, catering to children's feelings, and exalting a child's self-esteem has left parents feeling intimidated and uncertain when their disciplinary efforts cause their children to become upset and angry. Consequently, in far too many homes across America, it is the children who lead the parents and who control the landscape of family life, and they are making a royal mess of it.

I have come to understand that the symptoms children so often exhibit today, from unruliness to anxiety, are the result of how much power their parents have turned over to them. Sara's sleeping in her parent's bed every night; Dylan's relentless requests and full-blown tantrums when things don't go his way; Jacob's fear of storms and requirement that his parents plan life around the weather forecasts—these are but a few of the endless examples of the distortions that result when children have the power that should be exercised by their parents. These children are deeply loved and have their parents' complete devotion, yet they are out of control because their parents are not in the lead. What I have seen time and time again is that when children run a family, they ruin a family and themselves along with it. It is an epidemic that is heartbreaking to watch.

In this book I offer innovative ideas that challenge the prevailing parenting culture; I show why power and authority are as essential as love and good intentions to effective parenting. My observation is that while parents have long accepted *loving* and *leading* as the twin pillars of effective parenting, most parents have the loving down, but not the leading. Consequently, parents have too little power and kids have too much, and children across the country are suffering the ravages of this imbalance of family power. But simply understanding the phenomenon of IFP isn't enough. What parents really want and need are practical answers about what to do and what to say to resolve their children's problem behaviors. Stay with me, parents, because at the same time that I have been honing my appreciation of power in the parent-child relationship, I have been developing practical and effective parenting strategies based on my insights.

Specifically, I will teach you the Ladder—a clear, easy-to-follow, five-step action program for behavioral change to use with your children. For almost two decades, parents have relied on the time-out method, despite the fact that it rarely works. Time-out is particularly useless in quelling the more intense protests, where children's behaviors escalate out of control. The Ladder strengthens and expands upon time-out and reliably takes parents all the way to effectiveness. I will teach you how to use the Ladder to address a wide array of behaviors across many situations, including the thorny issues parents face most often: tantrums, fears, sleep difficulties, and toileting troubles. Best of all, you can use the Ladder both as a preventative tool and as a corrective one.

The Ladder allows parents to protect their children from the turmoil of too much power. It also helps parents correct an existing power imbalance before it gets worse.

All of this is good, but we can't really succeed in helping kids without helping their parents too. In my work as a child psychologist, truth be told, I often spend more time with parents than with their children. During this work, I ask parents to look at themselves and to identify their own parenting styles. Such self-reflection is not always easy, but I have found that not only are parents up to the task, they are clamoring for practical understanding and help. They are desperate for relief, not just for themselves, but for their children, who they hate to see in such states of struggle and distress.

To help parents focus on their role in their family's troubles, I have identified four main parenting styles that can lead to IFP: Pleasers, Pushovers, Forcers, and Outliers. You will learn about them in this book as well. Often, parents are shocked and disconcerted to learn how their own responses and patterns of communication have inadvertently turned power over to their children and created the troubles of IFP. Recognizing and acknowledging how their particular parenting style is affecting their children often has a crystallizing effect and motivates parents to learn to use the new tools they will need to correct their children's problem behaviors that have resulted from IFP. Once parents understand how they have gone astray and have learned what to do about it, the results are dramatic, rapid, and lasting! Parents who have learned and have applied my strategies for strong, loving, effective parenting are now successfully raising self-controlled, respectful, cooperative children. They are amazed and overjoyed at the rapid improvement in their children's problematic behaviors and thrilled by the goodwill and harmony that have replaced distress and turmoil.

As you read this book, I hope you will begin to see your relationship with your child and your role as parent through a new lens. By understanding the role of power in the family hierarchy and by learning to climb the Ladder, you too will transform the life of your family. Besides, you won't need me or another therapist in an office setting to succeed. Most children don't need therapy; what is making them unruly, anxious, angry, or confused is their parents' ineffectiveness and failure to lead. You can do the real repair work at home.

I have been surprised and heartened to learn that grandparents who hear these ideas are equally enthused and eager to shed light on their own family dynamic. They are strongly motivated to help their adult children break the ineffectual and negative patterns they witness, and they want to help them create a healthy and effective parenting environment for their adored grand-children. With the philosophy provided in this book, I hope that educators, childcare providers, and clinicians can also affirm and strengthen their leadership roles as they teach, help, and care for our children.

It is the struggle of today's parents that has most motivated me to write this book, and my concern for their children, whose futures are largely shaped by how they are parented. It is a book whose ideas and practical answers could not be more timely in light of the epidemic mayhem and madness that are derailing our families today. But it is more than a response to current trouble; the ideas in this book identify basic concepts and core truths about healthy parent-child relationships, and are thus timeless.

Parents, Children, and Power

Look around, it's hard to miss: unhappy, anxious, unruly children along-side unhappy and at times equally anxious and unruly parents. Kids are whining, crying, demanding, having tantrums, and flailing around with startling frequency and what seems to be a new level of intensity. Parents, in turn, are explaining, begging, pleading, negotiating, bribing, and finally threatening and screaming—matching their kids' responses in frequency and escalated intensity. Even the basic business of everyday life—such as sleeping, toileting, eating, and getting kids off to school—have become monumental challenges for many families. Children's fears, tears, entitlements, and demands are regularly derailing their parents' resolve and effectiveness.

In the last few years there has been a rising cry of distress coming from children and parents across the country. Everywhere you turn, you see profiles of the plight of these families in print and on television. The popular press is filled with descriptions of family woes that are now recognized as epidemic. The covers of *Time* and *Newsweek*, the front page of the *New York Times*, and numerous recent books all describe parents, particularly mothers, as living in mayhem, perfect madness, and battlegrounds, where no one is having any fun or enjoying their relation-ships. Reality television for once seems to have actually captured a bit of true reality with the show *Super Nanny*, where the chaos and misery caused by wildly out-of-control children are shocking.

While parents are genuinely engaged in all manner of effort to learn how to improve their effectiveness with their children—participating in parent seminars, teacher conferences, home-grown parenting groups, pediatric consultations, frequent conversations with relatives and friends—the answers continue to be conflicting and confusing. Parents are left in a quandary. No one has put a finger on what is really causing children to be in such turmoil. Parents still don't have an effective, practical solution for their problems.

In fact, families are struggling so much today that most parents regard daily discord and upset as an inevitable part of raising children, or they blame their continual struggle on their child, saying he is difficult or strong-willed. Most common of all, parents brush off problematic behavior by saying it stems from a stage their child is going through. Yes, there are challenges inherent in parenting, and children have varying temperaments and go through developmental stages, but I promise you, parenting does not have to be this hard, and relentless struggle is definitely not inevitable or stage-related.

Chapter One

The New Epidemic: An Imbalance of Family Power

Let's Take a Look Inside Homes across America

It is morning, midweek on a school day, and . . .

- ✢ Tommy is relentless in his insistence that he wants to wear shorts, even though it is 45 degrees out, and runs away and hides when his mother brings out a pair of pants.
- ✢ Sarah is sitting in front of the television and has no motivation whatsoever to get herself ready for school. Her mother has even brought her clothes down to the family room for her to get dressed, but she is moving like molasses.

At breakfast . . .

- ✢ Ben continues in a pattern of refusing to eat his meals at the table. He wants to be served in front of the TV and insists on his blue plate, red cup, and spoon with the Batman handle or he won't eat.
- ✢ Lauren is beside herself because her brother has eaten the last of the Fruit Loops cereal. She is accusing her mother of not being fair and always letting her brother get his way.

In the car on the way to school . . .

- ✢ Jack refuses to get in his car seat. Finally, after his father wrestles him in, he keeps unbuckling the seat belt and settles down only

9

when his father promises to play his favorite song over and over on the way to school.

❖ David is having a tantrum in the backseat because his mother has told him she does not have time to stop for a doughnut. He is yelling, "But I'm starving; I want a doughnut!" When his mother continues to say that she just can't stop, he begins to kick the back of her seat and wail even louder.

Once at school . . .

❖ Lilly's bottom lip begins to tremble, and she becomes teary because she does not want to leave her mother. She is worried something bad will happen or that her mother won't come back for her.

❖ At school, Joey's teacher tells his mother how much she enjoys having Joey in class and what a well-mannered child he is. Joey's mother drives away feeling relieved but also annoyed, because Joey is so good at school, but such a handful at home.

After school . . .

❖ James immediately wants to begin playing video games, and the rest of the afternoon and evening consists of arguments and negotiations about how much time can be spent playing video games and watching television.

❖ Ian wants his mother to be right by his side as he does his homework. He gets stuck easily and looks to his mother for help. But when his mother does make suggestions, he whines and always has a reason why her ideas are no good.

It is dinnertime and . . .

❖ Andrew keeps interrupting when others are talking. He likes to be the director of the conversation and pouts if his parents ask him to give his brother and sister a chance to tell about their day. He routinely complains about the menu and refuses to eat unless his mother makes him one of his favorite foods.

❖ Michael won't sit properly in his chair; he prefers to eat while sitting sideways. He has a bad habit of using his fingers more than he uses his fork. His parents find it trying to eat meals with him, and more often than not, someone starts yelling at the table and Michael ends up crying before the meal ends.

It's bedtime . . ..

It is the end of the day and time for the children to go to bed. Parents take a deep breath because they are weary from a long day, but they know that bedtime is often the most frustrating event of all . . .

❖ Bradley fights taking a bath, argues about which pajamas he will wear, can't decide what book he wants his father to read, and then insists that his father not be the one to read it to him—it has to be his mother (who is putting the baby to bed). He then wants a night-light, drinks of water, a song, and after being tucked in yells out that he has to go to the bathroom.

❖ Emily wants her mother to lie down with her before she falls asleep. This usually takes anywhere from twenty minutes to a half hour. Forget sneaking out; the minute her mother moves a muscle, Emily is wide awake. protesting, "Where are you going? You have to stay with me!" More often than not. Emily's mother winds up falling asleep in her daughter's bed.

Finally, it is time to relax, and you are desperate for some quiet. You take an aspirin, put on your pajamas, and crawl into bed with a magazine, when . . . in comes Kelly, clutching her blanket, tears in her eyes, begging to sleep with Mom in her bed tonight.

If you have children or know children well, these scenarios are all too familiar. Kids have their parents over a barrel on ordinary, day-to-day issues. Often these struggles persist throughout the day, with negotiations that lead to arguments. After a while, these negative patterns begin to define all of the family's interactions. For some, the issues escalate and take on an even more serious quality:

❖ Joseph has tantrums every day, sometimes multiple times a day. He cannot tolerate it when his parents tell him no. Sometimes he will throw things, flail his arms and legs, bang his head on the floor, and cry so hysterically his parents say they are sure the neighbors must think they are torturing him.

❖ Claire has become a worrier, and recently she has developed a terror of the wind. She does not want to go outside at all anymore.

❖ Dylan refuses to go to school. His parents have tried coaxing him, bribing him, and even threatening him, but he completely collapses whenever it is time to go. He has already missed two weeks of school.

❖ Ellen withholds her bowel movements for days on end. Secondary medical problems have begun to arise as a result of her prolonged withholding, but still Ellen fights having a bowel movement.

❖ Randy tells his mother that he hates her and threatens to run away.

❖ Jonathan just won't accept no for an answer. He is rude to his parents, mean to his sister, and there seems to be no limit to what he will do or say to get his way. The slightest provocation can set him off. He has begun to get physical with his parents when they attempt to set limits, pushing and kicking his mother and striking his father with his fist. His parents worry what will happen when Jonathan gets bigger and stronger if he does not learn how to deal with his temper now.

Imbalance of Family Power (IFP)

The very common childish behaviors I've just described are played out with alarming regularity in homes across the country. They represent a wide array of issues and vary in their severity, but they actually stem from the same root cause and share a central dynamic: an imbalance of family power, or IFP, in which parents have too little power and children have too much. From the common, routine childishness of Tommy, who wanted to wear shorts in the winter, to the more intense challenges of Joseph banging his head in protest and Dylan's refusal to go to school, these behaviors are all examples of the distortions that result from kids having too much power.

For a majority of families across our country, it is actually the children who prevail, who have the lion's share of the leadership power, and who control far too much of the day-to-day landscape of family life. For example, hundreds of parents I work with and speak with say they intuitively know they need to be the authority, but when they try to be, their child "won't let them." One set of parents told me their eight-year-old son fell asleep on the family room couch every night. When I asked why, they said, "He won't let us put him in his bed; if we do, he makes us stay with him until he falls asleep." *Won't let us? Makes us?* Is there any question who has the power in this family? I can assure you, there was no question in the mind of their eight-year-old.

Power and authority are at the heart of the matter. Certainly love is right there, but love alone is not sufficient. I have seen children who are deeply loved and who have their parents' complete devotion but are suffering from the ravages of IFP. How do children tilt the balance of power in their direction? They do it through behavioral tactics and/or emotional ploys. When a child discovers emotional tactics that allow him to get his way, he will use them often. When these tactics are unpleasant, parents become very put out and call him "bratty" and "spoiled." On the other side of the coin are children who have a hard time with separation anxiety. They worry too much and are overly fearful. They too are often victims of IFP, and their anxiety has actually become a powerful tool in shaping their parents' emotional reactions and accommodations.

All of these behaviors, from unruly to anxious, are a child's way of telling us something is wrong and that he is suffering. Believe it or not, kids are just as eager as their parents to be free of their troubles, but sadly, they become wedded to them because they wield so much power and influence. Of course, these children don't have a clue as to what is going on, let alone what to do about it. Many of them come to believe they are bad kids who are intrinsically problematic because "What is the matter with you?" is the question they hear all too often from their exasperated parents.

Children cannot be expected to exercise good judgment reliably or to constructively learn from their mistakes. After all, a large part of childishness and immaturity has to do with a child's inherent impulse towards immediate gratification and getting his way. Your child needs the benefit of your experienced and wise judgment and your love, delivered in a calm, confident manner that also expresses your power and authority. Only when parents are strong and effective are children able to learn to be self-controlled, respectful, and cooperative. They are just as happy and proud of mastering these strengths as their parents are, and it is much easier to be with, enjoy, and love them.

Unfortunately, while the loving part of parenting comes naturally to most people, being effective and establishing appropriate power and authority does not. This is what accounts for the new epidemic of IFP— where parents and children are caught in the turmoil and oppressiveness that arise when children have more power than their parents.

What Power Really Means

The concept of power has been around for as long as people have been writing about parenting. Typically, power in relation to parenting has been associated with *might* or *domination,* or *oppression.* The more relevant concept of power with regard to parenting, as I see it, is that of a relational dynamic—one that is inevitable, inherent, and central in all parent-child relationships. Parents naturally have power, but all kids are wired to vie for it, and if they end up with more power than their parents, their well-being, and that of the entire family, is significantly compromised.

Power, by definition, means "being able, being effective." A person is regarded as powerful if he has the ability to act, to substantially influence others, and to produce an effect. In the context of the parent-child relationship, power is no different; it is the degree of influence a person has over another to shape his reactions, determine how things will go, produce a sought-after result, and set the terms of the relationship. Being an effective parent means that your agenda, based on your experience and better judgment, prevails despite your child's resistance and protests. After all, a parent's job involves not only socialization but protection and guidance on a child's way to maturity.

Power is not a friendly or warm and fuzzy concept in today's climate. It is certainly not a term commonly used when talking about parent-child relationships. Even though *power* is such a distasteful word to so many, the truth we must face up to is that being powerful has to do with being effective, and being effective has to do with how we use our power. The two are intertwined. We have to start getting comfortable with the word, and the fact that power is essential to forming a healthy parent-child relationship.

The reason so many of us are put off by the notion of parental power typically is that we associate power with oppression and domination. Applied to parenting, the word conjures images of overbearing parents trying to force their will upon their children in an endless series of power struggles. I want to be clear from the outset that this is most definitely not the power I am talking about. I am in no way advocating a "might makes right" approach. In the coming chapters I warn against domineering and harsh parental practices. My view of parental power is that it is natural, it is essential, and exercising it on our children's behalf is at the heart of our love and concern for their well-being. Controlling, punitive, and critical parenting is the opposite of parenting with respectful and effective parental power. Domination and harshness are expressions of some parents' attempts to be powerful, but the truth is, these tactics don't make a parent powerful at all. They simply make him a bully.

So, while it may make you initially uncomfortable, this is a book about reexamining your biases about power and seeing it through a new lens, not the prevailing lens of domination and oppression. Power is a core and organizing dynamic in all relationships, and nowhere is this truer than between parents and children. If we are to be successful in raising healthy children, it is essential to understand the centrality of power, and learn how to employ it lovingly and respectfully with our children.

Why Is It All about Power?

Why is it all about power? Because kids want power so badly. Children are born into the world innately wired to test their sphere of influence, and they continuously look to their parents to see how they are going to respond to their challenges. Remember, the definition of power is to have influence in a relationship, to determine how it goes—this is the power children strive to make their own.

By virtue of their experience, wisdom, and judgment, *parents* have all the power, thus leaving their children to continually vie for it. These impulses aren't malicious, and our children aren't devious. On the contrary, this is the normal way kids are put together. It is my hope that by understanding that all children have an innate drive for power, parents will be relieved of some of their frustration and resentment when dealing with their children's power strivings. A core feature of immaturity and childishness is wanting to have your own way and wanting it *now*. A gracious response to disappointment and being able to postpone gratification are not a part of the childhood repertoire—such self-control must be taught. This is a key job for us as parents, even as we struggle with it ourselves.

On and On It Grows

We can clearly see evidence of power testing in the toddler years, when the two-and-a-half-year-old stands with a magic marker in hand poised to draw on the dining room wall and looks to catch his mother's eye, clearly testing her reaction; or when the three-year-old deliberately climbs on top of the coffee table in the living room and looks over his shoulder to make certain his father is watching before he starts to jump. We see this when the six-year-old insists on falling asleep on the family room couch or in his parents' bed rather than in his own bed; or when the eight-year-old won't turn off the television and do his homework.

These behaviors continually pose a challenge to parents with the question of *"What are you going to do it about it?"* The scary thing is, every time parents ignore the question, don't know how to answer it, or fail to provide an effective response, power is transferred from them to their child. And the more power a child has, the more outrageous, defiant, and anxious his behavior becomes over the years.

What a dangerous imbalance of power can lead to became obvious to me a few years back when I visited a wilderness program. As you may know, some wilderness programs are designed to treat adolescents who display negative and destructive behaviors. The program I visited was in the mountains of Idaho. A program guide took me down a trail leading to the base camp clearing, and a scene that was played out there remains vividly etched in my memory to this day.

A boy, who looked to be about fifteen or sixteen, was in the midst of a full-blown rant. He was wearing a bright orange vest and knee-high yellow rubber boots. My guide told me the vests were for the kids who needed the highest level of supervision, while the oversized boots were intended to slow the progress of those who had decided to run away from it all. This orange-and-yellow-clad young man was fuming. He was stomping around, glaring, and punching his fist into his hand as he spewed forth a torrent of expletives. It was clear he did not like life on any terms but his own. This was a kid with monster power, and his rage was palpable even from the distance where I stood.

Two men, both experienced staff members, went quickly to his side. It was apparent they were fully engaged, and they emanated a calm patience. Their demeanor said clearly that they were competent, knew the ropes, and could handle anything this angry kid could throw at them. As he raged and stormed around, the men stayed right with the boy. As he continued to rant, using the crudest profanity I've ever heard, one of the men told him to stop swearing, and that's when I heard it.

Getting right up in the counselor's face, the boy challenged, "Yeah? Well, what are you going to do about it, huh?" He asked it again, sounding even more emboldened and defiant than before, "What the f*** are you going to do about it?"

This question, asked bluntly, nastily, and crudely, lies at the heart of the parenting matter today. It was asked with no holds barred, in a remote backwoods campsite in Idaho, by a teenager who had been allowed to be out of control far too long. It may not sound at first like the question your little one poses to you on a daily basis, but it is, in essence, the same question all children ask the adults who care for them: "What are you going to do about it?"

Think about it. That's what the two-year-old, the three-year-old, the eight-year-old asks of his parents time and time again. This question perfectly captures the push-me, pull-you of parent-child relationships that starts from the time infants have the capacity for deliberate, independent behavior. The more unbridled power a child has, the more outrageous and defiant his behavior becomes.

That's why establishing the appropriate power and authority before a child reaches the age of eleven is critical. The stakes change dramatically in the preteen and teen years. Because of their growing independence, acting out becomes more dangerous, and a parent's capacity to physically contain and stop them is basically lost because of their size and strength. The raging teen in that therapeutic wilderness program is an example of what a child with unbridled power can become. It certainly does not have to be the case with your child.

Having the confidence, competence, and agenda to prevail when your young child tests you is what you need: *No,* he may not draw on the wall or jump on the table; *no,* he may not sleep in your bed or on the family room couch for the night; *no,* he may not decide he does not want to do his homework. Parents instinctively know this should be their response, but how to answer the question "What are you going to do about it?" remains unclear. What's more, most of us are unaware of how critically important it is to our children that we set standards and maintain them.

The Perfect Storm

With any epidemic, it is critical to know how it began in order to keep it from spreading. I've noted that as soon as parents' eyes have been opened, inevitably they lament, "How did we get here?"

The Origins of the Storm

In my estimation, a perfect storm has been brewing for several decades, resulting in the current epidemic of IFP. First, a "warm front" was created by the child-centered parenting emphasis begun in the early sixties, where paying attention to feelings, mastering talking skills, prioritizing self-esteem, and offering unconditional love were championed as the keys to raising healthy children. This approach certainly appealed to the loving and nurturing hearts of parents who were still recoiling from the harsh parental culture of the forties and fifties, and it tapped into the idealized longing in all of us to have all-good, all-loving relationships with our children. Parents came to believe that their children's well-being required that they exercise an exquisite degree of patience, sensitivity, and empathy, and so they committed themselves to these ideals.

Concurrently, a "cold front" was formed by an array of sociocultural variables. Women had become more educated, were entering the work force, and had more disposable income than ever before. Soon social critics, religious groups, and political representatives began to broadcast warnings that children would become damaged in irreparable ways if they had mothers who worked and left them in day care centers for other people to raise. Scared, but economically tied to their incomes, and also feeling fulfilled by their careers, women remained at their employment, but scrambled to assuage their chronic worry and guilt about the harm they were supposedly causing their children. What did a frightened and guilty mother do? The very best she could. She sought out the latest parenting expertise and guidance, which told her to be patient, fair, empathetic, and protective of her child's self-esteem at all costs. To promote the democratic family ideal, she was coached to give her children lots of choices and to shift from parent-driven rules to an emphasis on family process and negotiation. She was given reassuring platitudes and told to avoid saying no, to pick her battles, and not sweat the small stuff.

Mothers were also told that the best way to compensate for being away was to maximize quality time, thereby ensuring that their children felt special whenever they did spend time with them. Women became obsessed with optimizing all areas of their children's development by exposure to and participation in every class, sport, and lesson possible. Because they were exhausted from working, running a home, and attending to their children's every need, on top of being scared and guilty, they bought whatever conveniences and products their money could buy, in order to make their parenting job easier and keep their children entertained and happy.

It's a tragic twist of irony that, given all the good intentions, time, energy, and resources spent, the result is an explosion of insecure, unruly children. Mothers, feeling afraid and guilty, were ready to overcompensate and indulge their children. From this position, they wholeheartedly embraced the inherently indulgent parenting practices being offered. This collision of guilt and indulgence has created the dominant style of parenting that leads to IFP.

While the perfect storm has created an army of parental overdoers, there are other parenting styles common today: parents who go beyond pleasing to being deferential; parents who mistake parental power with bully tactics; and parents who create power vacuums because they remain emotionally distant. What all of these parenting approaches have in common is the transfer of power to their children, which inevitably causes distress in their family life. The result is children who are high-maintenance and unpleasant to be around; mothers who are resentful because all their extraordinary efforts have not paid off; and dads who don't really want to come home in the evening because the kids are a headache and their wives are so stressed and frustrated that they have nothing but complaints and a sour mood to offer. Families are hard-pressed to find harmony and goodwill, not to mention humor and fun.

The truth is that all of this parenting madness is not only unnecessary but beside the point. If parents would do more to increase their effectiveness with their children, then they wouldn't have to routinely turn themselves into pretzels and engage in the exhausting cycle of cajoling and accommodation in which they are so frequently trapped.

Furthermore, the fear and guilt that mothers feel about working are largely unwarranted, in my clinical experience. Mothers who work and mothers who stay at home can be equally effective in their parenting and can enjoy healthy, loving relationships with their children. The key is not whether they work or not, but whether they have been effective in creating an appropriate hierarchy of power with their children. This is by far a more salient factor in children's behavioral and emotional development than if their mothers are home with them full-time, particularly when children are cared for in healthy, appropriate day care and preschools. In fact, because a child's power drive is more intensely focused on his mother than anyone else, day care and preschool experiences offer wonderful opportunities for a reprieve from the testing mode—for both child and parent.

The Role of Parenting Books and Child Experts

There is one other front in the perfect storm. For the past fifty years, most parenting books and child experts, including therapists, have been espousing parenting philosophies and principles that have compromised our authority as parents. After all, most of the child experts who introduced feeling-centered practices were themselves therapists who took analytic and therapeutic techniques out of their offices and into the home.

The bulk of parenting books have focused on advice and strategies that teach parents to turn over or share decision-making with their children, to collaborate with them on limit-setting responsibilities, and to let children learn naturally from their own mistakes. From Haim G. Ginott's classic book, *Between Parent and Child*, to Thomas Gordon's revolutionary *Parent Effectiveness Training*, to the widely loved *How to Talk So Kids Will Listen & Listen So Kids Will Talk* by Adele Faber and Elaine Mazlish, to the more current *Positive Discipline* series by Jane Nelsen, it is obvious that these bestsellers are all in service of leveling a parent's position of power to one more equal with his child. They aim to raise sensitivity and consideration for how children think and feel, which I agree is extremely important, but they fail to address what is equally important—strengthening parental leadership.

By and large, the central concern of these popular parenting books is how children feel: Are they happy? Do they feel unconditionally loved? Parents have interpreted the message of these books to mean that they must ensure that their child feels good, feels happy, and feels special and loved as much of the time as possible. To accomplish this, they feel they must avoid being disagreeable authorities or provoking distress in their children, and they go to great lengths to create a daily environment where they can be happy hour upon hour. This is a huge mistake. Parents who are too intent on making sure their children feel good all the time inadvertently hand them a potent emotional weapon—the expression of distress and rejection, which children quickly learn to wield to their advantage. Anger, tears, and anxiety very effectively motivate their parents to accommodate and please them.

It hasn't helped that the main challenge to this position has been an authoritarian one, spearheaded by Dr. James Dobson in *Dare to Discipline*, which advocates corporal punishment. There has been, and remains today, a tension between empathy and force, as if polarizing these approaches were our only options. Ironically, both of these dominant parenting approaches, even the one that champions force, lead to IFP: one through indulgent tactics that compromise parental authority and the other through bullying tactics that create power struggles rather than effective, respectful, loving power.

The Role of Therapy in IFP

A similarly distressing realization is that when families who face escalating difficulties go to the therapeutic world to seek professional help, they are usually met with feeling-centered advice that only reinforces the practices that got them into trouble in the first place. Generally, therapists are aligned with more passive, supportive, and empathy-based approaches. Many are uncomfortable with provoking negative emotions in children, let alone in adults. *However, being willing to set the agenda and hold it, even in the face of disagreement and resistance, and to tolerate the ensuing rise in negative feelings, is a necessary part of both effective therapy and effective parenting.* When both therapist and parent don't want to or are unable to do this, significant correction and change aren't likely to occur. Hundreds of families I have worked with over the years have given testimony to this. I am convinced that famlies will fare better when the issues of power and effectiveness find their way to the center of parenting education and therapeutic interventions.

Now we can understand why, at a time when parental involvement in the lives of children is at an all-time high, children seem more unhappy, more out of control, and needier than ever. Too many adults place the responsibility for this breakdown at the feet of their children and their temperaments. I believe that children are not the initial source of the trouble most of the time. While children certainly get pulled in and become part of a debilitating cycle of dysfunction, it is the parents who set the cycle in motion. Children get caught up in it and become the symptom-bearers of parental missteps; they're the unwitting accomplices rather than the architects. This is serious business, because the impact of this cycle on our children is significant. When discord and upset dominate the parent-child relationship, there is much more at stake than frustration, exhaustion, and headache: A child's development becomes compromised in serious and lasting ways.

I want children to be happy, but I am interested in the kind of happiness that grows from the inside out, not the outside in. It is not achieved through indulgence and moment-to-moment gratification. I want children to feel good in their relationships with their mother and father, not feel entitled to feel good because their happiness is their parents' ambition for them. If this book gives short shrift to the pillar of loving, it is only because it has been given too much attention already, and the pillar of leading needs so much shoring up. Parents don't need help with the loving; they need help with the leading.

Staying Open to the Message

When I present these ideas in lectures or in the course of professional treatment in my office, it is not uncommon for parents to initially bristle and balk. When I start to talk about how IFP is ruining our children and how parents have been inadvertently contributing to their ruin by transferring so much power to them, I see wrinkled brows and hear a lot of restless throat-clearing. Some parents protest, "Hey! Wait a minute! We've completely devoted ourselves to the well-being of our kids; we've given them our time, energy, and attention, and we have spared no expense. And now you're going to try to lay the blame at our feet? I don't think so." These are parents who have clearly been busy loving their kids, but who don't yet appreciate that if their authority and leadership are compromised, so is the loving. You too may experience some doubts about the ideas in this book, and that's why I am addressing the issues head-on, so as not to lose you. Stick with me: What I have to say will go a long way to counter the flow of ineffectual information that is so abundant in most parenting books. I want to put an end to the lament I continually hear that nothing seems to help. Once you have turned the corner, you will never look back, and the changes in you as well as in your child will be quick and dramatic.

This book departs from other parenting books because it asks you to honestly look at yourself and identify your own contributions to your children's troubles. Just as they have wanted to protect children from feeling bad, most books have similarly protected parents. To make it easier on you, experts blame bad culture, bad family values, bad work schedules, bad temperaments within children, and a whole array of other external causes for children's misbehavior. It may be hard to face up to the truth about your parenting style and adopt a new framework of understanding, but change is not possible unless you do. I will take you carefully through the process, all the way through repair, to success and the peace and joy that come with it.

Chapter Two

The ABCs of Power between Parents and Children

Five Core Aspects of Power in Parent-Child Relationships

From my clinical vantage point, closely observing the way families relate, I have come to appreciate five core aspects of power in the parent-child relationship:

1. Parents are naturally powerful
2. Children naturally want power
3. Children resist what they need most
4. A family is a hierarchy
5. Children with too much power never use it well.

Parents Are Naturally Powerful

When you become a parent, you take on not only an unprecedented responsibility, but you are immediately imbued with an unparalleled dimension of power in relationship to another human being. Whether you philosophically agree with it, want it, or feel prepared or equipped to exercise it, when you are a parent, you've got it. In fact, you are the most powerful person in the world to your child, because she depends on you for everything. What's more, children know parents hold the power, even when parents themselves may not know it or may prefer to prop up an illusion of friendly equality.

Parents exercise their power in a variety of ways, for better or for worse. Some people firmly believe that parents need to put their foot down with their children, but they don't know how to actually do this without becoming harsh or bullying. Others, seeing the conflict and endless frustration engendered by parent-child power struggles, say the best solution is for parents to simply share their power with their children; this will give the children (so the reasoning goes) room to learn from their mistakes naturally and free reign to experiment with their judgment and choices.

Advocates of democratic, feeling-based parenting who place a high priority on a child's need to feel accepted unconditionally will invariably talk about power as *domination*. They dismiss the assertion that parents need to lead with authority as being a power trip and warn that such parenting practices take away the voice and choice of children. These experts claim that parental discipline can readily damage a child's sense of security in the parent-child relationship and undermine her self-esteem.

Ironically, even making the decision to establish a democratic family style is, in fact, an example of parents' exercising their judgment and power. Such a choice represents a parent's decision about the way things should be. You just can't get around it: Being a parent naturally gives you power, including the power to determine what you will do with your power.

Children Naturally Want Power

Why is power so important in the parent-child relationship? Because it is so important to the child. Put simply, children are hard-wired to want their way and to want it right now. All children seek power in service of their immediate pleasure and gratification. Every child engages in a process of finding out how she can best influence her environment, particularly the people in it. Children naturally experiment to find out what gives them power—in other words, what helps them get their way.

This process begins at approximately five months of age, when infants first become developmentally capable of crying to bring you to them—not because they need you, but because they want you. They test and learn the degree to which they can influence what you do. Again, I am not attributing devious, deliberately manipulative machinations to our young ones, and I hope you won't either. They can't help it yet—it is a reflex. That is why your solid parenting guidance is essential. You will help them learn where their sphere of influence appropriately begins and ends. All children are wired to experiment with their power, and they do so in service of their immediate gratification, some more so than others. Some children have a very strong power drive, others have a more easygoing temperament, but all are instinctively motivated to assert their influence. This instinct is never more strongly expressed than in the relationship with their parents. Grandparents, babysitters, relatives, friends, and teachers may get tested a bit, but never to the degree that a parent will be tested. Moreover, if you are in a two-parent family, what you undoubtedly know from your own experience is that moms are the primary target. Understanding that children have a natural power drive can help relieve parents of the anger and resentment they feel when pushed and pulled by their children day in and day out. Children can't help themselves; they don't challenge you with their power and influence because they are bad or want to give you a hard time but because it is part of their nature.

The Central Paradox: Children Resist What They Need Most

The power drive in children sets up an inevitable tension in the parent-child relationship, and herein lies the paradox. While your power and authority are exactly what your children need, more often than not they will resist your efforts because of their inherent power drive. To provide children with the parental leadership they need, you must grapple effectively with this paradox every day. When parents really understand this central paradox and keep it in the forefront of their minds, it will be easier for them to hold the line when their child is unhappy and distressed by the limits placed upon her.

Parents and children engage in a continual dance for influence and power. Whose agenda will prevail? Can Johnny watch one more television show even when Mom has said to turn it off? Can Sarah convince her mother to lie down with her every night until she falls asleep? Can David wear his school clothes to bed because he does not like to get dressed in the morning? These are the small potatoes of power and influence, the likes of which are vied for on a daily basis between parent and child. Even when parents have the balance of the power, some degree of struggle is inevitable between parents and children. You will have disagreements, you will have conflicts, and you will cause temporary disappointments when you say no. I know all too well how parents rationalize that giving in to these day-to-day struggles is basically harmless and serves to keep a bigger outburst from erupting. Before long, however, with this practice you'll be mired in all the troubles associated with IFP. What your children will learn is that their protests and resistance influence what you do and usually result in getting what they want. Unfortunately, the judgment of our little power brokers is immature; their experience of what is best for them is limited. Nor do they have any sense of moderation. So if you accommodate them, your children usually lose the benefit of your better judgment. When you allow them to set the agenda, it is often not what is best for them.

The primary point is that, regardless of his level of maturity, intelligence, or judgment, in order to function optimally, be secure, and develop a healthy capacity for emotional regulation, a child must grow up in a family structure where parents are in the lead. This is ultimately why parents need to prevail in the majority of the daily struggles set up by the central paradox. The constant drip of parental accommodation, which in the short run can look insignificant, can in the long run seriously compromise the context of relational leadership that is so central to a child's well-being.

Do Kids Learn from Their Mistakes?

We'd like to think that children apply the lessons learned from their mistakes in a constructive and consistent way when making future choices. Parents sometimes think letting children make bad choices and then suffer the consequences is an effective way to teach them important lessons. While this can be true, I see it as tricky ground that needs to be navigated with care and selectivity. Learning from one's mistakes requires logic and maturity that isn't yet in place in the young child. Childhood is a terrain fraught with immature and magical thinking. You have to be savvy about child development and power dynamics for this kind of parenting strategy to work in your favor. Otherwise it can end up being mean-spirited and unnecessarily punishing. What sense does it make for a parent to set her child up for failure? In my experience, the practice of letting kids learn from their mistakes is often a ploy to avoid power struggles. Rather than fight about it, just let Jack stay up as late as he wants, and ultimately exhaustion will teach him the importance of a good night's sleep. Rather than fight about it, just let the rain ruin Grace's bicycle, and the rust on her once-shiny silver rims will teach her to put her bike away. Making a parental choice to let kids learn from their mistakes can lead to setting children up unnecessarily for failure and suffering. I prefer effective leading that cuts through power struggles, gets the job done up front, and leaves no harmful consequence.

The philosophy of letting children learn from their own mistakes doesn't really work anyway. Just because a child ends up exhausted does not mean she will learn to go to bed and get a good night's sleep next time. Her power drive gets in her own way because of the in-the-moment nature of being a child. Your children have to rely on you to provide limits and boundaries to counter their childishness and their relentless instinct to test you: "I don't want to wash my hair!" "I want to sleep with my light on!" "No, don't flush the toilet; I don't like the noise!"

Since you know better, since you are the mature one, you must lead your child, not accommodate her.

Not allowing your family life to become organized around childish refusals and insistences is, in large measure, what being a powerful parent is all about.

If children are not protected from themselves by competent parents who understand this, they will all pay a much greater price than a tantrum—and will end up with significant behavioral and emotional difficulties that compromise the well-being of the entire family. The irony is that the more power a child has, the more it derails her capacity for self-control, respect, and cooperation. Parents need to hold firm on a daily basis.

A Family Is a Hierarchy

There is always a hierarchy of power within families, whether it is one or more than one family member who assumes the power. Parents may proceed with the best intentions for equitable, democratic relations to prevail, but despite their due diligence, a power hierarchy cannot be avoided and will inevitably form. The only question is: Who is going to be at the top? The outcome of day-to-day challenges between children and their parents determines who will be in charge of the family. And if children sit atop the hierarchy, then a family's health and integrity will be in serious jeopardy. Because of the very nature of their childishness, young children are wholly unprepared and ill-suited to have power over much of anything. When kids rule a family, they will ruin a family.

Children with Too Much Power Never Use It Well

No child who is given the balance of power in the family will ever use it well or wisely. For starters, children with too much power become unruly, impulsive, disorganized, anxious, fearful, angry, and insecure. The more a child's power dominates the relationship with his parent, the more outrageous, and even destructive, his behaviors can be. Inflated power also produces anxiety and fears, as children find themselves in way over their heads as they try to direct how life goes. The burden of adults kowtowing to them, and the mess they make when they are permitted to run family life, really wear kids down. Parents have long known that children can be compromised if they do not form a loving attachment, but what has not been appreciated is that children will be equally compromised if there are not enough effective parental limits to their bids for power and influence.

Of course, there isn't a parent alive who has not succumbed to the pressure of a power-driving child. You can get worn down or just can't bear to start in on another go-round that seems futile. A parent beleaguered by ineffectiveness will say, "Forget it, I already have so many battles with this child, I am not even going to go there." It is from this place of depletion that parental accommodations are inevitably made. You accommodate the pleading and tearful child by lying down with him until he falls asleep, accommodate the angry child by letting him see a movie that has too much violence and sex, accommodate an anxious child by letting her sleep on the floor in your bedroom. You let an insistent child wear his Batman costume to the grocery store and restaurants even though it is now a month after Halloween, or you make a special meal for a whining child who refuses to eat what you have already prepared and served.

Once parents make these accommodations, they then have to rationalize their responses, because they know they are not exercising their best judgment. The most common reassurances are: "What is the big deal?" "What does it matter in the long run?" "It sure beats the fuss and fight and crying that would otherwise be inevitable." This is really a rationalization, which can lead you to miss the real issue: The problem with this kind of path-of-least-resistance parenting is that it creates a vacuum of parental authority and standards, putting both parent and his unwitting child on the slippery slope to IFP.

How to Tell if You Have IFP

How do you know if there is an imbalance of family power in your home? How can you tell if your child is starting to flounder under the burden of having too much power? For starters, the degree to which your child resists your authority is indicative of how much power you have given her. When you assert your power, a child with inflated power will automatically try to trump you. If you find that not accommodating your child's requests predictably sets off a show of crying, pleading, emotional histrionics, or even more wild and out-of-control behaviors, then you can be pretty certain she is higher than you in the hierarchy of family power.

Another general indicator of the existence of IFP in your family dynamics is that you find that upset, struggle, and discord are occurring in your parent-child relationship more than 30% of the time. When there is an appropriate balance of power—one tipped in the direction of the parents—family life should be peaceful at least 70% of the time. Parenting can be expected to proceed smoothly most of the time when parents establish and exercise respectful and effective power and authority.

The Root Behaviors of IFP

It has been my observation that children's opposition and anxiety are the primary paths that lead parents down the ever-slippery slope to IFP. This is because the behaviors happen all the time, across all situations, and most parents are very sensitive to the provocations of both opposition and anxiety. Children who whine, cry, and talk back really push our buttons; similarly when our children are frightened or worried and beg us not to make them face something they are afraid of, a parent's natural instinct is to save them from their distress. Here is where the slope gets slippery. When parents are too passive in the face of their children's oppositions or too reassuring and solicitous of their anxiety, children perceive a means of influence and power for themselves. Given their innate power drive, they glom onto whatever behaviors "work" and keep on using them, honing their skill so as to get the most reaction out of their parent as possible. By accidentally reinforcing them over time, parents can create powerful opposition or powerful anxiety in their children.

In fact, as I listened to parents describe the problematic behaviors of their children over the years, it became clear to me that, almost without exception, the behaviors were either an expression of a child's opposition or of his anxiety. For example, when there are sleeping problems, or toilet troubles, or eating issues, I can inevitably trace them to an oppositional struggle or an anxiety struggle. This is true for almost any childhood behavioral problem. The behaviors of opposition and anxiety are the two primary ways for children to refuse their parent's agenda and assert their own.

IFP Is Not Just a Stage

The more power a child has been given, and the longer she has it, the more detrimental the effect will be. The longer the power has been wielded, and the more power the child has, the more muscle and determination will be required of parents to return that child to the appropriate place. No one gives up the throne without a fight.

The notion that a child goes through behavioral stages is well established in our culture—and so is the tendency of adults to excuse their children's poor behavior as stage-related when they really don't know what else to say or do. We comfort ourselves with a strong reliance on the belief in our children's resiliency, and with the sense that children, when left alone, will simply grow up and out of their troubles. "It's a stage, don't worry; she will grow out of it." . . . "Oh, that is common for children at that age; there's no need for concern. Just give it time." Parents routinely hear these reassurances from relatives, friends, even pediatricians. Unfortunately, the advice is often not true.

Kids do grow out of many behaviors, of course. How many kids have you ever known to jump on the coffee table when they are fifteen or sleep in their parents' bed when they are sixteen? *What they do not grow out of is the IFP that motivated them in the first place.* There are plenty of kids who, as they grow older, continue to demand life on their terms, rather than comply with their parents' better judgment.

Whenever I take an initial history from parents who are seeking help for their teenager, I almost invariably find that some form of behavioral trouble has been ongoing from the time the child was young. The behaviors may look different at fifteen and sixteen, but generally they have their roots way back in a child's life. What's more, the problems associated with IFP tend to get more serious and entrenched as children get older, and they become significantly harder to remedy. These are often the young adults floundering on college campuses, unable to grab hold of maturity and independent lives.

In general, children in families with IFP often put so much of their psychic energy into their struggles that they don't have the energy they need for more positive, prosocial experiences. From the time they are young, children with IFP can get so mired in conflict and relational difficulty with their parents that even basic developmental tasks such as learning to use the toilet, sleep independently, and develop healthy, appropriate eating habits can get seriously distorted and derailed. Children cannot afford to be compromised or distracted as they are growing up by an overinvestment in the maladaptive behaviors that are the result of too much power too soon.

Are You Talking Instead of Acting?

While many variables contribute to the IFP epidemic, I have found that a tendency to talk rather than act is one of the most damaging culprits. Parents are under the assumption that talking is the key vehicle for influencing their children and producing change. Whether they give a reasonable explanation, make an appeal to the child's sense of guilt, plead, make harsh commands or threats, or give lengthy instructions, parents rarely shift from talking to acting until they get very provoked. Then their action is usually better described as blowing up and is often too scary and mean for it to have a constructive effect on their children.

Talking alone does not effectively counter a child's power drive; rather, it is best contained and directed through action. *What far too few parents grasp is that the essential lessons of self-control, respect, and cooperation are not talking-based lessons; they are action-based lessons.* The art of successful parenting and establishing a healthy balance of family power is more about what you do than what you say. It is not that words aren't extremely important, but in the end, the most perfectly constructed, reasonable, and fair-minded statement will not impel a child to cooperate unless it has been paired with effective action. You have to walk the walk, not just talk the talk. The intrinsic power drive in children is modified more by parental action than by parental conversation.

The families I have worked with over the years have taught me that, for the most part, parents have good judgment; they just don't know how to apply it effectively to influence their children. What is most needed is for parents to stop talking and get moving. Remember the raging teen in the woods? The key question all children ask, and must have answered, is "What are you going to do about it?" not "What are you going to say about it?"

When I talk to you about exercising your natural and essential power and authority, I don't mean that you should say a lot of heavy-handed things to your child, such as "I am the boss" or "I am the mommy and you are the child, so you have to do what I say." Talking about your power will not make you powerful. It just makes you sound bossy and tells your child you are hoping to convince him you have power. People who are actually leaders and authority figures do not have to tell people they have power; it stems from their conduct and their effectiveness.

One of the worst byproducts of talking too much is the mounting frustration that ensues when it yields little to no result. No one is exempt from the feeling of craziness that comes over us when we repeat the same thing over and over again, without having any impact. Being impotent makes every parent angry, especially when the power tycoon is only five years old! It is at this point that damage can occur: Parents can explode into shouting or cruel name-calling, and threats of punishment, bad things happening, and even of abandonment can occur. It is not easy to face up to our worst moments, but even the most dedicated parent can ruefully acknowledge having said things like: "You are the most spoiled, ungrateful brat. I don't even want to see your face right now." "That's it! You've just lost Halloween, and I'm going to throw away your Ninja costume." "I can't put up with you one more minute." "You never listen. I am going to take you to the home for bad children." "If you don't stop, I am going to put you in the attic where there are bats and spiders, and then we'll see if you learn your lesson." All too often, parents tell me with deep remorse about this sort of loss of control and their cruel responses. The good news is that when parents are effective with their children, they eliminate the provocations that lead to these damaging exchanges.

No Voice? No Choice?

I am not suggesting children should be totally controlled. There are times when it makes sense for children to be the decision-makers. For example, children can choose and decide in matters and circumstances where it is developmentally appropriate for them to have influence: what kind of birthday cake they want, what color raincoat they prefer, if they want to watch *Sesame Street* or *Dora the Explorer* before they take a bath. In this way parents extend respect for a child's choices and individual tastes. Parents are still guiding and leading these choices and remaining parental while being considerate and flexible.

In contrast, determining bedtime, establishing where they sleep, picking the family vacation destination, and assessing what constitute suitable movies and television shows are not matters for young children to decide. Distinguishing between decisions that require the judgment and experience of an adult from those that are child-friendly is a key job of parents who are in the lead.

If a child is given an appropriate choice but makes a mess of it by being indecisive, too demanding, or impossible to please, step in and put an end to the struggle. This is the parent leading and shaping by making it clear to the child that just because he has the ability to make a choice does not give him the right to make it. It is an important lesson for children: having influence requires exhibiting the appropriate manner and self-control. When a whiny child is more interested in a power struggle than in making a real choice, an effective parent stays in the lead by saying, "Oh my goodness, I can see you are having trouble deciding. You can wear the red shorts today and the blue ones tomorrow." Then the effective parent leaves the scene promptly, short-circuiting the tug of war.

What's Normal, What's Not

Many parents are too willing to tolerate and endure high levels of upset and distress in their child and in their family. While it is true that children express themselves behaviorally, and it is common for them to evidence tantrums, refusals, rejections, anxieties, and dependencies, there are times when such behaviors cross the line. Since all these behaviors are, to some degree, within the range of what is normal for children, it makes it confusing for parents to tease apart what to ignore and what to view as a problem. To help you assess what's normal and what's not, use the these three measures:

- ❖ Frequency. If the trouble is occurring often, this should be an obvious red flag.
- ❖ Intensity. If the behavior is intense in its expression and is not easily redirected, this is an indication that a form of correction is needed.
- ❖ Duration. If the behavior has persisted beyond a few weeks, then something is wrong; your child is telling you he needs your help. Acting out is a primary way for a child to tell you something is wrong.

PARENTING TRAP

"That's Just the Way Kids Are"

Just because a problem may be normal or common in children does not mean that the best response is to shake your head, roll your eyes, and let it run its course. A problem may be "normal," but it does not mean that the correct parental response is to do nothing. Parental passivity is a form of neglect and rarely is a good strategy.

When faced with their child's anger, anxieties, and fears, too many parents have been conditioned to immediately regard them as expressions of temperament and therefore as something to be accepted and accommodated. While children do certainly have different temperaments and makeups, many of their oppositions and anxieties are in service of power strivings, not personality, and require parental shaping and directing. Furthermore, if a child's temperament is characterized by a strong will, anxiety, or shyness, he needs his parents' help in ensuring that these tendencies become assets rather than hindrances. Temperament is there, to be sure, but parents can't hide behind it or shrug off any resulting inappropriate-ness as if it were a fixed piece of their child's character. The truth is, when parents fail to provide their children with the necessary shaping and directing, over time such behavioral expressions do become part of a child's character, usually to the detriment of the child.

Don't let your own excuse-making derail you from the actions you should be taking. If only I had a quarter for every time I heard a parent tell me that her child's aberrant behavior was due to his being hungry, tired, off-schedule, upset because his father was traveling, or having had too much sugar! I know these can be valid disruptors for children, but parents rely on them way too much. Children follow suit and soon learn how to exploit these excuses themselves so they can avoid being account-able for their own behavior.

When children are freed from the burden of too much power, they have the energy to focus on learning things, rather than becoming stuck in a perpetual struggle with their parents. In my practice, it is very common for children to report, soon after their parents have resumed the lead, that they've learned to tie their shoes, ride a bike, or even read. The peace and goodwill that replace bickering and upset lead to children feeling calmer, being more focused, and sleeping better at night. Freed from the dominating drive to keep ruling the family, and with new access to their self-control and a wish to cooperate and be respectful, kids burst into being more productive, happier, and affectionate people.

Chapter Three

What's Your Parenting Style?

When it comes to authority, many parents don't instinctively know how to create a relationship with their child that is effective yet mutually respectful. Now it is time to look more closely at ourselves as parents because, while children are certainly players in the vicious cycle of family power struggles, it is the parents who set the cycle in motion. The way out is by identifying, analyzing, and correcting your own parenting patterns. In my work with families, I have identified four distinct parenting styles that most often lead to an imbalance of family power (IFP). I call them Pleasers, Pushovers, Forcers, and Outliers. I'll describe them below.

As you read the descriptions of the parenting styles, you may recognize yourself in more than one category or perceive that you have some characteristics of all four. This is very common, but it is my experience that everyone generally has a dominant and defining style. In working with parents over the years, I have also observed that many marriages are made up of people with different parenting styles. When parents have opposite styles, the tendency is for them to push each other into extreme positions rather than moderating each other's style. For example, if one parent is more rigid with rules and harsh with discipline, but the other parent is more coddling and permissive, rather than taking the best of what each has to offer and meeting in the middle, these parents tend to encourage a more extreme position in each other. So the rigid parent, frustrated by his spouse's coddling, becomes even more demanding. The permissive parent, in turn, feels the need to protect and counteract her spouse's harshness, and accommodates and coddles even more. As you read about the different parenting styles, consider both yourself and your partner, and how your differences are affecting you as well as your children.

Sometimes parents use a different style with each of their children. A father may be a Pushover with his daughter, for example, and a Forcer with his son; a mother could be a Pleaser with one son and a Forcer with the other. Different temperaments and personalities affect us differently, and different kids bring out different reactions in us. The injuries and angers we carry from the way we were parented can inadvertently drive dynamics in our relationships with our children.

Pleasers

Pleaser parents are everywhere today and they represent the largest group of contributors to IFP. More than the other three styles, Pleasers are a cultural phenomenon. They have been shaped by the democratic, feeling-based parenting practices of the past forty years, which has been exacerbated by mother guilt and the culture of material excess. Pleasers consult the latest parenting books, attend lectures, have mother-child play groups where they talk about parenting, and consult with family, friends, and professionals to learn how to best serve their children. They invest a lot of themselves in the parenting role, and their self-esteem is largely bound up in being a good parent. While it is natural for all parents to feel distressed when their child is having trouble, Pleasers take it very personally. An uncooperative, struggling child threatens their sense of self-esteem and competence, often leading them to considerable over-reaction.

Pleasers are first and foremost dedicated to doing all they can to ensure their children are happy, feel loved, are nice, and become high achievers. The children are the centerpieces of their life to such an extent that almost all decisions and details of daily life and socializing are planned around them. Pleaser parents are involved with and deeply committed to the well-being of their children, but they go well beyond a realistic accommodation of their children's needs to an overconsideration of their wants. Pleasers go too far. They *over*parent. They overattend to feelings, overexplain their requests, overnegotiate, and overrespond—except when it comes to enforcing directives and holding their children accountable. A Pleaser parent is very conscientious about how she talks to her child, with great care given to being "fair" and "nice." The Pleaser is generous, considerate, and fully invested in a close and loving relationship with her child. So what could be wrong? With all of these adoring and well-intended efforts, it seems unfair and, in fact, can be hard to understand and accept that this parenting style can go so wrong. But it does. The problem lies in the inflated sense of entitlement and power that children develop when they are given such an exalted status.

Many Pleasers, after examining their relationship with their child, say that they had never really considered the possibility that there could be such a thing as too much love or too much caring. This is an important point to explore, because the distortion does not stem from the strength of their love. On the contrary, it is not about love at all, but rather about how Pleasers translate their love to their children. The error is in prioritizing, in assuring that their child feels unconditionally loved and happy at the expense of establishing appropriate parental authority and competence.

Pleaser parents feel that they have to proceed with great care and with complete understanding of their children's experience or their children will come crashing down. Pleasers feel they must micromanage both the internal and external lives of their children in order for them to be secure, confident, and successful. When their children balk or fuss or act hurt in reaction to a parental directive, Pleasers scramble to soothe, solve, and fix. They explain, reason, empathize, and strike bargains, all the while worrying that their children's well-being is hanging precariously in the balance.

Pleasers strive to fold their children into a feel-good cooperative, where learning the lessons of behaving involves little or no distress. Hesitant to assert their authority and power directly, they prefer to cajole their children into accepting it. The hard truth is that much of their extensive efforts and overparenting turns out to be ineffective. What's worse, they compromise their children's independence and capacity for inner reliance and self-regulation.

Pleaser parents pursue an idealized relationship in which their children are equal partners and exercise reciprocal consideration. Pleaser parents expect their highly reasonable explanations and fair, nice bids for cooperation to be met with equally reasonable, fair, and nice responses from their children. Unfortunately, that's not in the cards. When have you ever heard a young child, after listening to his kind and reasonable parent explain why he needs to go to bed, finally concede, "You know, Dad, you are right. Now I understand that I need a good night's sleep to feel good and that you are not being mean. In fact, you have my best interests at heart! I am going to get right into bed and go to sleep." What young child hears the parent's careful reasoning and concludes: "Mom, you are so right. Sharing is nice. Sorry I keep forgetting this." Young children do not have the maturity to join a democratic process based on fairness, reason, and empathy, nor can they reliably display good judgment or make good choices. These are abilities that form incrementally over time. In fact, it is a central task of parenting to help children develop these abilities.

It is hard for Pleasers to recognize that so much commitment to their own dedicated, insightful, generous, and loving ways could be contributing to their child's trouble. The Pleaser logic at work insists that the more parental sensitivities there are in the parenting equation, the luckier the child. This is a monumental setup for failure, however. Here's how it plays out: Pleaser parents become disappointed and disheartened when all their benevolence and fair-mindedness are not met in kind. Before long they turn angry and resentful, demanding of their child: "What is wrong with you?" The irony here is that the Pleaser rarely sees the possibility of her own contributions and readily lays all the trouble at her child's feet. The problem is not badness within the child; it is a parental failure to bind sensitivity and benevolence with authority and competence.

Pleasers and the Hierarchy of Power

Children of Pleaser parents assume a position at the top of the family hierarchy. Because Pleasers are wedded to tactics that are ineffective in countering children's natural power drive, they fall short in shaping self-control and cooperation in their children, who therefore become hard to manage. A Pleaser parent's primary investment in avoiding upsets and ensuring that his child feels happy and good continually results in compromises in which the parent transfers power to the child by letting the child's agenda prevail.

The road to the throne for children in a Pleaser family is paved with endless parental negotiations, accommodations, and too much empathy. In a pattern that repeats itself multiple times in a day, a Pleaser asks her child to do something or stop doing something. The child then responds with a reason why he can't or doesn't want to. This leads to back-and-forth negotiations that include the Pleaser's explanations and rather precocious counterarguments by the child. The Pleaser parenting approach encourages children to practice the art of negotiation and outlast their parents in debate. By mimicking their Pleaser parents' fair-minded wordiness in their many negotiations, these children often develop a pseudomaturity. Unfortunately, Pleaser parents are easily taken in by their child's display of lofty language and rebuttals. Often entertained and impressed by their child's sophistication and intelligence, they relax their standards and thus cede even more power to their child.

The important point here is that while Pleaser parents may be satisfied that by offering reasonable and fair discussion they have parented appropriately, in the end it is too often the child who prevails or is somehow accommodated. Thus the child is given the bulk of the power and influence in relationship to his parent. In contrast, effective parents give the benefits of their better judgment and self-control to their children by holding their position even in the face of resistance and distress. Effective parents lead children by retaining their power and remaining at the top of the power hierarchy. A family will always be a hierarchy. Equal power-sharing between parents and young children is impossible. When you try to achieve equality, it is the children who inevitably end up on top. There may be a hierarchy indeed, but it is upside-down.

The Language of the Pleaser

Pleasers are first and foremost inexhaustible talkers: they explain, reason, cajole, entice, beg, and threaten, and then, when all that fails, they explain some more. Pleasers give children too many choices and too many chances. They ask for their preferences too often and directly seek their children's advice. Pleaser parents ask their whiny and fussy little one: "Please, use your words and tell me what you want." They apologize too often and with too much deference for having to enforce a limit or cause their child disappointment, saying things like, "Honey, I am so sorry, but Mommy has errands to do, so she can't stay at the park any longer, okay?" They also have a practice of thanking their children for ordinary cooperation: "Thank you for being such a good girl and letting Mommy finish her phone conversation."

Pleasers allow their children to give their input and influence decisions and planning when it is totally inappropriate. On more than one occasion, I have witnessed a parent standing at a restaurant table as she asks her seated child, "Where do you want Mommy to sit?" The ebb and flow of day-to-day life is driven by the preferences of the child. Pleaser parents have a distorted sense of consideration that is more aptly called acquiescence.

Pleasers have developed a whole new array of phrases to use with their children. Topping the list is the word *special.* They go on special outings, enjoy special time together, read special books, and, of course, tell their children how special they are. They scold their child by telling him his behavior is "inappropriate," direct him to use an "inside voice," try to settle him down by saying "calm your body, please," and ask for "good listening readiness."

Another habit of Pleasers that reduces their authority is seeking their child's approval for cooperation by asking, "Okay?" For example, "We have to go to bed now, okay?" or "You have to wait for Mommy to finish, okay?" Asking a child not only to cooperate, but also to approve of the parental request, is NOT okay. It gives a child power over the situation. It invites him to have a choice when he really shouldn't have a choice at all—and since children always want their way, they typically take the offer and reject it. With an emphatic "No!" the young child throws down the gauntlet for yet another parent-child power struggle, initiating yet more talking, reasoning, and bargaining from the Pleaser.

Pleasers are uncomfortable with putting their authority directly into the parent-child relationship. They are in the habit of softening or hiding it, rather than asserting it. A very common example of this is when a parent gives a directive to her child using the pronoun *we* rather than *you*: "We have to get our pajamas on" or "It's time for us to brush our teeth," rather than staying true to their separate responsibilities and saying, "You have to get your pajamas on" and "It's time for you to brush your teeth." Pleasers try to coax their children into compliance through a false suggestion of partnership.

An Overfocus on Feelings

When Pleasers express disapproval, they focus on how the child's negative behavior is making others feel, rather than focusing on the behavior itself. The Pleaser might say, for example, "You hurt Daddy's feelings by not cooperating tonight" or "You are making the waitress feel bad because you didn't eat your dinner." Unfortunately, the developmental limitations inherent in children under the age of ten keep them from being particularly motivated by the empathic perspective that Pleasers are so invested in imparting.

Pleasers overprocess and oversympathize with both the positive and negative feelings of their children. They pour on the praise: "Oh honey, Daddy is SO proud of you; I love your drawing. Why don't you hang it on the refrigerator so everyone can see it? Maybe you will be an artist one day!" They spread sympathy with an equally heavy hand: "Oh honey, that is awful. I am so sorry that Mary was mean to you and hurt your feelings at school today. I am sure that must have made you feel really sad. Let Mommy give you a hug. I wish I could have been there to give you a hug when it happened. Are you okay now?" Offering empathy and understanding in spades has the unintended effect of exaggerating the importance of ordinary, routine events. Children of Pleasers fail to develop a realistic perspective about hurts, upsets, anger, and disappointment and their natural resiliency is short-circuited.

Pleasers also overcommunicate their own feelings. They provide too much information about their emotional states, particularly about how their child is making them feel. "Thank you, honey, for being such a good girl tonight. You got all ready for bed, brushed your teeth, and everything! This makes Mommy so happy." "Thank you for setting the table without a fuss! This is the nice girl that makes Mommy so proud. Don't you like it when Mommy is happy and not grumpy?" Comments like these suggest that that the well-being of the parent and family harmony is the responsibility of the child. This is a developmentally impossible burden for any child to carry.

Because they have an idealized concept of their relationship with their child, Pleasers often take noncompliance, whining, and childish ploys as personal rejections. "Your behavior is making Mommy very upset. When you talk back and are mean to me, it hurts my feelings. Did you mean to make Mommy feel sad?" or "After everything I do for you, you have to give me an attitude when I ask you to do one lousy thing to help out? Now you have a resentful mother; so don't expect me to do any more nice things for you for a while!" Rather than simply managing their children's attitude or behavior, Pleasers get caught up in it emotionally and make it all about them. They attempt to strengthen or correct their children's behavior with a focus on how it has made the Pleaser feel.

These parents are telling their children that their childish behavior has the power to make the parent feel good or bad, under the assumption that this knowledge will make their children behave better. Here is the setup for these little guys: When they don't shape up after one of these emotional outpourings, the parent often describes the child as a self-centered brat who doesn't care about anyone but himself. Yet that's exactly what he really is—a child. Children are not organized around how other people feel; they are organized around what they want and how much influence they can have. Parents who are wedded to communicating heavy emotional reactions in response to behaviors that should be taken in stride or managed with little fanfare actually reinforce their children's use of such behavioral antics.

Pleasers in Action versus Effective Parents in Action

If you recognize yourself as a Pleaser, a look at the following scenarios may help you learn how to modify your style.

SCENARIO ONE

A Pleaser in Action

In the grocery store one day, I heard a father trying to console his clearly distressed and angry preschool-aged son: "I am so sorry, honey. I know you really wanted to ride in one of the special kiddie carts today. But there are not any left right now, and Daddy can't wait for one because we have to get home to give Mommy the food she needs to cook dinner. Do you understand? Now, I need you to be Daddy's big boy and stop whining. Next time we come I promise you can ride in a kiddie cart, no matter what! This is really disappointing, I know. But Daddy just can't do anything about it, honey. Okay? You know that Daddy would get you a kiddie cart if he could, right?" The child, who was not consoled, continued to fuss and protest. The father went on, "Now, I don't want to hear your whining voice anymore. Let me hear your big boy voice. Daddy needs you to use your big boy voice and to cooperate. Okay?" When I passed the duo again later, the little boy was wiping his tears and holding a big candy bar.

What's Wrong with This Scenario?

This little boy was not learning to take day-to-day disappointments in stride. Instead, what he learned is that it is a big deal for him to be disappointed and that the loving parental response he could count on was to be protected from ever feeling that way. All the fuss was over a kiddie cart at a grocery store! This little boy is certainly not being coached to build resilience for life's ups and downs.

The Effective Parent in Action

The effective parent keeps the solace and support short and sweet. "Oh, darn, honey, there aren't any more kiddie carts left today. Those are fun to use when we're here. Oh well, we'll probably be able to get one next time." When the child begins to whine, the father quickly responds, "Hey, come on now. I know you're disappointed, but there is no need for tears. Let's start getting the groceries; we have some yummy things on our list!" If the child persists in the upset, the father does not collapse and buy candy to compensate for the disappointment but continues with the shopping. If the upset escalates to a tantrum, the father takes the child outside of the store until he calms down and then returns to resume shopping.

SCENARIO TWO

A Pleaser in Action

At a restaurant a five-year-old girl is having a hard time staying in her seat. She is hopping around the table, singing, and trying to get her grandparents to watch her do a dance she learned at school. Her mother and father are extremely patient, as they find her to be more cute than annoying, and very nicely ask her to keep her voice down and to be careful not to get in the way of the waitresses. They have to repeat themselves several times as her dancing and singing continue. They say, "Honey, Grammy and Grampy love your dancing, but the waitresses are carrying very heavy trays with hot food. We don't want an accident to happen and for you to get burned."

Finally the anticipated collision occurs, but the waitress is able to divert a spill. At this point the parents firmly direct the little girl to sit down and stay seated. She slinks to her chair and puts her head down in her arms with a visible pout. Her father says quietly to the adults, "Oh, now she is upset." He gets up and goes to her and kneels down. Stroking her hair, he whispers, "Sweetheart, we're not mad, but the waitresses have to walk through here and we can't have you getting hurt. Okay? Don't be upset, honey. Mommy and Daddy did not mean to make you unhappy. Come on, give Daddy a hug and then why don't you tell Grammy about how you were star for the day at school last week?"

What's Wrong with This Scenario?

The Pleaser parent is showing overconsideration and tolerance for inappropriate behavior. The little girl is acting in a typically childish way, but the parents are not acting in a parental way. The child's Sara Bernhardt performance after she is admonished clearly says that one lesson she has learned is that she has the power to make her parents scrape and bow to her.

The Effective Parent in Action

Effective parents bring a tote bag of coloring books and activities that will help keep their child busy while she's seated at the table. Before going into the restaurant, they tell her that she must stay seated and keep her voice quiet while she's there. When she starts to get up and show off her new dance routine, her father gets up and leads her back to her chair. He firmly states that dancing must wait until they are home and reminds her of their conversation about the need to stay seated. He tells her she cannot bother the other guests who are eating and that she is in the way of the waiters. He then helps her get interested in one of the hidden pictures games she has in her bag.

If she tries to get up again, the effective parent takes the child by the hand and without any more conversation walks her to the front of the restaurant. Only after he has acted does he explain that she must stay in her seat or they will not be able to remain in the restaurant. The effective parent does not cajole and is not intimidated by pleading or pouting; he does not apologize for expecting his child to exercise self-control, be respectful, and behave appropriately. Through his actions, he helps strengthen his daughter's internal muscles of self-control and shapes appropriate behavior.

The Children of Pleaser Parents

In true royal fashion, the children of Pleaser parents sit upon thrones of power supported by their parents' well-intended efforts. All of the over-focus on attention to every need, wish fulfillment, and "special" considerations leads to no other end but a child who feels entitled and is demanding. This is not to say that all the advantages, lessons, and educational exposure don't pay off. They do. The children of Pleasers are often impressively accomplished and have admirable skills. These accomplishments can make it even more difficult for parents to reconcile the ungrateful, whiny, moody, and uncooperative behavior they encounter so often at home.

When children are routinely catered to and accommodated, their appetite for "specialness"—to be treated in a special way—only increases and so does the work for their parents. These children develop an array of rather unlikable qualities, as they persist in a mode of me, me, me, and now, now, now. Pleaser parents often describe their children as high-maintenance. They roll their eyes, shake their heads, and use a tone that conveys that their children are totally beyond their control. They have no idea how big a role they play in this dynamic. These children come to have such unpleasant power because of their parents' distorted investment in pleasing them.

Children of Pleaser parents are overwhelmed with all the emotional power they have been given. Daily negotiations involve so much effort that both children and parents become drained. Left with little resilience for life's disappointments, these children can have big meltdowns and generally behave worse at home than they do socially or at school. The micromanagement that so pervades the Pleaser parenting style blocks the children from using and strengthening their own internal muscles, with the end result that their individualization and autonomy are sacrificed to the interdependence of the parent-child relationship.

The developmental trajectory of this style is that Pleaser parents become helicopter parents when their children go off to college. Talking every day to their parents, sometimes two and three times a day, the children of Pleaser parents continue to struggle mightily with independence. They have very little resilience, often suffer the hurts that accompany thin skin, and feel entitled to special considerations. They have a rather narrow, self-centered perspective and are immature in their interest in the world and behind in altruistic pursuits.

Pushovers

Pushovers are the cousins of Pleasers. Steeped in feeling-centered, democratic parenting philosophies, they also overattend and overaccommodate their children. They go beyond pleasing, however, to what can really be described as giving complete deference to their child's wants and demands. They too want their children to be respectful and cooperative, but they have chronic trouble holding to a standard under duress. Some Pushover parents lack assertiveness in all of their interpersonal relationships and reflexively accommodate to the preferences of others. Other Pushover parents experience a dissonance in their lives: they are confident and competent in their adult and career relationships, but not so with their children. Especially because they see themselves as powerful in many relationships, they can have trouble accepting the idea that they are powerless with their children.

It is their anxiety and tentativeness about what they should do as parents that puts Pushovers in a category of their own. Their anxiety is rooted in an inability to trust the strength and endurance of the bonds they have forged with those they love, particularly their children. The anxiety inevitably leads them to assume subordinate positions in their intimate relationships. My experience is that many Pushover parents have, in fact, experienced losses or significant trauma in their own parent-child relationships: the love of their parent has either been lost or compromised. This experience has left them questioning their ability to sustain loving commitments with their own children. A significant number of Pushover parents have had a considerable struggle reaching parenthood. Years of battling miscarriages and infertility, or the complicated road of surrogacy, artificial insemination, or adoption can set the emotional stage for a child to be so special and treasured that the parent becomes deferential rather than taking the lead.

Whatever their own background, Pushover parents want their child's love and respect very much, but somewhere deep within themselves do not feel their child will find them competent, lovable, or admirable. Consequently, they become very uncomfortable if they provoke strong displays of negative emotion from their child. Fearing that they will hurt or anger her or damage their relationship, the Pushover acquiesces and continually allows the child to have her way. The dominant feeling-centered philosophies of our current parenting culture, along with all the warnings about damaging a child's self-esteem, fuel the hesitancy of Pushovers and elevate their anxiety when their children express anger and distress.

Pushovers often perceive their children's temperament as being too strong-willed, too active, too smart, too sensitive, too sickly, or too something for them as parents to be able to implement and enforce limits. I hear Pushovers declare, "Oh, you don't know Trevor. He will scream and carry on for hours!" or "Oh, but Elise is so sensitive! She's always been this way. She gets herself so upset." In fairness to Pushover parents, these perceptions are often fueled by real characteristics of their children. True or not, Pushovers tend to hide behind these perceptions and use them as excuses for not taking action and holding their parenting position. Rather than helping to shape and modify their children's temperamental predispositions, the Pushover's lack of parental assertiveness and effectiveness only strengthens them. Although it is certainly true that children can be strong-willed, precocious in their reasoning, and prone to anxiety, this does not mean they are beyond parenting or that their behavior can't be modified. Temperamental children have a genuine need for wise, experienced parental leadership and authority.

Rather than leading their children, however, Pushovers follow. They see their child as emotionally powerful and are intimidated by this power. They literally ask their child to tell them what he needs and what he wants; in other words, they invite the child to show them the way. They tolerate a considerable amount of disrespect and maltreatment from their child as well and accept it with a resigned passivity. In a relationship in which they feel themselves to be quite impotent, they rely heavily on deference and pleas for cooperation, rather than on leadership and insistence on standards.

Pushovers and the Hierarchy of Power

From the time their babies are born, Pushover parents relate to them with emotional deference. This reflexive acquiescence immediately places their children at the top of the family hierarchy. There are actually no power struggles that the children of a Pushover parent need to win to get to the top! The fact that children have an inherent power drive makes an inverted hierarchy inevitable for these families because Pushovers automatically back off when power is exerted. While Pleaser parents pave the way to the throne for their child with consideration and fairness,

Pushover parents stand aside and let their children walk unimpeded to the seat of power. These children learn to gain influence and keep it by playing on their parents' solicitude. They exploit the considerations and anxieties of their Pushover parents, not out of deviousness or maliciousness, but simply because they have learned how well it works.

To some degree, all children fall into patterns of behavior that are maintained through their parents' reactions. Some children do it by exercising their strength of will (relentlessly pursuing their agenda), some by a strong show of anger and dramatic laments ("You're being so mean!" or "You're not being fair!"), some by a display of anxiety and fearfulness ("Will you come back?" . . . "I don't want the wind to blow me away!"). Whatever the presentation, the result is the same: Parents take their children's communications too literally and respond in a way that further escalates and reinforces the children's distorted responses. In this way, Pushover parents set the stage for tolerating a considerable amount of disruptive behavior and raise children who require a very high degree of energy and attention, which completely drains the parents. Pushover parents, when confronted by resistance and protest in any form from their children, characteristically end up giving in with an air of resignation. They shrug their shoulders, shake their heads, or throw up their hands as if to say, "There is nothing more I can do." It is not uncommon for Pushover parents to collapse into tears after their negotiations, bribes, and pleading don't work. They cry to their child that they just can't take it anymore. When completely done in, Pushovers will sometimes retreat behind a locked door, saying that they need time-out for themselves. When things have spun way out of control, Pushover parents may tell their child they are going to leave him because they have just had it and don't know what else to do. Done in by the childish tactics of whining and refusing, Pushover parents yield power, along with their rightful position atop the family hierarchy, to their children.

As with all kids, the children of Pushovers become experts at relating to their parents in ways that will continue to ensure the maximum degree of their power, and there is a lot of power up for grabs in the Pushover relationship. The children grab it by the handfuls! Remember, the more power a child has, the more destructive he will be—both to himself and to his family. This is so not because children are intrinsically devilish, but because they are driven by childish instincts and immature impulses.

The Language of the Pushover

Pushover parents are akin to Pleasers in their solicitous communication style, but there are a few hallmarks that distinguish them. Pushovers grope for power. Not feeling they have any of their own, they resort to the power and authority of others to gain cooperation. They warn of what will happen if their child doesn't behave: "I am going to tell your father, and he will be very angry" or "Santa won't bring you any toys" or "Grandma doesn't like a fresh mouth and she won't take you to the movies." They try to add weight to their parental directives by invoking authorities the child does respect: "You know the doctor said you have to eat your vegetables to be healthy."... "Your teacher said all children in the second grade should go to bed by 8:30."

Pushovers also tell their children a litany of things that could go wrong and a host of dangers and bad things that could befall them if they don't listen to their parents: "Wash your hands before you eat. Remember, germs can make you very sick." ... "Don't jump on the couch, honey; you could fall down and hit your head and have a serious injury." Unfortunately, a strong reliance on fear-based tactics doesn't increase cooperation. Usually there is one of two outcomes: Since most of the Pushover's threats never come to fruition (the child doesn't get sick from not washing his hands, and the child does not crack his head open), the child learns to tune out his parents' warnings and their focus on danger. The other consequence is that the child takes his parents' forewarnings to heart and actually comes to see the world as a dangerous place, thus breeding a hefty anxiety of his own.

In addition to playing on fear, Pushover parents play on guilt. Rather than simply managing the undesirable behaviors of their children with timely and effective actions, they routinely get tied up in guilt-inducing messages that the child's behavior will cause something bad to happen: "If you keep making Mommy late for work, her boss is going to fire her," or "You act like you don't even like to hold Daddy's hand. That really hurts Daddy's feelings."

The pattern of Pushover parents' behavior in relation to their children—albeit unconscious and inadvertent—reinforces the message that these parents have no real power. Consequently, emotional manipulation becomes a central dynamic in the Pushover parenting style. Pushovers are immersed in strategies of subterfuge because their tentativeness doesn't permit them to stand up to their children and directly assert themselves as the authority. Unfortunately, because playing on the emotions is the dynamic the Pushover parent so often relies on, this is the dynamic the child soon learns to perfect. Of course, none of these ill-placed communication patterns starts by design—they are born inadvertently, as adjuncts of a parenting style. Emotional manipulation is certainly not an effective way to socialize children's behavior. Instead, it produces agitated children, who in turn learn to use emotional manipulation to get their way. The irony is that in the end, it is the Pushover parents, not their children, who acquiesce to these devices.

Another hallmark of the Pushover style is the habit of attempting to leverage cooperation with messages of their own neediness: "Mommy really needs you to take a bath tonight without arguing or fighting. I'm exhausted. I have a terrible neck spasm and I'm in a lot of pain." Or "I really need you to be on your best behavior when we go out to dinner tonight. Please, will you just do this for me tonight? Please, honey?" These need-driven requests sound very much like the pleading of the weak to the strong. You can be sure that children hear it this way.

Along the same lines, Pushover parents often stress what they can't do, don't know how to do, or simply aren't up to doing. They say things like:

"Honey, I can't take it tonight." "I can't fight with you anymore." "I don't know what else to do. You have to tell me want you want; just tell me!" The message the child continually gets is that her parents are uncertain, anxious, and looking to her, the child, to use her strength and compassion to show them the way. To add insult to injury, when the child doesn't respond to their bid for empathy, Pushovers not only take it as a rejection, but see it as a reflection of insensitivity and poor character in their child.

Like Pleasers, Pushovers talk too much and have the same reliance on ending directives with "okay?" They give the majority of their directives using the pronouns *we* or *us* rather than being direct and saying *you*. This phrasing is a way to avoid directness and to sidestep being the clear authority. More often than not, Pushovers also ask their child for permission to do things: "Please let Mommy finish her phone conversation, okay?" . . . "Won't you let Daddy read you a bedtime story tonight?" . . . "Please, can I read the paper first?" Pushovers are quite direct in their language of subordination and will even ask their child to tell them what it will take to get his cooperation. For example, "Sweetie, Mommy has a very important meeting this morning and I can't be late, so tell me what it will take to get you in your car seat without a fuss."

Pushovers not only talk too much; they actually listen too much, too, and take what their kids say literally. They give what is really childish distortion enormous credibility by offering justifications and reassurances. Just because a child says something does not mean it warrants a parental response.

Children of Pushovers can frequently be heard blaming and insulting their parents: "You are so mean." . . . "You never play with me, and you promised you would!" . . . "You don't love me as much as you love my sister!" Rather than dismissing these statements as the childish ploys and melodrama they really are, Pushovers are quick to offer a rebuttal: "Honey, I am not trying to be mean. I did not realize that's what you wanted." Or "I did play with you, for about an hour this morning. Don't you remember us playing cards, and then two board games after break-fast? I did so play with you." ... "Oh, honey. Do you really feel that way? You know Mommy loves you both the same." Line for line, Pushover parents keep feeding the cycle.

Pushovers in Action versus Effective Parents in Action
SCENARIO ONE
A Pushover in Action
At a shoe store, a mother is shopping with her young daughter (who looks to be about four years old). The little girl is taking too many shoes out of the boxes, and her mother, bidding her to stop, says, "Honey, you can't take the shoes off the shelves like that or the store man will be mad." The little girl ignores her and keeps taking out more shoes. The mother tries again, "No, Sophia, the man will make us leave the store." With a grand pout, and giving her mother the cold shoulder, the little girl walks several feet away, turns her back and crosses her arms over her chest.

In response to her daughter's show of indignation, the mother asks in an obsequious voice, "Honey, I didn't mean to hurt your feelings, but we would get in a lot of trouble if I let you keep taking the shoes out of the boxes. Do you understand? Mommy has to say no to you."

The little girl only puts her nose higher in the air and takes two steps further away from her mother. Her mother then asks, "Are you mad at Mommy or do you understand? Do you love Mommy? Do you know how much Mommy loves you? You can't play with the shoes, but you can get an ice cream cone when we leave." When Sophia still doesn't warm up, her mother feels compelled to add: "Honey, do you know how lucky you are to have a Mommy who loves you as much as I do?"

What's Wrong with This Scenario?
The real lesson learned by the little girl is not about appropriate behavior in a shoe store, but about how anxious her mother is for her love. Furthermore, she has learned that the most effective means of staying on

the throne of power is a good show of disapproval. The mother tries to use emotions to motivate her daughter, but her daughter is little affected. Sophia just responds with a manipulation of her own, and unlike her mother's, hers works. The Pushover habit of pandering needs to be replaced with the straightforward communication of a parent in control.

The Effective Parent in Action

The effective parent goes to her daughter and instructs her to put the shoes back, giving her a one-sentence explanation about why. She tells the little girl that if she does not stop taking the shoes out, then she will have to stay right with her and hold her hand. She oversees and assists her child in organizing and cleaning up, and then moves her daughter along by engaging her in a conversation about their afternoon activity. If the little girl continues to be disruptive and inappropriate in the store, the effective parent then says, "This is the second time I am telling you to stop taking the shoes off the shelves. Next time we will go out to the car." The effective parent does not say this as a threat but as a statement of what will be. Once she says it, she holds to it. If leaving the store becomes necessary, the parent can either opt to end the shopping trip and go home or have the child sit in the car for a few minutes and then return to the store, after giving the girl clear instructions about appropriate behavior.

SCENARIO TWO

A Pushover in Action

After dinner a mother says to her nine-year-old son, "I need you to take a shower tonight. You had soccer practice this afternoon, and you can't go to bed muddy."

Her son immediately resists, "NO! I am not taking a shower. I am going to watch *American Idol!*"

The mother keeps trying. "I know, honey, you can. Just go real quick into the shower; you won't miss much."

"No way! You said I could watch the show! You are so unfair!"

The mother says, "Honey, I know I did, and you still can. I'm really not trying to be unfair. It's just that you got all muddy on the field. C'mon, will you just do this for me tonight without arguing?"

Her son really cranks it up and shouts, "Mom, shut up! Don't be stupid; I am not missing one minute of my show."

The mother, hurt and exhausted, sighs, "This is really hard on me when you argue like this, and I don't like it when you call me stupid."

"Mom, just go away, okay? You are so annoying."

The mother, with resignation and a hint of whining in her voice, says, "Now you are being so rude, you've hurt my feelings. I can't take this anymore. Why do you have to be so mean to me? I am going up to my room! So, fine, you do what you want."

What's Wrong with This Scenario?

After years of interactions with a parent who is permissive, weak, and ineffective, children of Pushovers become emboldened and don't hesitate to fling insults at their parents: "You're stupid," "You're mean," or "You drive me crazy!" It is also not uncommon for children of Pushovers to punctuate their verbal defiance with dismissive behaviors such as pushing and hitting. When Pushover parents throw up their hands, even though they are upset when they do it, they give their children the power to dictate how things go, not to mention letting their outrageous behavior go unchecked.

This scenario hints at how volatile things can become if a child with so much power were to encounter firm parental limits. The longer parents fail to establish effective and appropriate power, the stronger the child's display of power becomes, thus requiring stronger and stronger counterforce to effectively correct him. The sooner parents correct power imbalances, the easier it will be for all concerned, not just the child.

The Effective Parent in Action

A child growing up in a relationship with an effective mother might press her, but he would never speak to her so rudely. By the time he was nine years old, he would have established respect for his mother and a habit of cooperation. An effective parent would say, "Honey, when the show ends, it will be too late for you to shower, so you have to do it now. Your best bet is to be quick and miss as little of the show as possible." If the child continues to protest, the effective parent should say, "It is not negotiable. You have to wash the mud off your legs before you get into bed. Now, this is the second time I am saying it and, remember, I only say things twice. If you need a third reminder, you're going to wind up not being able to watch the show at all. Now, hop to it, real quick, without another word." A parent who has established a pattern of respectful and effective authority in relation to her child will need little more than this. He may grumble and drag his feet a bit, but he knows his mom means business, and he will take a quick shower.

The Children of Pushover Parents

Talk about kids being in over their heads! The children of Pushover parents are in the position of not only running the show; they're taking care of their needy and anxious parents, too. In the absence of reliable, competently enforced boundaries, limits, and parental expectations, the behavior and moods of these children are typically all over the place. They can be pleasant and loving one second and maddeningly fickle and impossible to please the next. Their moods are unpredictable, and their tantrums can be wild. This is why the children of Pushovers are often described by their parents as high-maintenance. Insulted and indignant when challenged, they have learned that they can wear down their parents, whatever their resolve, with perseverance and heightened displays of distress.

It literally makes kids crazy to be given so much control and power by parents who are so maddeningly subordinate and accommodating. Children of Pushovers can get to the point of actually pulling out their hair and often exhibit behaviors such as biting themselves, scratching their arms, pinching their skin, and banging their heads against the floor or the wall. These children are crying for help, crying for someone to show them the way. In fact, one Pushover mom, in describing her child's tantrums, told me that when she instructs her child to calm down and stop, her child cries out: "Help me, help me, I can't stop. I can't. I don't know how! Help me!" Sadly, this plea for help often elicits a classic Pushover response: "Honey, I don't know what to do for you. You have to tell Mommy what you need. I'll do whatever it is, but you have to tell me what to do."

The children of Pushover parents are tired. Day after day they walk in the shoes of the parent, clomping around and making a royal mess. Since Pushover parents are also notoriously poor at enforcing bedtime and creating healthy sleep patterns, their children are not only emotionally done in from all their power-mongering, they are often starved for sleep as well. The combination makes for very unhappy children. How IFP disorganizes and derails children from secure, healthy development is nowhere more apparent than in the anger, frustration, and tears of these unwitting lords of the manor. Their desperate bids for help and direction can be heartbreaking; these children are often misunderstood and misdiagnosed by teachers, parents, and even clinicians as having anxiety disorders, attention deficit disorder, or oppositional defiant disorders. But what they really have is way too much power.

Sadly, the anxiety that is the hallmark of Pushover parents comes to dominate the emotional experience of their children, who are in a panic because at some level they know they are being asked to be in charge, something they are completely incapable of. The parents' repeated communication that they are not up to the job of managing their child ("I just don't know what to do with you") terrifies the child. The almost daily upsets that occur between Pushover parents and their children understandably result in weary and fed-up parents. It doesn't take long before the unruliness and tantrums cause parents not to want to be with their children very much. The children are all too aware of how their parents "just can't take it anymore," and they worry that today will be the day their parents give up and leave them. In this way, Pushover parents pass on their abandonment anxiety to their children.

On some level, children of Pushover parents really do feel bad about their conduct and their emotionally manipulative ways. Time after time, when I am having a frank discussion with these children in my office, they very clearly acknowledge that the things they say and the ways they behave are bad and that they feel terrible about it. Recently, a six-year-old girl, who had been very disrespectful to her parents said, with her head down, "I know it is rude and not a good way to be. I don't want to be this way, but I can't help myself." This is not an uncommon confession and raises a very important point: These children really can't help themselves, and they can't be expected to parent themselves.

Pushover parents (in fact, most parents) operate from the notion that children who feel bad, whether it's out of fear or guilt, will be motivated to change their ways. But children don't work this way. Caught up in the force of their innate power drive, children will repeat the behaviors that give them influence and power, even when it is at their own expense.

Even when it makes people angry with them, causes guilt, or results in punishment, the children of Pushovers stay with behaviors that get their parents' goat or give them what they want. Young children can and do feel bad about their misbehavior, but remorse does not make them stop. Instead of trying to make their children feel worse and worse in order to gain their cooperation, parents need to understand that the lessons of self-control, respect, and cooperation are action-based: Pushovers need to stop talking and pleading and get moving!

Forcers

Pleasers and Pushover parenting styles are child-centered and feeling-based ones, in which parents are reluctant to act as authorities. Forcers represent the opposite end of the parenting continuum. They overtly scoff at indulgent, pandering, child-centered parenting approaches, but unfortunately their own parenting behaviors are wrong in a different, potentially more damaging way. Firm in their commitment that parents need to be the boss and children need to obey, they fail to understand the need to harness parental power and authority in an effective, more gentle and respectful manner.

Unlike Pleasers and Pushovers, Forcers are not so invested in how their children feel. They are more concerned about behavior. Their focus is on taking responsibility, following routines, compliance, and getting the job done. They have a different investment, that of top performance and all-out effort and achievement. They have a rigid need for their children to have self-discipline and a strong work ethic, to be neat and organized, and to do everything above average. Slovenliness, mediocrity, bad manners, poor attitude, disrespectfulness—these are the provocations of Forcers. Of course, there is nothing problematic about parents wanting their children to aspire to high standards and ethics. It is the process by which Forcers go about achieving their goals that is so flawed.

Forcer parents feel that children must be "broken in" and have their will molded into compliance. Intimidation is regarded as an essential tool to get the job done, and Forcers are closely aligned with the old-school tradition of "spare the rod, spoil the child." While there has certainly been a significant decline in the approval and practice of corporal punishment in the last three to four decades, Forcers still convey the spirit of authoritarian dominance in their parenting style. While all parents, regardless of their style, sometimes resort to spanking and slapping in moments of frustration and desperation, Forcers are more likely to incorporate hitting or physical correction into routine discipline.

One of the things that can be confusing and difficult for the children of Forcers is that, when they are not acting as disciplinarians, these parents can be dynamic and lots of fun to be with. They are often high-energy, rough-and-ready folks. Forcer parents are both easy to love and easy to hate. Their children develop a strong ambivalence, wanting to be close to them and, at the same time, wanting to hurt them back. While Forcers are often their children's harshest and most rigid critics at home, they can also be their strongest defenders and protectors from outside attacks. They will not hesitate to challenge other children and adults if they perceive their children to be unfairly or unkindly treated. In these instances, the children are drawn in by the strength and assertiveness of their Forcer parent but confused and angry when these same attitudes and behavior are turned on them. This creates a confusing and painful emotional experience for children.

Forcers are comfortable and confident in their methods, focused on doing whatever it takes to get the job done: "Kids have to learn." Many feel morally certain and justified that when they spank, they are doing the right and difficult work of parenting. Those who believe they are following the teachings of the Bible are even more righteously committed to their heavy-handed style.

Forcers don't engage in any sugar coating; they have a "that's tough" attitude in the face of their children's disappointment and an imperviousness to their tears. While Pleasers overempathize, Forcers don't empathize enough. Talking directly and frankly to children is a good practice, but Forcers go too far and often sound mean and scary: "You can cry all you want; it isn't going to make a bit of difference. You screwed up, and now you have to pay the price." Forcers routinely use intimidation and threats to motivate their children. They begin directives with, "You had better. . . ." "Look at me when I'm talking to you" is another common Forcer demand often underscored by a finger pointed in the child's face. Harsh, barking directives are standard fare: "Knock if off!" "Get over here!" "Don't give me any back talk!"

Forcers use intimidation and fear in an effort to influence their children, and because they are strong and aggressive about it, it has the desired effect. Forcers can be scary. This is very different from the weak, hollow, easily dismissed fear tactics used by the Pushover. The Pushover parent might say, "Please put on your seat belt, honey. You know not wearing a seat belt is against the law and a policeman might arrest you if you don't buckle up." To this statement, a child of a Pushover would probably pipe up from the back seat, "No he won't, Mom. I looked and there aren't any police around here." The Forcer, in contrast, would be more apt to say, "You know wearing your seat belt is the law. If I catch you not wearing it again, I'm going directly to the police station and tell an officer on you." The child of the Forcer might buckle his seat belt but in a retaliatory spirit quietly take his pencil and gouge little holes into the backseat of the car.

Forcers are little concerned that their actions will lose the affection of their child, and they do not entertain the idea of seeking approval or permission from their child for their parental directives. They feel they are right and that they know best. Thus their children do not have emotional leverage. For example, when a concerned mother tells her Forcer husband that their child is upstairs crying and saying that Daddy is mean, and that she is afraid of him, it would be typical for the Forcer to respond: "That's tough. She's seems to have to learn the hard way," or "Good! She should be."

In addition to threats and punishment, Forcers use retaliation to drive lessons home. They will play tit for tat: "You did this to me. Now I will do it to you, so you can see how it feels." This can start when children are quite young. A Forcer parent may hit or bite a child so she can see how much it hurts.

Most Forcers don't consciously choose to hurt their children, despite the harshness characteristic of their style. It is common for Forcer parents to be heavily represented in the military, law enforcement, and firefighting communities as well as in conservative religious communities, where giving and following orders are embedded in the authoritarian structure. Many Forcer parents are in fact repeating the way they were parented. As with parents of other styles, Forcers are terribly pained and feel guilty when they realize the damaging nature of their ways. They can connect to how much it hurt them to endure similar tactics at the hands of their own parents. Despite the fact that their style is not heavy on compassion or sympathy, Forcers have a lot of heart and care deeply for their children. Their style is not an outgrowth of a lack of love or concern.

Forcers teach us a different lesson about power and authority in parent-child relationships. While Pleasers and Pushovers clearly illustrate the necessity for parents to establish an appropriate authority with children, Forcers provide the important example that power, in and of itself, is not the answer. Forcers think that carrying a big stick and not being afraid to use it makes them the boss. Yet their reliance on control and intimidation creates a parent-child relationship dominated by power struggles, not effective power. Deliberately hurting children does not teach them anything positive or constructive. It is also very confusing for children when a parent does the very thing he is supposedly teaching them not to do! Forcers are unaware of how counterproductive their efforts are. The dynamics of power and authority that are out of whack in their relationships cause significant compromise in the development of their children. Power and authority untempered by empathy, respect, and caring are as ineffective and damaging as no power and authority at all—in fact, they may be more so.

When met with escalating defiance and anger from their child—a common reaction to Forcer tactics—Forcers do not question their own methods, but blame their child for being audaciously brazen and reason that even stricter and harsher measures are called for. It is their heavy-handed manner that makes this parenting style such a problematic one.

Forcers and the Hierarchy of Power

The Forcer believes in his power and would most certainly tell you he rules the roost and is at the top of the hierarchy. But the truth is, Forcer power is a lot of show. Rather than exercising effective power, Forcers use bullying tactics. Consequently, their children never come to genuinely embrace the authority of the parents; instead, they perpetually resist, resent, and struggle against it. Power struggles define the parent-child interactions, creating a battleground.

The Forcer parent is akin to a ruler whose subjects only pretend to be deferential while covertly engaging in all manner of subterfuge. The child of the Forcer says "Yes, sir" out of one corner of his mouth and "I'll show you" out of the other. No one responds well to a harsh and disrespectful leader, as everyone's natural instinct is to resist taking in what is forcefully shoved upon him. This brand of parenting creates an environment of intimidation and oppression—one ripe for rebellion and mutiny. As a result, Forcers do not have genuine power: their children are engaged, at some level, in railing against their dictates rather than genuinely internalizing a healthy code of conduct and moral character.

The children of Forcers act out in two ways. Either they are sneaky and secretive in their defiance or they go head-to-head in direct conflict with their Forcer parent. The latter stance, unfortunately, is very provocative and destructive for the children. When acting out in overt defiance, these children provoke harsh retribution. Once engaged in this kind of battle, they continue to fight the parent, yelling and screaming in protest rather than succumbing to surrender. This gives rise to volatile and ugly exchanges, because the Forcer parent applies more force to his children's resistance in order to achieve submission. Despite what is often a tough, loud, and fearless showing, the children are deeply wounded by these battles. They also come to harbor a powerful anger—ensuring more storm and strife ahead.

The Language of the Forcer

A dreadful irony exists in the parental style of Forcers. In their attempts to assert strong power and authority, they continually model the negative behaviors they would punish in their children. They are disrespectful, swear, call their children names, and demean and humiliate them. They even slap and hit.

Since Forcers are not interested in being understanding or accommodating, they do very little listening. Children need to do as they are told and not ask questions or talk back. When asserting their power, Forcers typically speak in clipped, declarative sentences. For example, they will bark: "No questions! You heard what I said," or "Because I said so." They lecture with a critical tone, usually making the child feel bad about himself, rather than expressing their views or decisions constructively or supportively. In the same vein, Forcers tend to attack the general character of their children in the face of wrongdoing or poor performance by saying things like: "You are being lazy," "You are completely selfish," or "You are such a brat." Where Pleasers and Pushovers try to motivate their children by targeting feelings of guilt, Forcers use communications that intimidate and humiliate their children: "You are acting like you're still in kindergarten. Well, act like a baby and you'll get treated like a baby." They strike at the core of their child's sense of confidence and esteem. By doing this, they actually undermine their child's competence in performance and achievement—the very thing Forcers are so intent on building.

When disciplining or correcting their children, Forcers usually use a loud, domineering voice. When provoked, it is not uncommon for them to slam down their hands, get up abruptly, throw things, stomp around, and point a finger in their child's face or poke his chest. They are not inhibited when it comes to grabbing their child by the arm and jerking, pushing, or shaking him. Their anger can be explosive and is almost always activated when disciplining. "DAMN IT! I said I didn't want to hear you two bickering. Now both of you SHUT UP!" No matter what else children learn from their Forcer parent, intimidation and fear are part of the lesson. Rather than a true spirit of respect and cooperation, these parents engender in their children a motivation to not get caught. The children get very good at learning how to circumvent their parents' wrath, rather than building a genuine internal standard of conduct.

Forcers confront and challenge their child with heated intensity: "You have got to think! You act like you have no clue. I mean it. Or maybe you just don't care. Look at me when I'm talking to you!" They speak in black-and-white terms and habitually make global pronouncements regarding the child's future. "If you keep this up, you are not going to amount to anything. You are nine years old now, and you've got to get with the program in a goddamn hurry." They often dole out punishments that don't match the seriousness of the transgression, erring on the side of excess. Or they punish their children when punishment has no place—for example, punishing a child who "looked like a slacker" on the ball field or made "stupid mistakes" on a math test. These troubles may certainly need to be addressed, but not with harsh reproach and punishment.

Such patterns of communication build what I have come to refer to as bad blood between the Forcer parent and his child. Eventually, children of Forcers become so raw and resentful, they lose connection to their natural desire to please their parents.

Forcers in Action versus Effective Parents in Action
SCENARIO ONE

A Forcer in Action

A four-and-a-half year old boy has been continually calling his parents "stupid head" and "poopy face." They have told him over and over again that he is not permitted to say such disrespectful things and that he had better stop. The child does not, and the father finally warns his son that if he has a potty mouth one more time, he will get his mouth washed out with soap. Sure enough, the little boy says, "You are a poopy head!" and his father says, "Okay, that's it!" He marches his son into the bathroom, pulling him by the arm, where he lathers a washcloth with soap and attempts to wash the foul language out of his child's mouth. A few weeks later, when the potty language is still not gone, he switches to putting pepper in the boy's mouth.

What's Wrong with This Scenario?

What this little boy is learning is just how dangerous his father can be—dangerous because he has a strong stomach for making his child suffer and endure pain. He not only can tolerate suffering in his child, but he seems to have a need to inflict it. Consequently, this little boy learns to fear his father, and every minute he stands there choking on the soap, his hateful feelings towards his father grow stronger. All of this has occurred because an exuberant and expansive four-year-old was testing some dicey words and saw what a powerful effect they had on his father.

The Effective Parent in Action

"Poopy head! Hey, wait a minute. If I am a poopy head, then what are you? You must be a bubble head. Yep, that's us, just a couple of poopy heads and bubble heads!" The effective parent can joke and laugh with his young son, knowing that his words and actions are the common and harmless fare of a four-year-old. He moves his son along by distracting him and not making a federal case out of a little bathroom talk. The more rigid and upset a parent becomes at these childish word games, the more frequently and longer the child will play them. A parent's big reaction tells the child these words are powerful. Since Forcer tactics elicit power struggles, the child will wield his newfound power with a vengeance.

The better parental tactic is to go with the flow, be casual, and if your child gets carried away with the silliness and fun of the words, simply direct him to his room where he can say them all he wants, but where no one else has to hear them: "Honey, if you're not done using that word, it would be best for you to go to your room. Have a poopy head party and say it as much as you want. But since I don't want to hear it anymore, you will have to stay in your room until you are finished."

SCENARIO TWO

A Forcer in Action

Shelley and her mother keep butting heads over daily chores and responsibilities around the house. "I am sick of telling you to clean your room! You are ten years old now, and if you can't learn to take care of your clothes, then you can forget about any future shopping trips." Finally Shelley's mother lays down the ultimatum: "Either you pick up your room, or whatever is still on the floor is going into the garbage!" Shelley cries, screams back, and fusses while she makes a quick attempt to straighten her room before running out to ballet practice. When she gets home, she eats dinner and starts her homework.

Later that evening while Shelley is at her desk, her mother comes in with a large trash bag, picks up the remaining clothes, shoes, and clutter from the floor, and stuffs it all in the bag. Shelley begs and cries, but her mother is stern and unyielding as she says, "You have to learn, Shelley. You can't live like a pig, and I am not your servant. You treat your things like garbage, so will I. They are a going out with the trash. You can say good-bye to your favorite pair of jeans."

What's Wrong with This Scenario?

There are multiple problems with this mother's approach. First and most obviously, there is a meanness that drips from the words and actions of the Forcer parent. Any child would be hurt and angered by such an interaction and would move farther away from the motivation to want to please and cooperate. Forcers think pain is the pathway to gain. While going for the jugular can yield short-term compliance, a high price will likely be paid from using these methods.

Second, the child still never cleaned her room—her mother disposed of her things before she got to it. Shelley learns that while her mother has the power to hurt her, she does not have the power to actually make her do things. No constructive or positive lesson is being taught. Children of Forcers develop an attitude that they can do what they want, putting their greatest energy into avoidance of getting caught. If and when they do get caught, they steel themselves against the pain of the punishment. These tactics further ignite a power struggle, and the child will naturally have feelings of wanting to hurt back—a dangerous cycle that will lead to ongoing damage for both the child and the parent.

Third, this is an example of the punishment not matching the crime. Kids and messy rooms go together. It is a rare child who prefers neatness and order. Parents should have standards, but being rigid about clean rooms is a prescription for frustration and headache.

The Effective Parent in Action

"Shelley, your room is really messy again. I know you are busy with school, homework, and ballet, and I know that cleaning is not your thing, but you can't let it get any worse. Today is Wednesday, and you will have to clean your room before you can go out on Friday evening. I know it's a sleepover party, so keep that in mind. You won't be able to go until your room is cleaned up."

The Children of Forcer Parents

When a parent's corrective methods are based on force and intimidation, what happens to a child? Not what the parents intend or are striving for! Primarily, the child becomes part of a vicious cycle of power struggles, beginning with the parent's bullying tactics and leading to the child being afraid, hurt, shamed, and ultimately feeling angry and resentful. The anger and resentment then spur an appetite for revenge, decreasing the child's motivation to cooperate and please the parent. Some children's energies are turned toward lying and being sneaky and dishonest. Others become passive and wind up with a heavy dose of "not caring," which in turn is very powerful and provocative. Both sets of behaviors inflame the ire of the Forcer parent even more, satisfying the power and revenge strivings of the child. This destructive, damaging cycle goes around and around.

Children of Forcers are often unmotivated and underachieving. The barrage of criticism and relentless corrections they endure undermines and constricts their natural drive for learning and achievement. Besides becoming sneaky and involved in subterfuge, these children commonly evolve into bullies themselves. They go after their younger siblings, pets, and vulnerable children at school. In addition, they often laugh at other people's accidents, particularly if they happen to their Forcer parents.

Most children of Forcers learn to be Forcers themselves. Over time, they internalize their parents' style of behavior and communication.

Among children of Forcers, there is a subset that simply crumbles under the onslaught of harshness and reacts by becoming passive, avoidant, and socially immature. Escapists, these children often turn to food and electronic media to soothe themselves. For younger children, the themes that dominate play are rough and battle-dominated, centering on strength and power. They complain of nightmares, and their fearful anxieties center on acts of violence befalling family members or bad people breaking into the house.

Children of Forcers endure so much finger-pointing and blame for being inadequate and bad that they develop a defensive rigidity, making it difficult for them to accept responsibility for their actions. They blame others and concoct all manner of external excuses for what they do. They tend to be explosive themselves, slamming doors, hiding, and running away from their Forcer parent. When they cry, they are usually quite hysterical. The reason for such passionate crying is that for these children anger is often channeled into tears. After all, even though their tears may elicit belittlement from their parent, tears are safer to express than direct anger, which only invites one more force from the Forcer.

Reading about these children in the context of the relationship with a Forcer parent makes it is easy to feel empathy and to want to help them. In their day-to-day lives, however, the residue of having a Forcer parent leaves children with behaviors that are quite unlikable, and they are often troublemakers. These characteristics do not endear them to people, so it can be hard for teachers and caregivers to have much empathy for them. These children start to hear from everyone that they don't try hard enough, don't work up to their potential, and are a problem in the class and on the playground. The life of a child with a Forcer parent can be lonely and difficult.

Outliers

The three parenting styles described so far are generally familiar to most people. The fourth style is more elusive. The central characteristic of this style is one of emotional distance; these parents remain on the *outside* of their children's inner experiences. I refer to these parents as Outliers.

Pleasers, Pushovers, and Forcers, while differing in many ways, all engage in high levels of emotion in their parent-child relationships. Pleasers try to win favor, Pushovers plead, Forcers intimidate. Outliers, in contrast, are active, involved parents in most ways, but they are not emotionally engaged with their children. They parent by attending primarily to the business, scheduling, and structure of family life. Typically good-natured, good-hearted people, they love and care for their children but from an emotional distance. When their children exhibit signs of emotional neediness, Outlier parents commonly minimize the significance of the distress and provide only a cursory response, if any at all. In fact, skirting deep emotional expression and connection with other people tends to characterize all their relationships. Contained, private, and usually emotionally controlled, they don't know how to move in and really involve themselves in an intimate, close way in their relationships.

Outliers tend to be highly intellectual people, often with careers in academia or highly structured professions such as engineering, accounting, and scientific research. Outliers beget Outliers, so many of these parents have Outlier parents of their own. While Outliers are more comfortable with doing rather than with relating, some have a warm and playful demeanor, while others can be distant and cold.

Planning, organizing, preparing, transporting, decorating, purchasing, teaching, fixing—these are the strengths of the Outlier. They are comfortable in these tasks, but not in the business of emotions and feeling. For these parents, attending to the business of the family is the means they use to relate to their children and their primary basis for emotional connectedness. They move away from their child and into the tasks of parenting rather than toward their child in a way that strengthens the emotional bonds. Because they are such able and invested managers, the infrastructure of the family looks quite solid. In fact, by all appearances, Outlier families and children seem healthy and high-functioning. Yet all is not well. Children of Outliers develop unevenly, because they are left to negotiate and make sense of the complicated world of feelings and emotions with little to no guidance or support from their parents. They have a well-shaped exterior but a contrastingly hollow interior.

Intense feelings are generally missing from the Outlier's relational mix, both on the positive and negative end of the continuum. Pleasure, joy, and love, as well as pain, fear, and sadness, are expressed in minimalist fashion. What's more, Outliers do not invite or tolerate the expression of their children's intense feelings. These are usually met with noticeable stiffening, a disapproving facial expression, or even no response—a complete lack of acknowledgment. Consequently, children of Outliers learn to see emotional expression as an undisciplined, messy affair. They learn to keep most of their feelings in—but when they do let them out, the result is often tumultuous. Emotionally unregulated and without modulation, they tantrum, cry, pout, and flail.

Outliers are the most difficult and elusive to identify because they are generally considerate, socially adept, proud, and morally grounded. Thus, children of Outliers remain in the dark longer than most in their developmental journeys into self and family understanding. When I give talks and presentations, it is this style of parenting that generates the most surprised recognition from the audience. People say things like, "Oh my gosh! My mother was an Outlier. I never got it before, but that is exactly my story. This helps me explain and understand so much about her as well as myself."

Adult children of Outliers tend to have a characteristic defensiveness and protectiveness toward their Outlier parent. They say things such as "She is such a good person" or "Oh, I hate to use the word Outlier. I mean, she did a lot for us kids." In fact, Outliers are generally viewed positively and are described with words such as *strong, stoic,* or a *rock.* But there is more to the story. Underneath the core of strength, there is an emotional constriction, distance, and unavailability that is far from positive in the relational life of their children.

To add to the conundrum, while they are emotionally inaccessible, Outlier parents are not devoid of feelings. In fact, they can have deep feelings, but they keep them to themselves, tightly under wraps, and they prefer not to get involved with other people's emotions, either. This is not to say that Outliers are without a nurturing side. They usually tend to the family business with much care and consideration. Outliers nurture plants and gardens with joy. One of the hallmarks of the Outliers' style is their strong affiliation to babies and pets. They often show their strongest feelings in these relationships, where deeply investing themselves is the most comfortable because it involves so little emotional complexity. This is all the more confusing for their children, who see evidence of their parents' feelings—their goodness and caring—yet can't seem to connect to it personally or in a way that is satisfying or fulfilling.

Of the four parenting groups, Outliers are the least aware of how they are contributing to their children's behavioral and emotional problems. They tend not to be introspective and their sense of themselves as good, moral, attentive, and hard-working exempts them from culpability, in their minds. Their children thus get a clear message that their trouble is of their own doing and they had better get it together. The problem is their Outlier parents don't give them any emotional guidance or support with their struggles. Rather, the children tend to get judged from a distance: "I don't understand how you could do this" or "What were you thinking?" If Pleasers are associated with guilt inducements, Pushovers with anxiety, and Forcers with intimidation, Outliers have a way with principled judgment and condemnation. They don't pass judgment lightly or often, but when they do, it hits the mark and can be tough to bear.

As one would expect from this profile, Outliers are not personally motivated by self-reflection or analysis. If they participate in therapy, it is typically in service of someone else or to gain assistance in managing a particular event. Sharing the most private parts of oneself and connecting to deep feelings are the underpinnings of therapy, and these are the antithesis of an Outlier's makeup. In fact, what I know about Outliers I know primarily from their children or because they have come to me for help with their children. Most Outliers prefer to leave therapy after three or four sessions. They are interested in quick fixes and prescriptions—there's no early childhood, deep-feeling exploration for them! If you ask an Outlier how she feels about something, she will invariably answer by telling you what she thinks.

The questions that still need to be answered are: Why are Outliers organized in such a well-defended fashion, and why do they insist on remaining outside intimate emotional experience? My hunch is that they erect walls around a core of powerful anger. At a very deep level they fear that if their anger were unleashed it would be hard to contain and destructive.

When Outliers periodically allow some of their anger to leak, it provides a glimpse into just how stormy and dark their feelings can be. In this way they are more akin to Forcers than any other parenting style because they both end up intimidating their children. Outliers are rather thin-skinned and extremely sensitive to humiliation so they can't take criticism. They have a hard time with the vulnerability that comes from being open and intimate with others. Fearing that they will either get hurt or hurt someone else, they stay on the outside of relational experience. They establish boundaries that are so clearly communicated that people in relationships with them learn to abide by the unspoken rule that you just do not ask Outliers to be emotionally giving beyond their comfort level.

Outliers and the Hierarchy of Power

Surprisingly, unlike other parenting styles we've discussed, Outliers usually succeed in establishing a hierarchy of power within their families in which children learn to respect their parental authority. It is their competence and standards that ultimately give Outlier parents their relational power, but it is a power built on performance, not on attachment or emotional involvement. Outliers don't like things or people to be out of order, and they use their competence to enforce standards of conduct in those around them. This extends to their children, who do not want to feel their disapproval and rejection. To the degree that a hierarchy exists in this parent-child relationship, it is really more like a scaffolding of power. It has an empty interior.

Outliers spend most of their psychic energy repressing feelings. They ignore a lot, choose not to pursue matters of emotional difficulty, and are slow to become provoked by their children's acting out. When they are agitated beyond a certain point, however, they can have a strong and very critical way of expressing their disapproval. Preferring the moral high ground, their anger and disapproval carry a heavy chastisement and can cut to the quick. Consequently, their children learn to steer a wide path around them and to be careful not to provoke disapproval when they are with them.

In Outlier homes, an appropriate hierarchy exists, with parents on top, because the children tend to be emotionally insecure and unsettled. In pursuit of the elusive emotional connection they crave, they are highly motivated to please their Outlier parent and avoid disfavor, hoping somehow to find a way in through the walls separating them from the emotional life of their mother or father. Unfortunately, their cooperation is more about external pleasing than true internal self-control and solid emotional regulation. For these reasons, Outlier families sometimes look better on the surface, but the real story, below ground, can be an entirely different matter, and often a very troubling one.

Inside the homes of Outliers (especially if the Outlier parent is the mother), you will find a juxtaposition of orderliness and chaos. There is a lot of mischief going on behind the parent's back, as siblings tend to have ongoing discord that often escalates to physical fighting, and one child or another is usually trying to get someone to listen to him. But, at the same time, the table is most likely set, there is the smell of a good meal coming from the oven, and things are generally neat and tidy. When the kids slide into their places at the dinner table, they give a show of good manners and politeness rather than provoke a rebuke from their mother. After dinner, though, they quickly dart back to resume their mischief, knowing that Mom will stay in the kitchen and not poke around looking beyond the surface of anyone's behavior. If problems are brought to an Outlier's attention, she responds logically, in a task-oriented, no-nonsense way. An outlier's competence is limited to the business of the family, leaving her children to get away with a lot because no one is paying much attention.

The Language of the Outlier

Outliers are generally informed, well-read adults, but when it comes to relating personally and emotionally to their children, their communication is sparse and stingy. Praise, gratitude, complaints—adjectives in general—are largely missing from their communications. They rarely use the language of emotions, and for all their competency and organization, they aren't very insightful when it comes to discussing or analyzing matters from an emotional perspective. They express little curiosity about their children's inner lives, and so this rarely becomes a forum for any conversation. When emotional dynamics are clearly involved in a problem, the common refrain of the Outlier parent (delivered with a quizzical tone) is "I had no idea" followed by "I just don't understand."

Unlike Pleasers, who analyze every nuance and talk about every angle of their children's lives, Outliers don't talk to excess. Ruminating and processing are not practical. Their language tends to be action-oriented and concrete. It is rare for Outliers to ask "why" when trying to understand someone's inner motivation; their interest revolves around what to do about it rather than what caused it. They are quite concerned about respecting people's privacy and boundaries. This characteristic is another example of their interpersonal retreat as well as their preference for the moral high ground, and it ultimately supports their comfort with noninvolvement.

For Outliers, communication is not in service of the emotional process that must occur for deeper levels of knowing and understanding to be reached. Rather, their language and communication patterns prompt their children to be self-sufficient and learn how to grow up on their own. Outliers are more readily available for solutions and practical support than for empathetic, reflective, or insight-oriented conversations.

There are some words and phrases that are hard to come by in the language of the Outlier. They are not very free with "I love you," "I'm sorry," "I'd really like to talk about it," "I'd like to hear about it," or "I am worried about you." Acknowledgment of moods and feelings is quite minimal, and when they are acknowledged, the response is heavy on the intellectual side. On a positive note, because Outliers limit their emotional involvements, their children are spared the confusion of the emotional games and manipulations that pervade some parenting styles.

Outliers in Action versus Effective Parents in Action
SCENARIO ONE
An Outlier in Action

A seven-year-old girl has developed the habit of sleeping on the floor outside her parents' bedroom door. At first, her mother asks why she chooses to sleep on a hard cold floor when she could be sleeping in a warm soft bed. Her daughter says she just likes to. Her mother shrugs her shoulders in response and replies, "Well, okay, but be sure to take your pillow and blanket back to your room each morning." The next morning, finding her daughter asleep on the floor outside the bedroom door, she simply steps over the child on her way to make breakfast. At dinner sometimes, the little girl's older brother and sister tease her and laugh at her for sleeping outside of their parent's room. Her mother doesn't intervene in this teasing.

When the little girl is grown up, the story of her sleeping in the hallway has become part of family lore, retold with amusement. Even at this point in time, no one relates to the fact that her behavior reflected a child in need, including the woman herself.

What's Wrong with This Scenario?

The Outlier parent is not alert to the fact that her daughter's behavior is communicating that something is wrong. Children routinely rely on behavior to communicate their feelings, but with an Outlier parent, this is rarely considered or understood. In this case, the mother doesn't attend to her child's emotions and views her behavior as quirky and just a stage. She makes very little of it. In fact, she is nonplussed, concluding that somewhere down the road the behavior will resolve itself, and that is that. She shrugs her shoulders and says, "I don't understand it, but I suppose it's harmless."

The Effective Parent in Action

An effective parent would be disturbed to find her child sleeping on the floor outside her bedroom door and would take it seriously, knowing that it meant something was wrong. She would never allow this pattern to run its course, but at its first discovery would move in and help her child deal with her anxiety and get her back into her own bed and back to sound sleeping habits. Appropriate questions and care would be extended in order to understand and help her child with whatever was driving the problem.

SCENARIO TWO

An Outlier in Action

A ten-year-old boy is playing touch football with a group of friends in the backyard. They are making quite a ruckus, yelling and screaming, shoving and punching each other as they tackle. The mother is busy preparing dinner in the kitchen, where the window overlooks the backyard. She has heard and seen their increasing wildness, but she remains nonplussed until she glances out the window and catches sight of one of the boys diving to catch the ball and landing in her flower garden with all the boys following. Now she is concerned. She is quickly out the door and says, "Boys, game's over, at least in this backyard. I'm not going to have you trampling my flowers. Now out you go." The boys file out through the gate to find a new place to play.

What's Wrong with This Scenario

As the escalating noise and the physicality of the game increased, adult intervention was needed to protect the kids from getting hurt and the neighbors from being disturbed by very loud play. This mother remained uninvolved, as if not registering the potential for harm. It takes the well-being of her flowers to motivate this parent's action.

The Effective Parent in Action

Hearing all the noise, the effective parent intervenes, both out of respect for the neighbors and to make sure no one gets hurt in the game. She tells the kids they can keep playing, but they have to keep the noise down, and it has to be touch football, not tackle. Then she calls her son over to her and says to him one-on-one, "James, I don't want anybody to get hurt. Come on, you've got to help keep things from getting wild. I am going to keep my eye out, and if the game gets out of line again, you'll have to find something else to do."

The Children of Outlier Parents

Rather than developing a truly rich and solid emotional life, the children of Outliers learn to keep their troubles hidden. Although they do act out and find their way into considerable mischief, it is usually not in view of their parent. Knowing that the Outliers won't come looking for problems, their children tend to get on a slippery slope that leads to more and more self-destructive behavior, with no internal or external brakes to stop the slide.

If the child of an Outlier is angry with his parent, the parental inter-pretation is that something is wrong with the child, because certainly there could not be any reason for him to be angry at his good, hard-working parent. Because Outliers are not organized to think relation-ally or dynamically, their children internalize the message that their temper tantrums, anger, and misbehaviors are due to being rambunc-tious and high-strung. The Outlier parent shakes her head, shrugs her shoulders, and looks askance, as if to say: "There he goes again; that's Johnny for you!" The message is clear that the badness is inside the child, and there isn't much to be done about it. Due to this hands-off style, children of Outliers tend to become unregulated in feeling and action. They can be easily frustrated, have tantrums, and find it difficult to settle down.

To some degree, the children of Outliers can't help becoming Outliers themselves. They have a difficult time accounting for their feel-ings and are not very reflective about the feelings of others. Because they were given little relational empathy as they were growing up, they, in turn, have not developed much empathy themselves. Children of Outliers frequently answer feeling-centered questions in my office with "I don't know" and a lot of shoulder shrugs. They are rather nonplussed about their own troubles and are hard to reach at an emotional level.

Children of Outliers usually do not get enough touching and hugging. They are emotionally needy, but they learn rather young not to seek comfort or understanding from their Outlier parent. It is somewhat of a consolation that these children disconnect early from their emotional experience, because it is a rather lonely and disturbing one. But it doesn't stop there; the disconnection follows them into young adulthood because they simply don't have the capacity to acknowledge or address their emotional needs. Consequently, they have a hard time with the mutuality and consideration that are at the very heart of partnership. They are independent operators, not because they want distance but because that's what they know.

Addictive behavior, whether it involves alcohol, drugs, work, or exercise, is a common feature of adult children of Outliers, as they keep turning to something external to regulate and repress their feelings. In true Outlier fashion, however, they have very little connection to the fact that whatever it is that they are doing in excess is a form of compensation. If you ask an alcoholic Outlier what he is trying to drown out with so much drinking, he would probably say, "Drown out? I'm not drowning out anything; I just like my beer." Children of Outliers have learned to stay out of their own feelings. They heed the warning: Do Not Trespass.

The tragedy of the Outlier parenting style—and all the others described above, for that matter—is that in each case parents are doing what they think is right, doing the best they can on behalf of their children, whom they love very much. They don't realize the harm they are causing and can't see the vicious cycles of relationship in which they are trapped.

The Good News about All Parenting Styles

As a parent, you may find it hard to believe that you are falling short in your role as an effective authority figure and may be surprised to hear the echoes of your own voice as I've described the various parenting styles. We hope you will have experienced moments of recognition as you've read this chapter—the "Aha!" that so many others in my practice have had. These identifying, crystallizing moments are the foundation upon which you can build new strength and effectiveness as a parent. Despite the broad-reaching impact of ineffective parenting styles on our children, the good news is you don't need to undergo a total personality overhaul to make things better and to reverse the imbalance of power in your family. Regardless of your temperamental inclinations or how you have been relating to your child, by understanding the dynamics of power in

The Ladder: Five Steps to Raising Self-Controlled, Respectful, and Cooperative Children

How do you stop turning over power to your children and learn to stem IFP—the tide of power imbalances in your family? Understanding the problem is key; what to do about it is really the heart of the matter. Parents and children need help.

In the next three chapters, I will teach you the Ladder, an easy-to-follow five-step *action* plan that effectively counters the protests and oppositions of young children and establishes you as a respected leader and a loving parent, sitting comfortably atop your family hierarchy. The Ladder is designed to keep parents firmly but lovingly in the lead, which is just where their children need them to be. It prevents IFP from developing and corrects it if it has already taken root.

With its step-by-step guide on what to do and say, the Ladder makes time-out more effective. It goes beyond the traditional time-out method by giving parents definitive responses to manage the more intense, out-of-control behaviors that are so common in children today. Regardless of your parenting style, the Ladder will give you the help you need.

I developed the Ladder over the course of many years of working with children and families in my private practice. Parents were telling me they had read every book they could find and had tried every technique they knew of to help restore some semblance of order to their chaotic households and topsy-turvy relationships with their children. I listened carefully to the stories parents repeated about how their children were beyond their control: "He won't sleep in his own bed." "He won't poop in the potty." "He just won't listen." In particular, they lamented how time-out did not work. Their children were refusing to stay in the time-out chair, the naughty corner, or in their bedrooms. From what I was being told and seeing myself, kids were spiraling out of control as their parents tried to be firmer with them and hold the line. Situations were going from bad to worse.

As I listened to these parents' stories about how their children protested and acted out, the details became increasingly familiar and even predictable. As a result, the Ladder took shape as a means to help parents know what to do and say so as not to get run over and done in by their children's protests and refusals. The success parents had using the Ladder quickly became apparent. It works, and it generally works in short order.

No matter what your parenting style, you will be able to achieve effectiveness by climbing the Ladder. Of course, when parents are effective, so are their children. Much more than a discipline strategy, the Ladder helps create healthier, more secure parent-child relationships. It puts kids right where they want to be—in the safe harbor of parental competence and leadership, where kids thrive.

Chapter Four

Preparing to Climb the Ladder

The Ladder is a discipline sequence that effectively contains the natural drive within children for influence and power. It is an essential tool for effective parenting that generates confidence in the parents who use it and establishes them as respected authorities with their children. It is an antidote to parental tentativeness, accommodation, and impotence. The Ladder goes a long way toward reducing the frustration and blowups that destroy the loving and good feelings between parents and children. Once you begin using the Ladder, your children may not be pleased at first that things aren't going their way, but all kids yearn for parents who are competent—and they actually like being reined in. As a result of using the Ladder, your child will become secure in the certainty that you are up to the job of managing him, and it is in this relational context that he will be calmest, most assured, and self-controlled. As if that isn't good enough, your child will also be happier and more affectionate! And so will you.

How the Ladder Works

The Ladder Goes Beyond Time-Out

Time-out has dominated the discipline efforts of most parents for over twenty years, yet it has not completely addressed children's resistant behaviors. Why are so many parents still using time-out and failing? The short answer is that parents have not understood the dynamics of power in the parent-child relationship or the pitfalls of an imbalance in family power (IFP). Each primary parenting style shapes how a parent implements discipline and employs time-out. Pleasers talk too much and want to make time-out nice and agreeable; Pushovers plead for adherence to the program, but can't hold it and wind up taking the time-out themselves; Forcers use too much force, making time-out more like jail time; and Outliers are too often involved in other things to use time-out, let alone make it work.

Furthermore, time-out is a technique that is limited in addressing the needs of frantic, out-of-control children. It only offers one response—to put your child in time-out and hope he stays in it. The only variations in time-out are *where* you put your child (for example, the time-out chair) and for *how long*. For many children, being left alone offers no help and only serves to disorganize them and rev them up more, with no parental containment or help nearby. In addition, now that IFP is so common, very often it is the kids who determine the course of time-out: where they go and how long they stay. The Ladder brings parents into the process and teaches them how to confidently assist their children in settling down. Since the Ladder entails an incremental progression of responses, it provides parents with a way to match their responses to what their children are doing.

The Ladder incorporates time-out but it also goes beyond that. It provides parents with the details that have been missing about how to effectively implement the technique, as well as two additional steps that respond to their children's refusals to cooperate. The existing protocol for time-out is incomplete. There have never been fully developed guidelines on how to use or enforce it, so parents often get stuck because they don't really know what they are supposed to do. I am always asked myriad questions by frustrated parents about how to use time-out: How many times should you ask for cooperation before you actually put a child in time-out? Should you count to three as a warning? How about ten? Should children sit in the corner or in a chair or go to their rooms? How long should a child stay in time-out? Should you use a timer? Once you get your child to the time-out spot, what do you do if she screams and yells? What do you do if a child won't stay in time-out? What if a child gets really angry when you exercise your authority and the situation escalates to the point of being out of control?

You may say, "Time-out just doesn't work for my child." Well, the truth is, it doesn't work for most kids when they have too much power. All of these unanswered questions about time-out, its limited scope, and the fact that it has never been taught within the context of power dynamics help explain why it has been so ineffective. The Ladder goes beyond time-out. It guides parents to effectiveness by filling in each of these gaps.

The Ladder is effective because it teaches children in an action-based context, which is how the lessons of self-control and cooperation are learned. Talking and conversation are limited while using the Ladder, but what parents do say is perfectly targeted to take power away from their children's negative behavior. The Ladder arms parents with the tactics and know-how to address the wide array of oppositional, negative, and escalated behaviors that children commonly use to test parental power. Since you will have learned how essential it is for your authority to prevail in the face of his protests, mastering the technique of the Ladder will prepare you to handle whatever your child throws at you. At the same time, the Ladder will help you strengthen a warm, secure bond with your children, which is equally important.

The Ladder Is a Strategy, Not a Punishment

The Ladder is not a punishment. It is not to be used as a threat or a means for parental retribution. It is not meant to teach children a lesson through fear or suffering. All four styles of parenting are too focused on providing a punishment for bad behavior, rather than addressing the more important task of proactively teaching their children while establishing their own parental leadership and authority.

Punishment, by design, makes kids feel bad, so it leaves some toxic byproducts: hurt, anger, and revenge. While I know children never like to have their agenda thwarted, they won't store up anger and resentment when you climb the Ladder—and neither will you. In fact, because it is respectful and supportive, the Ladder breaks the vicious cycle of bad blood and returns goodwill to children, as well as motivating them to please and cooperate. If the Ladder is distorted and used as a punishment or threat, it will backfire, reinforcing the problems and bad feelings between you and your child that you are so pointedly trying to correct. The Ladder cannot be seen as a last resort to use when parents are gripped by the fury of mounting impotence. The Ladder is a controlled and respectful form of parental help for containing and redirecting the drive all children excercise to have it their way.

PARENTING TRAP

Using Harsh Discipline Instead of Respectful Discipline

Misunderstanding the difference between discipline and punishment is a common parent pitfall. Discipline is about teaching, directing, and correcting, while punishment is about delivering an unpleasant consequence to unwanted behavior. Too many parents rely on punishment and have the notion that the more their children dislike a consequence, the more corrective the punishment will be, i.e., the more they suffer, they more they will learn. They often have a knee-jerk response that says: Hit them where it hurts. They lash out, taking away television for a week or making children stay in their rooms for the rest of the day, saying, "I don't even want to see you!"

Sadly, a punishment orientation can escalate to startlingly cruel measures. For example, parents have told me of making their child throw a favorite stuffed animal into the fire; throwing away clothing that was left on the floor; making a child sit in the bathtub for a time-out because it is uncomfortable; biting a child so he can "see how it feels"; and squirting soft soap into a child's mouth and making him hold it there for thirty seconds. When parents are the overt and deliberate architects of their children's suffering, the lessons of self-control, feelings of respect, and the motivation to cooperate are lost altogether.

Climbing the Ladder Does Not Leave Love Behind

Loving your children is not related in any way, shape, or form to letting them set the agenda. Always playing the music your child wants to hear in the car, letting him sleep in his clothes if he really wants to, serving meals only in the dishes he likes best, lying down with him until he falls asleep every night—these indulgences are not indications of committed or loving parenting. Giving unconditional love to your child does not mean you have to suspend standards and expectations.

Parents have asked me, "But what is so wrong with my seven-year-old sleeping in her clothes? They don't wrinkle and it makes the morning rush less hectic." Or, "I really don't mind lying down with my four-year-old until he falls asleep! I actually enjoy the special time with him." The point is not how these behaviors affect the parents and whether they mind doing them or not. The significance lies in the relational importance of parents being in the lead and not compromising their better judgment. Let's be honest: no parent initiates these practices, having decided they are the best practices for their child; they come about because parents collapse wearily into them in the face of their child's incessant demands. Then parents rationalize and try to convince themselves that doing so really isn't such a big deal after all. But it is.

Climbing the Ladder does not leave love behind as it gives children what they need most: the loving with the leading. It supports the twin pillars of effective parenting, not just one. The Ladder harnesses the natural power within parents, rather than relying on external sources.

The Ladder is not a gimmick or a quick fix. There are no timers, bells, charts, notes to write, or M&M's to be earned. There is nothing to post on the refrigerator. The Ladder does not ask parents to rely on external props, bribes, threats, or rationales to manipulate children into compliance. The Ladder is simply a vehicle for the parent to exercise his natural authority and competence directly with his child. Children respond quickly and positively to its use because they really do prefer a competent parent who will show them the way, rather than one who goes through endless rounds of begging and pleas for cooperation.

The Ladder Prevents and Corrects IFP

If your children are very young and you are just establishing yourself as a parental authority, the Ladder will ensure you do so successfully, one small step at a time, keeping pace with your child as he tries to expand his boundaries. If you are among those families in the midst of a power imbalance, the Ladder will provide the answer you have been looking for to stop the upset and restore the peace. If you are already, by instinct, on the path to effective parenting, the Ladder will be a complementary tool that you can use to hone and reinforce your skills.

Using the Ladder to *correct* an imbalance of family power will likely be quite different from using it to *prevent* an imbalance of family power! Prevention is always easier than correction. When correcting IFP, you will be breaking the grip your child has on the power and influence that should be yours. Don't expect him to let go of it easily—no child ever does. In fact, children often ratchet up their protests in reaction to parental strength. No child gives up her power willingly—the longer she has occupied the family throne, the bigger the struggle when her regime is overthrown. It is also true that some children have a more tenacious power drive than others, and so will not give up the fight without a fairly dramatic struggle.

As a parent on the front line of change, you should have a realistic expectation of the resistance and protest your child may kick up as you assert your authority and leadership in a stronger, more effective way. What makes this approach manageable is how quickly children start to respond. Typically, after only two or three times of climbing the Ladder with your child, you will see her exercising more self-control, more respect, and more cooperation. Ultimately, the Ladder will allow you to protect your children from the turmoil of too much power and also help save them if they already have it.

Entering the Correction Phase

When a family hierarchy is characterized by an imbalance of power (IFP), where the kids have too much power and parents have too little, shifting children out of their power positions typically causes increased struggles before things settle down. Parents need to anticipate this and be primed and ready for what is to come. I refer to this initial period of change as the *correction phase.* I recommend that parents be thoughtful and practical about when they are going to start their correction program.

As I've stated before, no child gives up his power willingly, and the more you have given him, the stronger his reaction will be when you take it away. In particular, Pleasers and Pushovers will be bombarded with loud cries from their children of how mean and unfair they are being. Princes and princesses like to admonish their mom or dad with threats of their own, such as "You are not my friend anymore," or "I will not give you a hug until you say you are sorry," and "You are not my best Mommy anymore." Don't forget that in translation, all these dramatic exclamations are your child's way of saying, "I don't like what you are doing." It is nothing more frightening or serious than that. So hang in there! Remember, your child won't be accustomed to your steadfastness as you use the Ladder, so he will think if he just pushes harder, or protests louder, or gets sadder and acts more injured, you surely will give in, just as you have done so many times in the past. I know you are not going to collapse, but he won't know, until you prove it to him.

Over many years of teaching the Ladder to parents, I have identified four preparatory steps that will optimize your effectiveness, as well as your child's receptiveness, to the correction phase:

1. Make the commitment
2. Set the tone for cooperation
3. Choose the when and where
4. Hold to the structure and the script.

Make the Commitment

You are going to embark on a program to modify your parenting style and secure your position as a leader with your children. Understanding the central role power plays in all parent-child relationships has informed you why this change is necessary. This holds true for both parents. A thorough rebalancing of power will not occur if only one parent has mastered the philosophy and made the commitment to strong and effective parenting.

Because the correction phase can be a time when the cure temporarily worsens the problem, it is important for you to make a commitment to hold fast. Old habits die just as hard for parents as they do for children, so don't be tempted to revert to your old scripts. Once you have started climbing the Ladder with your child, you must not step out of the sequence until *you* have prevailed, not your child. Take heed: If you go halfway and then give in, you reinforce stronger and stronger displays of protest in your child. Essentially, you will be teaching him that you have a breaking point and that all he has to do is keep up the fight until you reach it. If this is what he thinks, he will try more and more outrageous measures to keep up the protest, thinking it will ultimately work. That is why making a commitment to see the process through to the end is essential.

Set the Tone for Cooperation

Maintaining a tone free from irritability and anger is critical when implementing the Ladder. Children become more agitated and out of control if you treat them harshly and disrespectfully. If you are tentative and have little confidence in your authority, your child will know it in a minute and will quickly take the power you cede. You want to create an environment where cooperation is most likely to thrive. Your children will want to please you the most when they respect and admire you. If you are competent and strong and also loving and respectful, then your child's motivation to cooperate and work with you will be at its highest.

Many parents, because they do not move quickly enough into action, become fed up with repeating themselves over and over and not getting cooperation. This leads to parents using time-out as a threat. Through clenched teeth they threaten: "If you don't stop it and start listening right now you are going to get a time-out." Or, they may wait until they blow up, and then yell, "That's it! You have pushed me too far. Now, you have to have a time-out!" This is not the emotional stance you want when redirecting and correcting your young children.

Communicating in a serious, respectful, matter-of-fact tone is best. You want to convey clearly and in a good-natured way that you are your child's biggest supporter but that you are also comfortably in charge: you are the leader and he is the one that needs to follow, without exception. The Ladder will help you exercise parental control and remain calm, so that you do not need to resort to a bullying style. The steps of the Ladder always keep you in the lead, effectively responding to your child's challenges. They leave little room for your child to doubt whether you are up to the job of parenting him. You want your child to learn to be confident of your authority, not feel threatened, shamed, or harshly criticized by it.

Choose the When and Where

It's essential to make a realistic assessment of how much volatility will be provoked in your child when you begin to hold him to a line of standards and expectations. Parents who know their son or daughter will dig in can expect the initial days of the correction phase to keep them very busy. If this is the case, or if you prefer to be totally focused, I recommend that you start the correction phase on a weekend when your schedule is free and without other diversions. If the IFP is pronounced or your child has a strong power drive, it can be helpful to ask family and friends to take your other children on an outing or to their homes to play on the first day or two, just to make it easier on everyone.

The evening before you begin the correction phase, sit down with your child and let him know you have something important to tell him. You might say:

> "Honey, there has been a lot of arguing and upset between us lately, and neither of us enjoys these struggles. One of the most important things in a family is for children to learn respect, self-control, and cooperation. That includes our family, and that includes you. So, beginning tomorrow, we are going to be making some changes. Together we will change things for the better, and the whole family will be happier."

Notice how saying less is more and how the message remains positive. This is classic powerful parenting in action. If your child presses you for more detail, simply tell him you are not going to discuss it any further, but you want him to be reassured that things will be improving. Remember...

- ✤ **PLEASERS.** This is not an invitation for you to sit down with your child and launch into a discussion about the imbalance of power in the family or to ask her if she feels secure in your parenting.
- ✤ **PUSHOVERS.** Do not tell your child that "the doctor in the book" says parents have to be the boss and you really need him to cooperate.
- ✤ **FORCERS.** Keep your tone soft and friendly. Don't make the new program sound like a prison sentence.
- ✤ **OUTLIERS.** Stop what you're doing and go over to your child. Take his hands in yours and tell him you are going to help him make some changes that will make everyone happier.

Hold to the Structure and to the Script

In the beginning as you use the Ladder, your child won't be accustomed to your steadfastness and will challenge it. The interventions and script at each step of the Ladder have been carefully constructed to ensure that parents will prevail, no matter what their children try. You will discover, as so many parents have reported to me in the past, that the sequence will unfold with your child just the way I say it will. The Ladder anticipates their reactions and is designed to respond effectively to them. Stay focused and stick to the script so that you do not fall back into old habits while you are strengthening your competence and authority. You must continue to implement the Ladder without giving your child any wiggle room. The correction won't occur efficiently or effectively if you are inconsistent in employing it. After a few weeks, or when you have hit a comfortable stride, you will naturally start making this technique your own.

Once you have achieved your child's cooperation, you can loosen up a bit and be a bit more flexible in what you say and do—as long as he remains respectful and is willing to comply. The correction phase ends once you have reestablished your power and authority and harmony begins to characterize your relationship. At this point, keep paying close attention to your child's behavior and tighten or loosen your adherence to the Ladder as needed. Realistically, you can expect to see the beginning of a change in your child's behavior by the end of the second day. At this stage, while they might still have a long way to go, most parents report feeling very excited and empowered by what is happening in their relationship with their child. We hope you will feel this too, and it will help you maintain your dedication to the program.

Chapter Five

The Five Steps of the Ladder

To ensure that you keep your resolve and do not falter on the way up the Ladder, be thoroughly familiar with what to do and say at each step. Read through all the steps first and make sure you know them. You don't want to get stuck once you've started climbing and risk compromising your authority all over again.

Step One: A Friendly Bid for Cooperation

The starting point of most disciplinary interactions is when a parent asks a child either to do something or to stop doing something. This request may pertain, as well, to what a child is saying and how he is saying it.

Here, as at every step of the Ladder, the words you use and the attitude you convey by the tone of your voice will be of central importance. Your Step One directive should be given in the manner of a friendly bid for cooperation. Because so many parents are frustrated by their previous experiences of impotence and ineffectiveness, their first bids for cooperation are often anything but friendly. Too often, their words and tone convey irritation, harshness, and the feeling that they don't really expect their child to cooperate. What the child hears is a bid for battle, rather than cooperation. This is why it is so important to get rid of your anger and irritation and pay attention to the tone you use. Maintaining a good-humored, supportive, and confident tone is especially important if you've been caught in the trap of being too harsh and too negative with your child. If this is the case, it is imperative that you make a conscious effort to reestablish a good feeling between you. To start off on a positive note, use a cheery, upbeat tone in Step One. Using a pet name or term of endearment when addressing your child helps soften your request. The script for Step One is:

> "Hey, buddy, it's time to turn off the TV now and wash your hands for dinner."

Or

> "Sweet pea, it is time for you to pick up your toys and begin getting ready for bed."

Don't be put off if your child is negative and surly in response to your good spirits. Remember, this is only Step One, and chances are you have been tussling for a while. Be patient and don't collapse into negativity. Staying positive, supportive, and good-humored, especially when dealing with a child who doesn't seem to deserve your goodwill, is an important part of the correction effort. These are the little ones who actually need your positive tone most.

Once you have delivered your bid for cooperation, pay attention to your child's response. If she does not comply within a reasonable amount of time (it could be anywhere from twenty to sixty seconds, depending upon the circumstances surrounding your request), it is time to move on to Step Two. If your child does cooperate, you can bask in the glow of effective parenting and family harmony! Your work this time around is done.

Step Two: An "I Mean Business" Reminder

Step Two is both a reminder and a statement of consequence. A different tone and posture are required from those used in Step One. Your child has not responded to your authority, so now it is time to let him know that you mean business and his failure to cooperate is not going to be accepted.

Before saying anything, though, take a few steps closer to your child. Or, if you are already standing next to him, move or bend down so you are more directly in his line of vision. For example, if you were standing in the doorway of your family room during Step One, before saying the script for Step Two, take a few steps into the room towards your child. Then change your tone from upbeat and friendly to attention-getting and businesslike. This time, don't address your child using a pet name; use his full first name. The script for Step Two is:

> "Will (or Jennifer): I just said that it was time for the television to be turned off and your hands washed for dinner. This is the second time I am saying it. If you need yet another reminder, then you will be heading to your room."

I prefer using the phrase "if you need yet another reminder" instead of "if I have to tell you again" because it is more pleasant and respectful. You don't need to be heavy-handed when referring to the consequence of failing to comply at this step. Being both helpful and matter-of-fact, you are telling your child what your actions will be. It is important not to sound threatening with your word choice or tone. Instead, you just put it out there: "You'll be heading to your room."

If your child has developed a habit of ignoring your requests, then it will be helpful at this time to change your body language as well as your tone. Cocking your head to one side, raising your eyebrows, and focusing your eyes directly on your child—while at the same time raising your hand and pointing your index finger up in the air—will help underscore that you mean business, and that your child needs to take notice and act.

For some children, the reminder and foreshadowing of consequence in Step Two will be all they need. For many others, more action and direction will be needed from you. If you do not get your child's cooperation after giving your "I mean business reminder" only once, then proceed to Step Three.

PARENTING TRAP

Off-Putting Attitudes

Do not insist that your child look at you or acknowledge that he has heard you. Not looking at you in no way interferes with your child's ability to hear you, and besides, he needs to learn that it is his responsibility to tune in when you are speaking to him. You don't need to make harsh demands such as, "Look at me when I'm talking to you!" or "Did you hear what I said? Answer me!" These demands are too heavy-handed and aren't necessary. Parents with a Forcer style sometimes step right into a power struggle by insisting that their child look at them or acknowledge that they have heard them. This is counterproductive and moves the focus away from your child's primary responsibility, which is to comply with your request. Worse, it sets the child up with the power to dismiss you.

On the other hand, don't rely too often on reasoning and being nice as a primary strategy to persuade your child to respect your authority. Democratic parents and permissive parents are often tempted to keep repeating their child's name, or asking politely for their attention, for example, "William, William? Please will you look at me, honey, when I am speaking to you?" or "William, honey, Mommy needs you to do something important, so I need you to listen to me. Okay, honey? Will you listen to Mommy?" This is being too deferential to your child. Do not dilute your authority by talking, explaining, or asking your child to look at or to listen to you. Stick to the script of the Ladder, and stay calm and on task. You must give your child the opportunity to learn that your authority has to be respected and that you will settle for nothing less.

Step Three: To the Bedroom

Always allow your child two opportunities to work with you, but after that there are no more chances for your child to follow your request without going to his room. Remember, in Step Two you have just said, "If you need yet another reminder, you will be heading to your room." So that is exactly what must happen next. No more talking, it is time for action.

Remember, cooperation is an action-based lesson first and foremost. The action of having your child go to his room is essential to underscore that your words are not empty ones. There must be an action-based consequence for noncooperation, not just louder or nastier words or threats. Also, it is counterproductive to linger—it just gives your child more wiggle room, and the interaction inevitably gets messier. Your child needs to go to his room now, and it's up to you to make it happen.

The instructions for Step Three are divided into two parts. Read through the entire lesson before you start, because it covers a host of parenting traps to avoid.

Step Three, Part 1: Take Your Child to His Room

Step Three begins with action, not words. It is very important that you walk over to your child, so that you are right next to him, before you say anything. In this step, as in all the others, your demeanor should never be threatening or angry: Your tone and body language should be supportive and convey an "Oh well, so be it" attitude. Or use a tone that communicates that you are a bit surprised that your child hasn't chosen to cooperate, but that's fine; off to his room it will be. Once you have walked over to your child, use the following script:

"Okay, that's it, off you go to your bedroom."

While delivering this directive, place your hand on your child's arm or behind his shoulders and guide him towards his room.

PARENTING TRAP

Don't Repeat Yourself of Threaten

Do not repeat yourself a third, fourth, fifth, or sixth time before you act. If you do, the message your child will hear is: "I know you probably will not cooperate because I have no real authority, but I'm going to keep trying." With every repetition of the same request, you underscore your impotence. Instead, your child should be offered one friendly bid for cooperation, and then one "I mean business reminder." And that is all. This is a key sequence in the Ladder: say it once, give a reminder, and then act. One, two, *act*.

Do not use going to the bedroom as a threat by saying, "Okay, you will have to go to your room. Did you hear what I said? Do you want to have to go to your room?" By reverting to threats in order to get his cooperation, you are telling your child that you really don't know how to enforce your authority and are just hoping you can threaten him enough to get him to cooperate.

HOW TO HANDLE PLEADING AND BEGGING

Don't give in when your child begs to be given just one more chance. Often the children of pleasers and pushovers will play to their parent's good-hearted sense of fair treatment and plead: "I was just going to—please, please let me have one more chance, it's not fair!" or cry, "I will, I will! Okay, I will! You have to give me more of a chance!" When this protest occurs, the best response is to say with a positive and supportive tone:

> "That's good, honey, you were just about to! Next time, I am confident you won't wait quite so long, because you will remember I only ask twice. Now, come on then, this time you do have to go to your room."

Say no more.

Don't respond negatively or defensively to children who say things along the lines of "You can't do this! You're being so mean! Stop it! Go away!" With a very light tone, set your child straight, and keep the interaction on your terms by saying:

> "No, sweetie, I am not being mean or unfair. I asked twice, and you did not cooperate. Now it's off to your room you go."

Say no more. If your child tries to derail you by saying angry and mean things, or by pleading and begging as you take him to his room, do not respond. It is important not to let yourself get pulled into any of your child's verbal efforts to engage you in his power ploys. Once you have started escorting your child to his bedroom, don't say anything further until he is on his bed.

If your child won't go to his room under his own steam, and you have to carry him, move quickly and deliberately. Speed is of the essence, as it is part of demonstrating your effective power. It also helps prevent the situation from becoming more out of control and keeps the fanfare to a minimum. If his verbal protests escalate into flailing, then bring one of his arms close to your body and with your free hand, gently but firmly hold the wrist of his other arm down at his side.

TWO DON'TS WHEN YOUR CHILD NEEDS
TO BE IN HIS ROOM

1. Don't think that for your child to be effectively disciplined, he has to suffer in some way. This perspective leads parents to question whether it is an adequate deterrent for a child to spend time in his bedroom. In other words, will it be an effective setting for punishment if it is filled with toys and things he likes to do? There is no need to worry about this. Remember, you are the source of the corrective power, not the number of minutes or the setting. It is actually a positive outcome if your child spends his time in his

room being self-controlled, calm, and playing appropriately by himself. You have successfully responded to his noncompliance on your terms, and he is not combative or out of control. Nor are you making him feel bad. If, however, you have put a television, a computer, and/or an electronic gaming system (e.g., Nintendo GameCube) in your child's bedroom, I would recommend you remove any and all of these items as your first course of action. Electronic entertainment, as a general rule, is highly stimulating, and for many children it can have an almost addictive quality. These entertainments require parental monitoring and regulation and will definitely detract from the effectiveness of using the bedroom as a place to foster self-control and self-containment. Otherwise, consider it fine for your child to go to his room and become absorbed in a self-directed activity such as reading a book or playing with a toy that interests him.

2. Don't override the recommendation of using the bedroom and opt for bringing your child to a corner, the basement, or the garage, thinking these locations will make a stronger statement that you really mean business. While it is true that your child requires firm and consistent consequences, it is certainly not true that you need to make your child suffer before he learns to respect your authority. And this is precisely what will happen if you bring your child to one of these locations. If we routinely erode and break down the way our kids feel, how can this help them grow up strong and secure, let alone want to cooperate?

Step Three, Part 2: Set the Terms

Once you have walked or carried your child to his room, sit him down on the bed. Say matter-of-factly:

> "Now you need to stay in your room until I tell you that it's time to come out."

You have now set the terms. This is all that needs to be said. Do not explain further, provide justifications, or get caught in a back and forth with your child. Ignore his protests and bids to keep you hooked into an argument with him and simply walk out of the room.

It is very important that you do not let your child decide when he is ready to leave his room. For example, don't say, "Now stay in here until you can behave," or "You must stay in your room until you can cooperate and be a nice boy." Using this language is a classic mistake for two reasons: First, by saying this, you are transferring power back to your child. The key to having power and authority is that you remain in charge from the beginning to the end of every disciplinary interaction you initiate. When you instruct your child to stay in his room until he thinks he can behave, you are in essence saying, "I am now putting you in charge of deciding how long you need to stay in your room so you can have some introspective time to think about your behavior." This sets up more trouble because young children don't have a clue about reflecting on their readiness for cooperation. No child is going to sit and think about the bad thing he did. On the contrary, his thoughts will be full of how unfair you are. So, stick to being the leader. This is what really gets the job done.

As you leave the room, be sure to leave the door open. Do not go far, though, because your child may still need more assistance from you to gain appropriate self-control, in which case you will need to go to the next step of the Ladder. Remain close to the doorway, but position yourself in such a way that your child cannot see you. It is time to leave him to do the work of exercising self-control, respect, and cooperation.

Let's recap the script for Step Three:

Part 1: "Okay, that's it, off you go to your bedroom."

Part 2: "Now you need to stay in your room until I tell you that it's time to come out."

Step Four: Shut the Door

At this stage of the Ladder, one of three things will invariably happen. Your child will either (1) stay in his room and complete an appropriate time-out, (2) stay in his room but act out by screaming, wailing, and being verbally obnoxious, or (3) dismiss your directive altogether and run out of the room. This is the step where parents feel at a loss and where traditional time-out has failed to guide an effective response. The Ladder teaches specific responses to each of the three scenarios.

STEP FOUR, SCENARIO 1: YOUR CHILD REMAINS IN HIS ROOM APPROPRIATELY

When your child has been in his room for the time period you have designated, and has kept within the boundaries of acceptable time-out behavior, end the disciplinary intervention by simply poking your head into the room and saying:

> "Okay, honey, your time in your room is finished. You can come out now."

Parents are often uncertain about what constitutes appropriate behavior from a young child who has been taken to his room for a time-out. As long as your child remains relatively calm and quite, this is sufficient. If he is on his bed crying softly, or muttering to himself about how unfair you are, or that he was just about to do what you'd asked him to do, this is perfectly fine as well. There is no need to intervene further.

If your child's refusal to perform a task (such as picking up toys) led to your using the Ladder, then it is time for another bid for cooperation. For example:

> "Come on, let's go. Now, where were we? Oh yes, you have some toys to pick up."

Have a smile on your face as you give this directive and keep any tone of anger or irritation out of your voice. Really, there shouldn't be any: You are dealing with a little child after all, and a child's failure to comply is hardly anything for an adult to get worked up about. Keep your perspective and your cool—and remember that teaching and disciplining your child is at the heart of your job as a parent. Don't let it get to you.

Having a good-natured demeanor when ending the disciplinary interaction is particularly important if frequent battles have dominated your interactions. You don't want to give your child the message that you are overwhelmed or angry about having to parent him. So, start with a clean slate and a respectful, fun bid for cooperation. If your child still fails to cooperate with your directive, start climbing the Ladder again:

> "Oh my, this is the second time I am saying it, I thought for sure you would be ready to cooperate. Well, just remember, I only say things twice."

PARENTING TIP

How Long Should a Child Stay in His Room?

As a rule of thumb, I recommend that you add two or three minutes to the age of your child. Don't fall into the trap, however, of thinking that if seven minutes will work, well then, twenty minutes will work even better. If you make too long a time demand on your child, you will set him up for failure. Some parents like the idea of using a timer to keep track of the passing time and frequently ask me if they should. The answer is no, definitely not. First of all, it overemphasizes the importance of the actual time. What your child learns should come from you and through your ability to prevail. There is no corrective power in a timer or in a certain number of minutes. The time a child spends in his room does not need to be exact. Also, when you set a timer and then leave, this takes the parent out of the discipline process, which is the opposite of what is corrective. The effectiveness of the Ladder comes from the parent setting and holding the agenda every step of the way from the first bid for cooperation through to the end.

THREE DON'TS FOLLOWING TIME IN THE BEDROOM

1. Don't launch into a post-discipline analysis after your child has completed the designated time in his room. In other words, don't go and sit next to your child and ask questions such as, "Honey, do you understand why Mommy was mad at you?" "Do you understand what you did wrong?" "Do you know why Mommy had to put you in a time-out?" These questions are problematic for several reasons. First, if you have disciplined appropriately, then your child's awareness of what he did is a given. Secondly, the correction happens because you are enforcing limits, not just talking about them. Such a discussion is too democratic, and if you ask if your child understands why you had to put him in time-out, it communicates to the child that you are a reluctant and almost apologetic authority. It's almost as if your real message is, "You know, honey, if it were up to me, I would never assert my authority and put you in time-out, but you make me have to do it." Emotional processing gives routine childishness, and the necessary parenting it requires, far too much weight and importance.

2. Don't feel the need to reassure your child of your love for him when you let him out of his room. Some parents want to say, "You know Mommy loves you, don't you? It is just that sometimes I don't like the way you behave." There is no need for your child to be reassured, let alone to be reassured of your love. Nothing traumatic has happened. You have simply held him to a standard of cooperation and let him know there is no wiggle room in the matter. This is standard, run-of-the-mill parent-child fare, and asking your child if he is still certain of your love makes this interaction seem anything but ordinary. What your child will hear loud and clear is that you are anxious and uncertain in your role as his parent and authority. Stick with the script of the Ladder.

3. Don't take the bait and enter into a struggle if your child responds to your statement that he can leave his room with more protest:

"No! I don't want to! I am not coming out." Your child obviously has remained angry and defiant while in his room and is still invested in regaining the upper hand and rejecting your authority. Your response should be simple and straightforward: "Okay, that's fine. I just wanted to let you know that as far as I am concerned, the time when you have to stay in your room is finished." That's all. And then go about your business. With these words you remind your child that you are in control. And if there is a task that still has to be completed, redirect your child to it when he comes out of his room.

STEP FOUR, SCENARIO 2: YOUR CHILD REMAINS IN HIS ROOM BUT ACTS OUT VERBALLY

It is not considered reasonable time-out behavior if your child is yelling loudly and carrying on obnoxiously while he remains alone in his room. When children scream and yell at this step of the Ladder, most often it is in protest against what they claim to be the great unfairness being done to them. They will cry and scream, "I don't *want* to stay in my room! This is not fair, just give me one more chance, please, Mommy! Don't make me stay in here." "How long do I have to stay in here? Come back here! Mommy! You are so mean, I want Daddy!" If your child resists in this way, it is best not to let his yelling go on for longer than a minute or so.

What to do? A bit of cleverness is required here, because the truth is there is no acceptable way for you to actually make your child be quiet. After all, gagging is out of the question. So it is important for you to learn how to sidestep getting into power struggles you cannot win. Fortunately, while direct control is not possible, indirect control most definitely is. Here's what you can do.

In response to your child's loud yelling and protests, stick your head back in the door of his bedroom (don't walk over to him), and in a loud whisper deliver the script for Step Four, Scenario 2:

> "Shhh! Don't forget, honey, the work of time-out is done quietly, and with all of this screaming and carrying on, the time you have to stay in your room hasn't even started yet."

With these words your tone should convey that you are giving him the best tip of the day! You are not angry or frustrated at your child's reaction because you understand your child is young and struggling, and, being his best ally, you are reminding him that settling down will get him out of his room sooner.

Whispering in the face of your child's screaming is an important variable in this response. First of all, whispering is extremely effective in prompting someone to want to hear what you are saying. Also, with whispering you are demonstrating that you are calm and in control of yourself and not taking the bait your child is offering. You are not struggling; your child is. You are disciplining, leading, and not having any trouble with it. Your calm demeanor helps establish you as the competent authority, and your effort to help him reinforces that you are not at odds; it is just that your child must learn how to be in your family, adhering to certain standards of self-control, respect, and cooperation (SRC). Your tone and your calm demeanor convey to your child that his big loud demonstration of protest simply doesn't have any real impact or power over you.

Don't worry that your child won't be able to hear you, because even when he is screaming and carrying on, he will focus in on your whisper. He should be able hear you just fine, and if by chance he doesn't, he will learn to pay more attention the next time you whisper. Once again, all you need to do is very softly say:

> "Honey, hey, hey, Shhh! Remember, the work of time-out is done quietly, and with all this carrying on, the time you have to stay in your room hasn't even started yet."

Then add this finishing touch:

"And because your screaming is so loud—and I don't want this obnoxiousness to fill the house—I am going to close the door as a way to help remind you that you need to be quiet."

Now it is time to shut the door. Be certain not to have any discussion with your child or respond directly to his protests. After you have closed the door to your child's room, don't leave just yet. Remain outside the door to see if your child needs further help to settle down.

Don't converse with your child. In fact, this is a rule of thumb when engaged in the Ladder correction with your child: No back-and-forth communication should take place. Effective correction requires that you give directives and instructions and enforce them without getting derailed or distracted by your child's resistance. As a parent, you must establish and maintain your place as leader and authority. In this context, ignoring your child has an important place—an essential place, in fact. If you feel compelled to respond to everything your child says, to give all of his childish utterances the respect of a response, then you are sunk. Children are masterful at protest and exerting relentless pressure to get their way. You must learn to dismiss these antics and not reinforce them as strategies that have any power. If your child cries, "But Mommy please wait! No, no, don't close the door!" remain even-tempered and do not say anything to answer your child. Simply back out of the room and close the door, just as you said you were going to do.

It may be that your actions in Step Four will be enough to help your child find his self-control and calm down. If this is the case, then there is no need to climb to Step Five. Remember that the time-out actually begins when your child is appropriately quiet and controlled. If his behavior remains appropriate for the designated number of minutes, then you can open the bedroom door and let him know his time-out in his room is finished. Follow the script to end a time-out:

"Okay, honey. Your time in your room is finished. You can come out now."

STEP FOUR, SCENARIO 3: YOUR CHILD RUNS OUT OF HIS ROOM

If, at the end of Step Three, your child promptly jumps off the bed and runs out of the room, after you have instructed him to stay put, what does this tell you about the degree of authority you have in relationship with your child? I'm afraid it says that you have very little of it, and his behavior is a clear indicator of an imbalance of family power (IFP). His behavior means that he needs you, more than ever, to bear down and find the strength and resolve to hold to the limit you have established. That is why you remain positioned at his door: If your child does run out, you are right there to stop him. Make sure you act quickly so as to catch him before he gets more than a foot or two out the door. Turn him around and walk him back into his room and onto his bed. The script for Step Four, Scenario 3 is:

> "Whoa, hey, where are you going? I just said you have to stay in your room until I tell you it's time to come out, and I haven't told you it is time yet."

Stay in complete control of yourself, keeping your voice steady and free of frustration. Remember, an even and calm demeanor is central to effective and respectful disciplining. This may be a bit challenging if the intensity of your child's protests are ratcheting up, but the higher you climb the Ladder, the more important it is to stay calm. Keep your frustration in check and don't fall into the parenting trap of becoming as worked up as your child. If you're out of control yourself, you won't be able to help your out-of-control child.

Once your child is back in his room and on his bed, look directly at him, eye-to-eye if possible. Raise your index finger as a way to underscore your seriousness and in a firm tone, using your child's full name, say:

> "William, I mean business about this. You need to stay put. Now, when I leave, I am going to close your door as a reminder to you

that you are not to leave your room until I say it is time for you
to come out."

Without engaging in any further discussion, turn and leave the room,
closing the door behind you. Once again, stay at your child's door in case
further intervention is required.

This is the end of Step Four. At this point, either your child will accept
your direction and remain appropriately in his room, or your authority will
have provoked him into a full-blown tantrum. If your child becomes cooperative, then complete the time-out routine, but if you are met with
increased tantrums and out of control behavior, proceed to Step Five.

Step Five: The Parent Hold

Children who have been parented with few effective limits—and who are
suffering from IFP—haven't learned to act in a self-controlled, respectful,
and cooperative fashion. They have had little experience with resolute
parental authority or regulating their feelings of disappointment appropriately, and they've had little experience in *not* having their power prevail.
This is the step on the Ladder where parents must remain unyielding in
their expectations—and where children can go over the edge and become
unglued. Your child's behavior may deteriorate into out-of-control
banging on his bedroom door, kicking, throwing things, stripping the
blankets and sheets off his bed, and screaming and crying in a full-blown
rage. This is the point where, in my opinion, your child needs you most.
Step Five offers parents and children a response that effectively and sooth-
ingly meets the needs presented by out-of-control behavior.

Unless you are a parent who has a child between the ages of three and
ten, you may think that out-of-control behavior is manifested only by
emotionally disturbed or traumatized children. This is not the case at all.
Children who have no underlying psychiatric or psychological distur-

bances can and do exhibit significantly defiant, oppositional, and unregulated behavior. This is not to suggest that you should consider extreme acting out behavior as normal, however; it often reflects the degree of behavioral and emotional disruption that is caused by an imbalance of power in the parent-child relationship. When you are met with out-of-control behavior, it is time to move in closer to your child, rather than walk away from him. He needs you to hold him, soothe him, and provide the emotional regulation he cannot find on his own.

When other children are present and you need to go to Step Five of the Ladder, don't worry, it is still manageable. Simply tell your other children that you will be focusing on helping their sibling to cooperate and learn self-control. Tell them that when you are in the bedroom with him, they must find something to do. If you have a toddler, use a playpen or crib for temporary safe containment so you can attend to the needs of your out-of-control child. This may not be easy, but remember, the stakes are high, and you're the only one who can do this. Your children are counting on you to get the job done. The first time you use the parent hold, it will require the most effort, but your child will reap the benefits quickly, and each successive hold takes less time and energy. The work you do now will soon yield enormous payoffs.

Don't All Children Have Tantrums?

Because children's tantruming has become more and more extreme in so many families today it is important to talk about the implications this has for a child's development. When a child suffers intense tantrums and experiences emotional chaos, it is not simply a benign or temporary disturbance. Each one of these episodes impacts a child's sense of himself and his sense of security in relationship to his parents and encourages a perception that his "badness" is too much for adults to handle. Certainly all children have tantrums now and then, but tantrums that are frequent, intense, and disruptive of family life signal a more serious problem.

For some children, the vicious cycle of their negative behavior, and their parents' inadequate management of it, is an incubator for anxiety and developmental compromise. They become vulnerable to a much broader range of behavioral disturbances. Paradoxically, the children who have the most power in the family are not confident and self-assured but are suffering the most emotional volatility and anxiety. Their out-of-control behavior affects not just their family relationships but compromises peer relationships, school performance, and emotional maturation. With the passing of every month and year in which these emotional storms continue, children are put at higher and higher risk for more serious trouble, not only at home, but at school and in the larger community as well.

What Is a Parent's Responsibility When a Child Loses Control?

When a child's tantrum behavior escalates to the point of being physically out of control, what is your responsibility? Is it best to back away and wait until your child has raged himself out of energy and the tantrum finally subsides? Or is it better to move in and provide the containment, soothing, and regulation your child is unable to muster on his own?

Without hesitation, I can tell you that as long as you are sufficiently bigger and stronger than your child, it is far better to provide the containment and control your child is lacking. When his behavior is the most off-putting, and your instinct is to turn away, this is when he actually needs you the most. You may not realize it, but by backing away and leaving him to flail and thrash on his own, you are in effect saying, "I can't help you; you're too much. You are now on your own." This means your child is lost because it is completely unrealistic to think that an out-of-control child will somehow, from out of the midst of emotional chaos, find the capacity for self-regulation and self-control. Either we move in— not back away—and hold our children close, soothing them, grounding them, and telling them we are there to help them (which lets them internalize their emotional regulation and control) or they will suffer increasing states of emotional and behavioral disorganization and harbor more and more anger and fear.

Parents Holding On

When you use the Parent Hold, you are going to enter into a whole new relationship with your child where he will be grounded and will be much more secure in your competent ability and authority. As you go through this correction together, you will move from chaos to calm to the deep-felt love and tenderness that binds you as parent and child. You will both feel so much better as you let go of the struggle and bad feelings that have been weighing you down and putting distance between you. After just one or two holds, even though your child may struggle mightily, he will end up feeling relieved by your loving containment and grateful for your leadership. You will be pleased as you see him quickly becoming happier and more affectionate.

While they may not show it, or directly admit it to their parents, every child I have ever worked with who suffers from emotional outbursts and disruptive behavior has been terribly burdened by shame and guilt over what he knows is his "bad" behavior. Very often, when children start to use their self-control, show respect, and act with a spirit of cooperation, I concurrently see them burst forth and master new skills that they did not have enough energy and focus to master before. With less emotional volatility and disorganization to drain them, and with new levels of self-control, they take real steps forward.

Although designated as Step Five, the Parent Hold can actually be done at any step of the Ladder where your child is out of control. It could occur, for example, at Step Three, as you begin to direct your child to his room. He may resist by hitting and kicking you, in which case you will need to harness all your strength and get your child into his room. If he hasn't settled down, but continues to flail, then implement the hold. The privacy and containment of the bedroom makes this the optimum place for the hold, but if you can't get him there due to the force of your child's struggle, hold him where you are.

Practically speaking, implementing the Ladder and seeing it through to the end, especially if you have a highly unregulated child, takes a bit of time. You can count on it taking twenty minutes to a half hour in the beginning correction phase. Don't despair: Your focused parental effort and close adherence to the guidelines of the five steps will yield results in a matter of days. It won't be long before your child will be cooperating by Step Two, and when he does need to go to his room, he will do so with little fuss and behave appropriately, while exercising his newly found self-control. Until then, you have to prioritize the time, attention, and energy it will take to tip the balance of power back into your hands.

While you are holding your child, remain supportive and reassuring. You want him to feel your commitment to helping him. I always remind parents: You are not against your child; you are on the same team. You are there to help, support, and teach him, and while he may not like learning certain lessons, trust that his anger will only be temporary if they are learned, but lasting if they are not.

The Parent Hold is an extremely powerful and effective technique that helps children correct their behavior, develop better self-control, and regulate their emotions. It also strengthens the parent-child bond. After using the hold three or four times, you should see notable improvement. If this is not the case, and your child continues to struggle intensely, becomes angrier or more oppositional over time, or seems to need the hold even more frequently, then discontinue using it. If you have embarked on the correction phase without professional help, this is the time for you to stop using Step Five until you have further specific directions from a professional on how to proceed.

When Is a Parent Hold Indicated?

A parent hold is indicated if a child hits, kicks, bites, throws or breaks things, knocks over furniture, trashes his room, or acts in a way that may cause harm to himself and others. The parent hold is intended only for use when a child is truly out of control.

When Is a Parent Hold Not Indicated?

Every parent must decide what is best for his or her child and family based on individual characteristics and specific circumstances. Using a parent hold effectively, respectfully, and safely ultimately requires that a parent have more calm, understanding, strength, and endurance than the child. Therefore parents who are limited physically or who suffer from emotional troubles of their own may not be up to the rigors of this technique. Similar consideration of your child's physical health is appropriate as well. For example, before using the parent hold with a child who has a physical condition such as cerebral palsy or a pulmonary disorder, consult with your physician to assess whether or not it is an appropriate and safe technique for your child. If you have doubts or hesitations about either your child's suitability, or your own, for the parent hold, be sure to consult with a professional first.

The parent hold should not be used at home with children who have suffered sexual abuse or any other form of intrusive psychological trauma. A parent hold may trigger a form of posttraumatic stress reaction in these children. If you are dealing with out-of-control behavior in your child and he has been traumatized, consult an experienced mental health professional for guidance in how to help your child.

Staying Calm and in Control

When disciplining your child, assert only the degree of power and physical strength required to maintain your authority and control over him. It is also imperative that you do not hold your child if you feel out of control yourself. Anger, frustration—these emotions will only distort the warm and safe feeling intended by a parent hold. Stay calm, in control, and steady, and always convey a reassuring and competent manner. If your own behavior is out of control, ask your partner to take charge or wait until your inner stability has returned so that you can calmly move in and hold your child.

The Five Steps of the Parent Hold

There are five steps to follow when you're using a parent hold with your child. The intent of a parent hold is to give loving, respectful, caring support to children who are out of control and who cannot help themselves in moments of extreme distress. The aim is to give the child safe and secure containment.

Going through a parent hold with a child establishes a firm power structure. Holding your child when he is in the throws of a full-blown tantrum is a powerful and intense experience. As you ride out the storm with your child, a very strong, intimate, and corrective bond develops. This is at the heart of the therapeutic value of the process, and it will propel you and your child into a healthier and stronger relationship with one another. This is an experience most appropriate for a mother and her child or a father and his child—not nannies, grandparents, aunts, uncles, or siblings.

STEP 1 OF THE PARENT HOLD

Moving toward your child, say in a gentle and understanding tone:

> "Honey, you are out of control, and of course I am not going to let you hurt me or hurt yourself or any of the things in your room. It is not good for children to be out of control. I am going to hold you until you calm down."

With your child facing you, reach out with your dominant hand (whether you are right- or left-handed) and take hold of the wrist that is diagonally across from you. If you are right-handed, you will reach across to your child's right wrist. If you are left-handed, you will take hold of his left wrist. From this position, hold onto your child's wrists (not hands, because your child can wiggle free too easily), and cross her arms over her chest in the form of an X, holding her wrists close to her waist. Your child's left wrist should be resting on her right hip, her right wrist resting on her left hip. This safely immobilizes your child's arms.

STEP 2 OF THE PARENT HOLD

At this point, your child's out-of-control energy will move from her arms down to her legs, and she will start to kick and try to get loose. Therefore, the next step in the restraint is to contain leg mobility. This is accomplished by pulling down on your child's wrists to bring her to the floor. Go down to the floor with your child, sit down behind her, opening your legs and pulling her body in as close to you as possible. You will be positioned so that her back is against your chest, and you will still be holding her wrists at her waist.

While maintaining the hold on her wrists, cross your legs Indian-style over your child's flailing legs. If she is little or requires only minimal physical containment, then only use one leg. *Never use more force than is required to contain your child's physical struggle as she fights the process of self-control.*

STEP 3 OF THE PARENT HOLD

Now that your child's arms and legs are contained, she may begin to bang you with her head. Put a throw pillow or something soft between your chest and your child's head. (Some preplanning—having a pillow close by in the bedroom—is helpful.) You will have to let go of your child's wrist momentarily to position the pillow, so try to do this quickly and get back to the holding position. The pillow won't stop your child's head from bucking, but it will help buffer the impact for both of you.

STEP 4 OF THE PARENT HOLD

Now that your child is physically contained, continue to hold her in this position through Step 5 until she has calmed down, gone limp in your arms, and the struggle, physical and verbal, has completely subsided.

Given that children are already in an agitated emotional state when a hold begins, the experience can be intense and hard on both the child and the parent. During the hold, *be careful to respond to her rhythms of struggle with only the degree of strength required to hold her safely and securely. Never use more strength than is necessary.* Tighten and loosen your hold on your child throughout the process without letting go until she is completely calm and fully relaxed.

PARENTING TIP

Taking Care to Be Careful

It is important for you to maintain a vigilant eye and ensure that the hold always progresses in a manner that will be soothing, reassuring, and calming to your child. Never follow your child's emotion and become angry and provoked yourself. Should this happen, it is better to have your spouse take over or to discontinue the parent hold until another time. While no child has ever been hurt or suffered any adverse effects in the fifteen years I have been teaching this technique to families, the potential obviously exists for injury or harm due to the escalated physical nature of the intervention. Since most children will protest when in the Parent Hold by yelling, "Let me go, you're hurting me!" be certain to do your own careful and clearheaded assessment of how your child is doing. Are you holding too tightly? Can your child breathe freely? The child's breathing must be monitored all the time. Are you keeping calm and using a soothing tone? Be sure to monitor your energy and the strength of your hold, as adrenaline can make you stronger than you may realize. Don't attempt to hold a child who is too big or too strong for you to manage by yourself. Also, if your child behaves bizarrely, or persists in laughing during the Parent Hold, you should discontinue the hold and consult a therapist.

The average holding time for an out-of-control child is twenty minutes. Once your child is calm, sit together for a minute or two before getting up.

STEP 5 OF THE PARENT HOLD

Once you have your child in a proper hold and she can no longer offer up effective physical protests, she will go through an escalating sequence of verbal protests. The following are the various verbal protests and the desired parental responses to them.

Protest Phase 1: "You're Hurting Me!"

"You're hurting me! I can't breathe; let me go. You're hurting me!"

> "No honey, I am not hurting you. I am holding you firmly because you are out of control."

"Let me go!"

> "Of course I will let you go, but not until you have calmed down. I am going to hold you to help you calm down."

Your child may continue to protest along these lines for a few more minutes. Do not overtalk in response, and only repeat this reassurance a few times.

Protest Phase 2: "I Hate You!"

This phase of your child's protest will be the most intense—here she will really let the full force of her anger and resistance come out. During this time she may say rather extreme things, such as:

"I hate you; you are trying to kill me! You are the worst mother, get off of me!" or "I am going to jump out my window and run away and you will never see me again!" or "You can't do this to me; I'm telling on you! I'm going to tell the police that you are hurting me! I am going to sue you!" or "I'm going to kill you and chop this house down and you won't be able to stop me!"

Respond in a very soothing, quiet, loving, reassuring tone:

> "I know, honey; you are very angry. I hear you. But it's okay, because Mommy's here, and I am going to help you. I've got you,

and I'm not going to let you go. Mommy's right here, honey, and
I'm going to hold on and not let you go. You're okay."

Protest Phase 3: "I Have to Go to the Bathroom!"

This is your child's last-ditch effort to regain her power. "I have to go to
the bathroom. I have to go really bad!"

"Okay, honey, you can go, just as soon as you have calmed down."

"But I have to go *now*, I can feel it coming out!!"

"That's okay, you may have wet pants, but we can get some dry
ones in a moment. The most important thing right now is that you
are calm and no longer out of control."

While children may readily revert to bathroom urgency as a last-ditch
effort to get you to let go, it is very rare for child to actually wet her pants.
If you have a child that does, be prepared and put your child on some
towels, and proceed as before. Your child must have the help of your firm
guidance and containment.

Be prepared for variations on this last-ditch effort to have the upper
hand. Your child may say "I am going to throw up" or "I have to blow my
nose" or "I need a drink." Regardless of your child's pleas or threats, use
the technique described above and make certain your tone remains
compassionate and supportive.

If you are faced with unplanned interruptions of this sequence, such
as your child wiggling free, the most important thing for you to do is
remain calm; don't collapse your air of authority. Resume the hold as
soon as you can, responding to whatever level of protest your child is in.

ENDING THE PARENT HOLD

Your child will finally cease her struggle and go limp in your arms. Many
times, particularly if the phases of protest have been intense, your child
will dissolve into tears. It can surprise parents that their child's crying is

not angry or combative but deeply felt and cathartic. Most likely, your child will turn to you for comfort. Wrap your arms around her and while holding her gently offer reassurance by saying:

> "It's okay, sweetie. You are just a little girl and you're still learning. All children need to learn. Don't worry; Mommy and Daddy are going to help you. It's okay. You are fine, and we are fine. I love you very much."

After you have sat together for a few minutes and all emotions have passed, say:

> "Okay, sweet pea, let's go put some cool water on your face, and you can blow your nose and get a drink."

Take your child's hand in yours and go together to the bathroom. While in the bathroom, say with a rather light tone:

> "My goodness, you were really angry, huh? That was a lot of feeling that came out. I don't think that lesson will ever be so hard for you again."

Move into your next phase of activity by once again reaching out your hand to your child and saying:

> "Now where were we?"

Suggest that you go and do whatever the requested task was "together as a team." Do not offer any further verbal reassurances, explanations, apologies, or corrections. This ends Step Five and completes the Ladder.

You did it! Not only have you been an effective parent, you have started on the path of reclaiming the course of your child's development and the well-being of your entire family. I trust that you feel a deep sense of accomplishment and gratification. You should!

A Summary of the Ladder

STEP ONE: A FRIENDLY BID FOR COOPERATION

In a friendly, upbeat tone, referring to your child with a pet name, give a directive:

> "Okay, sweetie, time for you to turn off the television."

Wait a reasonable amount of time to see if your child complies. If he fails to comply, climb to Step Two.

STEP TWO: AN "I MEAN BUSINESS" REMINDER

Shift from a friendly, light tone to a more businesslike voice; drop the pet name, and refer to your child by his proper name:

> "William, I just said it is time to turn the television off now. This is your reminder. If I need to say it a third time you will be heading to your room."

It may be helpful to punctuate your reminder with your index finger pointing up and at a slight angle. If your child does not comply, climb to Step Three.

STEP THREE: TO THE BEDROOM

Step Three, Part 1: Take Your Child to His Room

Begin this step with action, not words! Move towards your child before you start to speak. Then, as you are walking towards your child, say:

> "Okay, hon, that's it, off you go to your room."

Do not engage in any conversation or respond to your child's protests or begging. There is only one exception to this: If your child says, "But I was just going to, please, please, I was about to; it's not fair—," you may say with a positive and supportive tone:

> "Good, honey, you were just about to! Next time I am
> confident you won't wait quite as long, because you
> will remember I only ask twice. Now, come on then,
> this time you must go to your room."

Then without another word, and with speed and deliberateness, get your child to his room, either following behind if he goes on his own, or carrying him. If your child becomes physically out of control while trying to resist being taken to his room, move on to Step Five: The Parent Hold.

Step Three, Part 2: Set the Terms

Place your child on his bed and then say with a firm but nonthreatening tone:

> "Now, you need to stay in your room until I tell you it
> is time to come out."

Having said that, *say no more.* Turn and walk out of your child's room, leaving the bedroom door open. Stay close to the door, but out of your child's view.

STEP FOUR: SHUT THE DOOR

One of three things will happen next. Respond accordingly.

Step Four, Scenario 1: Your Child Remains in His Room Appropriately

If your child stays in her room and behaves appropriately, stick your head into her room after a few minutes (add two minutes to the age of your child to give you an idea of approximately how many minutes to wait) and say:

> "Okay, honey, you may come out of your room now."

If your child says, "I'm not coming out!" in an attempt to still have the upper hand, then simply say:

"Okay, that's fine, but as far as I am concerned you
can come out of your room now."

Then walk away.

Step Four, Scenario 2: Your Child Remains in His Room but Acts Out Verbally

Your child stays in her room but is yelling and screaming too
loudly to be tolerated. After a minute, stick your head into the
room (do not go all the way into the room) and in a loud
whisper, say, with a very supportive tone (as if you're giving the
best tip of the day):

"Hey, sweetie, Shhh, shh. Remember, the work of time-
out is done quietly. With all this carrying on, your time-
out hasn't even started yet. As a way to help you
remember the need for quiet, and because I don't want
all this noise and obnoxiousness to fill the house, I am
going to close your door."

Then close the door, but do not walk away. Stay close to the
door.

Step Four, Scenario 3: Your Child Runs Out of His Room

Your child shows no regard for your direction to stay in her room
and attempts to run out the door (this is why you have stayed
close by). Putting your hands out to catch and stop your child as
she tries to flee, say:

"Hey, hey, hey! Where are you going, sweetie? I just
said you have to stay in your room."

Turn your child around and direct her back to bed, or pick her
up if it is necessary. Once your child is sitting back on the
bed, say:

> "Now, I mean business, Melissa. You need to stay put
> until I tell you your time in your room is over. As a way
> to help you remember, I am going to close your door."

Saying no more, turn to leave the room. Again, remain outside the door in case your child still needs you.

STEP FIVE: THE PARENT HOLD

Standing outside your child's closed door, speak to your child through the door, in a calm, grounded tone:

> "Honey, you are starting to get out of control. I want
> you to go over to your bed now and sit there so you
> can calm down."

If your child can't calm down and becomes emotionally or physically out of control, open the door, go to your child, and follow the procedure for the Parent Hold (page 127).

Chapter Six

The Ladder Out and About

So often over the years, after I have instructed parents on the steps and script of the Ladder, they've said, "Okay, great. We get that, but what are we supposed to do when one of our kids acts up and we're not at home? This question is perfectly valid, since it isn't necessarily obvious how you can adapt the Ladder for use in the car, in restaurants, when shopping, or during visits to friends and family. But it's completely workable, as you'll see in the pages that follow.

First, a brief comment about the difficulty of correcting your children in public: It can be very hard to rise above the scrutiny you feel directed at you from relatives, friends, and other onlookers. Also, your child's behavior may at times require that you cut an outing short. This is never easy, especially if you really want to be there. Public corrections require more adult maturity, confidence, and self-control than when you are at home. Make your social plans with forethought and be honest about whether you and your child are up to it.

If you are addressing an imbalance of family power (IFP) with your child and he has little regard for your authority, it is best to go through a few days of correction at home in order to realign the power dynamic before going on outings again (see Preparing to Climb the Ladder on page 93). It is helpful to begin the correction phase on a Friday evening or over the weekend, when work and school obligations are less likely to interfere and your partner is more likely to be around to assist you. You need time to teach your child that life is not going to continue to be on his terms, and to do this effectively, you can't watch the clock.

The lessons you are teaching your children are rooted in common sense and matter-of-factness. The basic message you are imparting to your child once he has reached four or five years of age is that a set of manners and behaviors is required if he expects to go out in public places and be with other people. He needs to exercise self-control, be respectful, and cooperate in a reliable way to have the freedom to go out and about.

Taking the Ladder on the Road

The car, where most outings start, can be the toughest setting in which to achieve effectiveness because the responsibilities of driving limit what actions you can take. In large measure, you are relegated to using just words, and words alone don't often compel children to cooperate, particularly if you are dealing with IFP. Having said that, there are steps you can take to increase your effectiveness. If being in the car has posed a big problem for you and your children in the past, then for your first venture or two, make teaching your children, and not the destination, the primary purpose of the trip (without letting your kids in on this little secret, of course!). If you are not obligated to keep an appointment or shop for groceries, you will feel freer to turn around and go home if need be.

Follow the Five Steps of the Ladder

Before you actually start driving, tell your child what your expectations are of his behavior while you're in the car. Turn around and say:

> "Okay, sweetie, let me go over a few quick things before we get going. A few basic rules apply whenever we are in the car. First and foremost, you must buckle up and keep buckled until we arrive where we are going and the car stops. Second, the noise level cannot get too high, because then I can't concentrate. That means your voice, the radio, or any movies, games, or things like that. And of course, you must keep your self-control, which means not hitting or kicking the seats or your brother, for that

matter. You must be respectful and cooperate. If you do not follow these basic rules, then the car ride ends. Pretty simple, right? Okay, high five, now off we go."

A message like this gets the basics across and sets the stage so that if your child does act up, you don't get sidetracked into any sort of explanation. You can just get right to it, and say, for example:

"Hey, I told you the rules for the car, and that's too loud."
"Whoops, keep that seat belt on! You know that's my rule."

Such a direction represents Step One of the Ladder. Remember not to overtalk or overreact to any show of inappropriate behavior.

Step Two is the friendly reminder:

"Maggie, what did I just say? This is the second time I am reminding you of the car rules. You know I only say things twice, so if there is a need for a third time, I will pull over and stop the car."

Again, keep your cool and use a positive tone. Don't let frustration leak through; your emotion feeds your child's power drive.

Step Three is in fact pulling the car over and stopping. Act before you talk—by pulling over. Don't address your child until you are actively and safely turning the car off the road. Again, keep your cool—don't indulge in aggressive driving or abrupt stopping. A show of anger does not teach your child anything about self-control. Simply find an accessible and safe place to turn in, and park for a few moments. If you are on the highway, this most definitely means exiting or pulling off into a rest stop. Once you are pulling off the road, say:

"Okay, we have to stop. I am not going to continue driving until you buckle your seat belt (stop screaming, playing loud music, etc.)."

If your child protests and refuses to listen, tell her that you are getting out of the car because you don't want to hear all of her fussing and that you will get back in and continue on your way once she has settled down. Whatever you do, don't put your child out of the car and threaten to leave her. This prospect is too scary and mean-spirited and, in the end, an empty threat, because of course you would never really leave her. (A parent or two has confided that she did in fact drive down the road forty or fifty yards in order to prove she really meant business. This, of course, is not a parenting strategy anyone can recommend. You can avoid such desperate, damaging tactics by knowing how to be effective in the first place.) Stay on top of the situation by keeping your child contained in the car instead. If you have to get out, then stand with your back to the window, leaving your child inside to carry on with her fussing. (Child safety locks that control both the backseat windows and doors are very helpful features—be sure to use them.) Periodically you can open the door and say:

> "Oh my, still fussing? We can't get going until you are calm and quiet."

Don't add any fuel to the fire with emotional pleading or threats. This represents Step Four.

Step Five is the Parent Hold. It becomes necessary if your child's tantrum spirals out of control and grows potentially dangerous—for example, if she is kicking, thrashing, hitting the windows, trying to push her way out of the car, gouging holes in the seat cushions, or doing anything that could potentially harm her or damage the car. Get into the backseat with your child, positioning yourself behind her and the seat as best as you can, and use the parent hold. Do not let go until your child is no longer fighting you in any way.

These recommendations require significant effort on your part, but you have to look at them as an investment. You don't want your child to grow up using her childish power to spoil good times and outings. Once your child learns that you mean what you say, your car trips will be much more enjoyable. If your child never adequately settles down, or her behavior is way out of control, it is best to turn around and go back home. The lesson your child will learn from your response is that her unruliness does not give her power or influence—in fact, it actually diminishes it. If you have not gotten very far from home when your child starts to break your rules, simply say:

> "Uh-oh, you've already forgotten what I said about the car rules. I am going to turn back and take you home. I was looking forward to your company on this outing, but you (keep the emphasis on the child here) can't go out and about if you don't follow the basics."

There are no second chances and no threats. In order to be effective, you must commit to the action and follow through. Be calm and maintain a supportive tone as you tell your sobbing little one that you trust she will remember the rules next time, and that you can plan another outing for tomorrow, but for today she will be staying at home. Here your child's distress is constructive: She is reacting to your authority and leadership rather than your being the one who's getting angry and upset while reacting to her childishness.

Being cooped up in the car can be hard on kids. Games, songs, lollipops, pretzel sticks, and so forth are helpful. But don't overdo it—distractions are not a substitute for effective parenting. Nor do you want to give your children the message that they have to be entertained and catered to at every turn.

What About Subways and Buses?

If you live in a city and your outings include subways and buses rather than cars, the same basic rule applies. Provide your child with a preview of the behavior you expect before your outing gets underway. Then, if your child acts up, give an "I mean business" reminder that ends with this direction:

> "Remember, I only say things twice, so if you need a third reminder, we will be getting off the train (or bus) until you find your self-control."

Yes, action on the subway translates into getting off. While this is a nuisance, your effort will pay off in a way that is well worth it. Pick up your child or wheel him out the door, buckled into his stroller. Explain to him that he can't be on the train without behaving appropriately. Let him know you will wait until he has found his self-control and willingness to cooperate before reboarding.

Keep your head held high all the while you are climbing the Ladder in public. I know it is not easy to manage child misbehavior when all eyes are on you, or when it feels like it's too much of an inconvenience and effort to carry through an effective action. I can't underscore enough, however, what an invaluable service you will be doing not only for your child but for other parents, who learn from your example, and for fellow travelers who will gratefully be spared from your child's disruptive outbursts.

At a Restaurant

Realistically, toddlers and preschoolers are just not going to be able to exert enough reliable self-control to adhere to the manners and decorum of eating out—except at fast food or family-style restaurants, perhaps. It is a gamble when eating out with young children, so plan wisely before taking them to dine where they will have to remain seated quietly for longer than thirty to forty minutes. The more active and power-driven your child is, the greater the challenge. If your child is five years or older, you should be able to count on her to hold up reasonably well for an hour or so in a restaurant. For a child with IFP, however, age doesn't matter: You will be taking a gamble any time you go out.

Troubleshooting

A little preparation is in order for all children before they eat out. When young children will accompany you to a restaurant, bring along some things to occupy them—coloring books, drawing games, or whatever you think your child will enjoy. Just be mindful of activities that might disturb those dining around you. An older child who is not comfortable waiting or making small talk might also appreciate some quiet take-along activities.

Before you go into the restaurant, talk to your child for just a moment about your expectations. While being friendly and upbeat, let her know that good manners in a restaurant means staying in her seat and keeping her voice down. If you are going to put parameters around what she can or cannot eat, such as no soda, hot dogs, or dessert, then be certain to establish this before going inside. Above all, don't turn your directives into a question by ending them with "Okay?"

Pull Out the Ladder

If your child protests when you make your expectations clear, wait until she has calmed down and stopped fussing before you go into the restaurant. You may need to climb the Ladder at this point, saying at Step Two:

> "Look, Jane, if you cannot settle down and get over your disappointment that you will not be having soda, then you will have to leave the restaurant and we will go home."

Never say this as a threat, but as a matter of course. There may well be times when your child just doesn't have the patience or frame of mind to be in a restaurant. Be honest in your assessment of this, and be willing to go home if necessary—even if what you really want is to go in, sit down, and eat. Sometimes you are better off changing your plans and picking up a pizza instead. Why set yourself up, or your child, for a bad experience?

If you are already seated in a restaurant and your child begins to make demands or starts fussing, you have to get busy. Beware of the temptation to pacify your child, thinking it may be better to accommodate her than to let the situation deteriorate. It's hard to avoid doing this, but if you do it often your child will know that being disruptive gives her the power to set the terms when eating out and you will be creating a restaurant bully. I recommend that at some point before the meal you give your dinner companions a heads up that you may have to interrupt the conversation to attend to your child, should she require your attention. Strive for a comfortable balance. While you cannot ignore your child, she must learn that she does not have to be in the spotlight all the time and must learn how to occupy herself while adults are talking.

Let's say your child says, as you order, "Okay, Mommy, I want spaghetti and a soda." You can reply with:

> "Remember, honey, there's no soda this evening; how about juice or a glass of milk?"

If she continues to plead, "No, I want the soda. Please, Mommy!" keep a supportive tone as you answer:

> "I know you do, sweetie, but soda isn't good for you to drink very often, and I said before we came in that there will be no soda tonight. Now, let's not get stuck here. I will order you some juice."

Then change the subject and see if you can shift her attention away from a struggle. Keep any distraction low-key: An overblown effort has a ring of desperation to it, and children pick up on this. With their power antennae signaling loudly, they will go full steam ahead.

If your attempts to change the subject don't work after a few moments, climb up the Ladder to Step Two, since you've already told your child what your position is on the soda (Step One). To manage her protests, start by saying:

> "Jane, I have said no soda. I am not going to have any more conversation about it. This is your last reminder. If you keep fussing, you will have to leave the table."

Climb to the next step if you have to.

The key component of Step Three is to start with an action: Get up, pull out her chair or lift your child out of the booth, and escort her by the hand or carry her out of the restaurant. Once you are engaged in the action, you can say:

"Okay, out you go."

You can take her to the restaurant foyer, outside the entrance, or to the car. Once you have appropriately removed your child, let her know that you will return to the table in a few minutes, after she has stopped insisting on the soda.

If your child starts screaming or physically protesting as you move her along, get her swiftly out of earshot so as not to disturb other diners. Similarly, if your child gets overly loud or rambunctious, act quickly. There's no time for the ineffectiveness of explaining and reasoning. Pick up your child and leave the dining area—no questions asked, no bids for cooperation. After you have exited, you can address your child:

"You may not be so loud and unruly in a restaurant. No way. You have to use your self-control and remember your manners. We will go back and join the others once you have calmed down."

For tantrum behavior, the same need for quick action applies. It is best, if the car is handy, to proceed there for privacy so your child can let off her steam. You may need to get in the backseat with her for a Parent Hold, depending on how out of control she becomes. Remember, always let your child's behavior determine what level of response you counter with: If your child is crying and angry but not out of control, you do not need the hold. Time spent in the car is sufficient.

If your child will not settle down after you have left the dining room, you obviously can't return to the table. Cell phones are a godsend here, allowing you to phone the remaining party to make a

Plan B. Either change your order to a carryout or, if your party has already been served, ask that everyone else finish their meal and have your food and your child's boxed up for taking home. Or, if you were close to finishing your meal, ask another adult to relieve you so that you can return to the table.

Use this same basic response for any protest, back talk, untoward silliness, or verbal shenanigans that you encounter. One important note here: Once you get the Ladder out and go to Step Two, don't fail to make the climb! I can't tell you how many times I have heard parents say, "Do you hear me? We will leave, and I mean it. I won't care, I will tell the waiter, and we will go." But then they don't do anything! They just keep threatening. This is classic ineffectiveness in action. Take real action and finish the job so that your agenda prevails.

PARENTING TIP

Who's in Charge?

Parents often ask: When a child is acting out in a restaurant and you take him outside, or even take him home, then isn't the child winning? The answer is no. Handling restaurant unruliness the way I have mapped out is not done with heated emotions or a throwing up of the hands. You are leaving because you have taken charge and made an executive decision about what has to happen next, given that certain behavior is simply unacceptable. Your child will absolutely know the difference between when you are in the lead and when he is.

If you have had a series of particularly unpleasant times dining out with your child, then it is time to tell him calmly, on your way home from a spoiled dinner, that the next time there is a dinner outing, he will be staying at home. He will need to work on his self-control before he can join the family at restaurants again. Then make arrangements for a babysitter, so that the next one or two times that you go out, the child isn't included. Stick to a matter-of-fact tone when you tell him, "In order to go out with other people, manners and appropriate behavior are a must. These are simple rules that apply to everyone."

Similarly, if you are out and about and the idea of stopping at a restaurant comes up, be clear that you can't go because Tyler has not been using his self-control at restaurants recently. Say that you trust he is working on it, and you can try again soon. Be kind but clear and unyielding about this.

Visiting Friends and Family

Parents are often thrown for a loop when they are faced with their child's unruly or uncooperative behavior during visits to friends and family. If you have just begun an effort to address IFP with your child and are in the correction phase, postpone social visits for a week or two until both of you have gotten used to your new roles as leader and cooperator. If you must visit family or close friends, talk to them ahead of time about your focused efforts on correcting your child's unruly behavior. Let them know that if your child acts up during the visit, it would be helpful to take her to a room where she can be alone and regain her self-control, respect, and cooperation. Agree on the best place in their home to do this.

Speak with your child before going out and make it clear what behavior you expect of her while you are guests in someone's home. If a problem arises before you even leave your house, or if it has been a rough day all the way around, you as the parent must make a decision about whether it makes sense for your child to even go on the visit at all. It's always better to parent preventively whenever you can. It takes a lot of self-discipline to make this type of hard call, but taking such action is not only preventive, it also teaches a powerful lesson.

PARENTING TIP

Find a Room

The instructions for using the Ladder specify the child's room as the best place for her to regain her self-control and spirit of cooperation. This is also true when visiting someone else's home. If you put your child on the front steps of the house for a time-out, for example, it is likely other people will be visible and within earshot, which can be embarrassing for your child. It is not respectful to make a spectacle of your child, and it can be irresistible for a concerned grandparent or aunt or uncle to chime in, try to help, or, conversely, for your child to try to get everyone else involved in the drama. The privacy, quiet, and containment that a bedroom offers is always preferable.

Putting the Ladder to Work

If your child forgets her manners in a social setting and begins to act up, be discreet with redirections. Keep your voice quiet and your corrections as private as possible. With mild transgressions, sometimes a silent expression of disapproval, such as a raised eyebrow or slight shake of the head, will do. If not, then it's best to get up and go to her, bend over, and in her ear with a low voice, give her a short and clear direction about her behavior. This represents Step One of the Ladder.

Don't immediately resume your conversation with the adults. Remain standing close by your child, as a way to punctuate that you mean business and will be monitoring her compliance. If she does not correct her behavior, go to her again and use a shortened version of the script for Step Two:

> "Suzie, you must stop running and being so loud. This is the second time I am saying this. If you need a third reminder, I will take you in the other room for time by yourself."

The key components to effectiveness in social situations are to stay steady and calm, remaining focused on your child. Also, act deliberately and without delay. A lot of parents feel they don't want to cause a scene at grandma's house or in front of their friends—but we've all observed how a scene becomes worse when it's compounded by parental ineffectiveness. You must teach your child to exercise self-control, respect, and cooperation no matter where she is.

If you do not feel comfortable climbing the Ladder where you are, then you will have to let your host know that if your little one continues to act up, you will have to cut your visit short and take her home. Quietly inform your child of the same plan:

> "It is time for you to use your self-control, or we will end our visit for today and return home."

Then, of course, you must do as you have said. If the situation requires your departure, gather your things quickly and take them out to the car so you are all set to go. Make your apologies for having to leave abruptly, say some quick goodbyes, and only then go to your child. Pick her up and say:

> "With you acting this way, we are not going to stay any longer."

You will of course be met with a wail and probably some flailing once you have picked her up. Keep a firm hold on your little one. If she has been playing with another child, tell the playmate that you are sorry to have to cut the visit short, but you will arrange another time to get together soon. Then go out to the car. Do not overdo your anger or upset; the fact that you are leaving is statement enough. There should be no shows of eye rolling to a friend, or berating your child once you're in the car, either. These things happen with children occasionally, and while the tasks of effective parenting can be inconvenient and annoying, it is your job, and it must be done. Once home, escort your child directly to her room in keeping with Step Three of the Ladder. Climb as high as you need to go.

Be Respectful

When away from home, don't let your own discomfort motivate you to speak disrespectfully about your child to your friends: "Oh, she is impossible. I just can't take her anywhere. Can you believe what I have to put up with?" This isn't fair to your child, and besides, chances are she will overhear your disrespectful comments. Exercise your own self-control and show respect by bypassing such commentary and getting on with effective action. Deliberate, calm, effective parenting action is not embarrassing.

At the Mall and in Stores

As always, a bit of preplanning is in order. For store outings with young children, it is helpful to pack a small bag with a few snacks and a toy or two. Young children have little patience for sitting and doing nothing; being strapped into a stroller or shopping cart quickly loses its appeal. They will do much better if you provide something to engage them.

Plan the Outing Together

Be sure to give your child a quick preview of what he can expect—i.e., what you are shopping for, how long it will take, and what he will be allowed and not allowed to do during this particular trip. For example, if you are going to the mall, let him know whether or not he will be able to pick out something for himself on this outing. If you are in the grocery store, advise him as to whether he can select one or two food items himself, or pick a candy bar from the checkout line. Thinking out a plan and communicating it ahead of time helps everyone.

PARENTING TIP

If Johnny Would Rather Run than Shop

A word about impulsive children, or those with a propensity to dart off: I am sure most parents of two-, three-, and four-year-olds have experienced at least once that terrible, sick feeling when, for a moment, your child slips out of your sight. For some parents, this can be an all too frequent occurrence. Parents ask me what to do when their child chronically bolts away from them or wanders off. My best answer is to limit the number of times you take the child shopping until he matures a bit. When you really have no other option, using a child-friendly harness and a lead will ensure safety. You can purchase these online and in stores that sell children's gear. While the practice of putting children on a lead is not all that common in our culture, it can be an invaluable safety option for children who have a tendency toward high levels of activity and impulsivity. Try not to be bothered if other shoppers look askance at your child's lead. Hold your head high and know you have made a good decision on her behalf. Chances are someone will ask you where she can buy one for her own child!

If your child is going to get a treat, do not connect it to a bribe or threat: "If you are a good boy and listen to Mommy, then you can have a candy bar." A better approach is:

> "Okay, today we are really going to load up our cart because we will be buying food for each day of the week. Let's get some ice cream today, too. How about you pick what kind? Hey, and you know what? Today will be a good day for a treat at the checkout as well. That will be something to look forward to as we do our shopping."

Then don't bring up the candy again or use it as a weapon. If you have trouble during the trip, use the Ladder. If your child responds well to your discipline, resuming your shopping and buying the candy is fine. If he does not settle down and you have to abandon your trip, then of course there's no candy. You don't need to mention this unless your child wails, "What about my candy?" You can answer:

> "With all your fussing today, the candy will have to wait for another trip."

He will learn with certainty that his self-control and cooperation are the keys to getting such treats. This lesson will be much more solid than one in which you tolerate annoying, disruptive behavior, all the while threatening that he will not get his candy if he isn't good.

Once in the store, if trouble starts to brew, use distraction as your first line of defense. Try to engage him in a counting game or "I Spy," solicit his opinion on something you are looking at, or offer a snack from the bag you have packed ahead of time. If distraction isn't working, then it is time to take out the Ladder.

Start Climbing Again

Give your first directive regarding what he needs to stop doing, and/or what he needs to start doing:

> "Sweetie, don't put any food in the cart without asking me first."

If this does not do the trick, it is on to Step Two of the Ladder.

To really get your child's attention and emphasize that you mean business, push your cart to the side or walk your child to an out-of-the-way spot. With your hand holding his arm, give him a reminder in a calm but businesslike tone:

> "Okay, Mike, I just said you can't put food in the cart without my permission. This is the second time I am saying it and I mean business here. If you need a third reminder, you will need to get back in the cart."

Step Three is of course action first, talking second. If your child fusses or is too big to ride in the cart, it's time to push your food basket to the front of the store, park it to the side and carry him out. Once your child has calmed down, you can return to the cart and resume your shopping. If you are in a mall, it is the same instruction: Head for the exit promptly. Quick and deliberate action is best for teaching your child you mean what you say.

Once outside the store, if your child has already calmed down in response to your action, then it is okay if you don't go all the way to the car. You can say:

> "Good, you have found your self-control. We will wait out here for a few minutes to be certain you really have a hold of yourself, and then we can go back in and finish shopping. You know you must use your self-control to be in the store."

If you have to go all the way to the car, follow the advice outlined on pages 145 to 147.

If you are dealing with a really wild tantrum, you may need to make the decision to abandon your trip altogether and get your child home. Again, remain as calm as you can and don't berate him as you are driving home. Just let him know that he cannot act like that ever, and certainly not in a store. Your tone, body language, and action should express disapproval, but you should refrain from directly putting him down. If you have had two or three incidents of trouble when out shopping, you can let him know that he will not be going on the next few outings, as he clearly has not been using his self-control.

Since you may have to leave the store and even abort a shopping mission, it is always best to plan realistically. If you have an errand that must get done and your child has not been using his self-control reliably, then it is best not to take him. Get a sitter or wait until your spouse is home and you can make an evening run to the store. On the other hand, if your child has consistently acted up in stores, then do as you did with car rides: Plan a shopping outing or two that are specifically designed as correction trips, with the deliberate intention of climbing the Ladder, if need be, while you're there.

Again, this type of parental response takes effort and self-discipline on your part. In contrast, if you never put in the effort, and keep relying on ineffective, talk-based responses, your child's unruliness will go on and on and on. Tolerating bad, inappropriate behavior takes real effort too—and it's dreadful. Keep a longer-term perspective in mind and find the will to act on behalf of your child's well-being.

Now you are ready to take the Ladder on the road. Remember: Making an effort in the beginning means less effort in the long run, and the time you spend with your child will be that much more enjoyable.

PARENTING TIP

Be Realistic

No matter how sound your discipline strategy, it is no replacement for good planning. Be realistic and don't set up your child—or yourself—for failure. For example, taking your seven- and nine-year-old boys to the mall on a summer afternoon while you try on clothes is probably not a good idea. And think twice about dragging your hungry five-year-old to an eight o'clock dinner reservation at the new steak house in town. In all likelihood, you'll get so frustrated that you'll really want to hit your child with the Ladder instead of climbing it! Let's be honest: misbehaving children are a drain. But blaming them all the time really isn't fair either. Effective parents are effective planners.

Opposition and Anxiety: The Kingpins of IFP

Opposition and anxiety play a key role in the development of an imbalance of family power (IFP) because very few parents today seem to know how to effectively counter and contain them. Consequently, when a child asserts himself with, "No, I don't want to" (opposition), or "No, I am afraid to" (anxiety), too often it is the child's protest that prevails. When this happens, the better judgment and leadership of the parent is lost, the child assumes more power than the parent, and IFP takes root.

Together, opposition and anxiety form the central and all-important power drive. Remember, a child is hard-wired to find out where he has influence. He quickly learns that expressions of opposition and fear are very powerful influencers, and influence means power. He will perfect the use of whatever gives him power. This means that when the whining of opposition and the weeping of anxiety succeed in influencing you, they will only intensify and get worse. Soon your children's protests and distress, not your better judgment, are determining how things go, and the balance of power shifts from you to your kids. The dual roles of opposition and anxiety are so central and can be so detrimental to the parent-child relationship that I've named them the kingpins of IFP.

The knowledge that when behaviors are reinforced they will be repeated and strengthened has been around for a long time. This insight, formally called the Law of Effect, is at the heart of behavioral learning theory.

The new news is that power serves as a salient reinforcement for children. Parents can become very confused when they try to make sense of the quagmire they find themselves in with their kids. They think of how unpleasant yelling, tears, and upsets are and wonder how any child could want to keep provoking such misery. Parents fail to appreciate that the true engine that keeps the negative cycle of interaction going around and around is their child's growing power in his relationship with them. It doesn't help that the way he is wielding his power is making everyone miserable. Think of your own strong reactions as a parent in negative interactions. Your child has a strong influence over you and for him this is very heady power indeed.

Although it is true that self-assertion and protest are normal, healthy responses for all children, such responses fall outside of the normal range when they start to color more than 30% of a child's interactions with his parents and begin to have a disruptive influence on family life. At this juncture, it becomes necessary to address the power dynamics in the parent-child relationship.

The pull and force of opposition and anxiety are inescapable. In fact, all of the common behavioral challenges that parents face when raising young children are fueled by one or the other. For example, when our children have trouble going to bed or sleeping independently, their protests are either motivated by opposition or anxiety: Either they resist staying in their own beds or they are too anxious to sleep in them. The same goes for toileting issues. Kids are either willfully noncompliant or too frightened to use the toilet.

The impact of children's anxiety on us as parents is powerful and readily motivates us to make all kinds of accommodations to our children in order to reduce their distress. This is what gives anxiety its kingpin status. The fact that anxiety can exercise such a powerful role in our relationships with our children can come as a real surprise to parents. While it is more obvious that opposition and defiance are characteristics of kids with too much power, we tend to associate anxiety with helplessness and powerlessness. But the Law of Effect holds true for anxiety just as it does for opposition. Whatever children do, if it is successful in influencing their parents, it is powerful for them, and therefore reinforcing, and so they will keep doing it.

During a consultation, one of the parents of an anxious child put her finger on the heart of the matter when she commented, "If my daughter had been angry, demanding, and screaming a lot, I would have known that I had to stop accommodating her, but since my daughter was afraid and crying a lot, I felt so bad and wanted to do whatever I could to help her feel better. I never realized that what I intended as support and consideration was actually strengthening her anxieties."

As parents, we need to stay on our toes when managing anxiety and opposition. If not held in check, they can take on such a tenacious power that families soon find themselves held hostage to their dictates. Fortunately, when you parent with an understanding of how power dynamics work, and as you use the Ladder, you can respectfully and lovingly correct opposition and contain anxiety. This will restore the balance of power in your family and will result in strong, secure children who know and accept their appropriate place within the family hierarchy. The next two chapters will give you all the tools and strategies you need to diminish and extinguish the unwanted effects of anxiety and opposition.

Chapter Seven

Opposition and Defiance

It has become particularly popular of late to pigeonhole children into a variety of niches as a way to help parents get a handle on understanding and dealing with them. We now have the difficult child, the strong-willed child, the explosive child, and the spirited child, to name just a few. The common denominator that runs through all of these labels is opposition and defiance, which can be very annoying and challenging to parents, no doubt about it. In fact, uncooperative, negative behaviors can be extremely powerful and can upset the life and harmony of a family. Opposition occurs in direct relation to a parent or other authority figure, when a child is resisting, opposing, or pushing in some fashion or another. Defiance refers to opposition that is characterized by a bold or provocative attitude, such as when a child says, "You can't make me" or "You're not the boss of me." Both opposition and defiance are fundamentally resistances to authority and bids for power.

A point of distinction worth noting is that not all annoying and challenging behaviors are forms of opposition or defiance. Sometimes children's idea of adventure and fun involves crossing limits, being annoying, causing damage, and doing dangerous things. These mischievous behaviors and play are not about power challenges per se, but about children asserting themselves, satisfying their curiosity, and testing themselves and their experiences of the world. Nor is impulsive play motivated by opposition and defiance. There are times, however, when normal mischief can set the stage for a power struggle and ignite an oppositional or defiant reaction. For example, a child having fun squirting a garden hose can get out of hand and need a bit of parental redirection. How a parent asserts that redirection can inadvertently shift a child's motivation from ordinary childish play to reactive defiance. For example, if a parent barks out, "What are doing? You squirt the windows one more time, and you're done." A child's spirit of "But it's fun!" can quickly turn into the stubborn stance of "Yeah, you watch me" or "You don't scare me." Suddenly, the interaction is about power, and the child defiantly keeps on squirting.

Self-Control, Respect, and Cooperation (SRC)

Behaviors that comprise opposition and defiance go against the three primary requirements for appropriate social conduct and healthy relationships: self-control, respect, and cooperation. Because I use these important terms so often, I use the acronym SRC. The words *self-control, respect,* and *cooperation* are at the very heart of the matter—they resonate with children and encourage a mature level of interaction. So when parents address oppositional and defiant behaviors with their children, they need to use these three words directly. It is important to make very clear to children what you want and expect from them. For example, in a situation where there is potential for a power imbalance to arise, you might start by saying:

> "Honey, remember—self-control, respect, and cooperation. I know my decision is not the one you wanted and you are frustrated, but I expect that you will keep your self-control and continue to be respectful."

Of course you will say this in concert with whatever action is necessary to ensure your child's compliance.

During consultations, when I ask children to contribute their thoughts on what happens when people live without SRC, none of them have any doubt that it leads nowhere good. Many of these children, who are a real oppositional and defiant handful at home, do not cause any trouble for their teachers at school, but when I ask them how they would feel if their teachers and classmates were to see a video of their behavior at home, they invariably look ashamed and acknowledge that they wouldn't like it at all. On several occasions, children have said that the way they behave at home is not a good way to be and is their secret, which they would never want anyone to know about. They readily agree that they are capable of more self-control, respect, and cooperation, but just haven't been exercising it at home.

These kids genuinely feel bad about how they are behaving, but they don't know why they keep acting the way they do, or how to stop it. But we know why—they are caught in the trap of IFP in their relationship with their parents. Kids will never figure this out, nor can they break the pull of their power drive on their own. They need their parents to lead them out of this trouble. Towards that end, I also ask children to assess their parents on the same three qualities of self-control, respect, and cooperation. Most of the time the children are very clear about where their parents fall short. Children will never exercise more self-control, show more respect, or extend more of a cooperative spirit than their parents do. SRC must be a foundation for everyone in a family, parents as well as children. Yelling, bullying, disrespect, crying, pleading, and threatening are all evidence of family members not working effectively and respectfully with one another. There's IFP in these families and they'll need the Ladder to climb up and out of the hole they have dug for themselves.

The Top Ten Parental Missteps That Fuel Opposition and Defiance

Parents usually have more than just one or two behaviors in their repertoire that fuel opposition and defiance in their kids, and they tend to make these missteps at different times as they scramble to be effective and have an impact on their children. The message here is not that missteps cause outright damage in and of themselves. However, when they are relied on too heavily, as a means to gain their children's cooperation, they wind up fueling the very behavior parents are trying to stop. The following list of top ten parental missteps is followed by a more detailed discussion of how they fuel our kids' opposition and defiance:

1. Overexplaining, reasoning, and negotiating
2. Apologizing too often
3. Seeking a child's permission and approval
4. Not owning parental decisions and directions
5. Being overly focused on parents' needs
6. Manipulating with too many bribes and threats
7. Repeating the same direction over and over
8. Blaming the child and looking to him for answers
9. A dismissive and disrespectful manner
10. Being too heavy-handed and using corporal punishment.

Misstep 1. Overexplaining, Reasoning, and Negotiating

Overexplaining, reasoning, and negotiating are the hallmarks of the Pleaser and Pushover parenting styles, but there isn't a parent alive who hasn't overdone all three. As with most things, explaining, reasoning, and negotiating are not intrinsically bad or damaging, but if they have come to dominate the way you communicate with your child, you are either already in a heap of IFP or well on your way. Unfortunately, some parents these days equate smart, patient, thorough, reasonable talking with top-of-the-line parenting. Of course it is good to talk to your children, and teach and explain, but not when what is needed is action and solid parental limits, direction, or correction. Simply talking when action is needed compromises your effectiveness.

Leave the overtalking out of correcting. Keep it short and to the point. Avoid putting too much emotion into your words. And then, if your words aren't effective in eliciting your child's cooperation, get moving.

The key point to remember is that by overexplaining and reasoning you are providing the perfect setup for your child to join in the word game, bait you into a negotiation or debate, and ultimately prevail. You are thereby reinforcing your child with loads of power.

Misstep 2. Apologizing Too Often

The widely adopted communication practice of apologizing for disappointing your child's expectations has come out of the prevailing democratic, child-centered parenting culture. The idea is that offering empathy and consideration for a child's wants and feelings during times of correction or discipline will reduce a child's distress and make him less inclined to protest. The more salient effect on the child, however, is that it exaggerates how important it is that a child always feel considered and happy. A typical apology goes something like this: "Honey, I'm really sorry, I know you are having fun, and I promise you can play with your dolls again tomorrow, but we have to take a bath now and get ready for bed. I know it's hard, and I hate to stop your fun, but it really is getting late, and tomorrow is a school day."

The truth is, when parents make a habit of apologizing for having to provide leadership, children understand it to mean that anything that thwarts their happiness is most regrettable. This exaggerates their sense of specialness and makes it seem like not being able to do what you want—or having to delay or interrupt fun—is really a hard thing to do. Rather than learning how to cooperate with parental direction, children learn to turn up their distress when they hear "No" followed by an "I'm sorry, honey."

Another reason that routine apologies are so ineffective and serve to inflame opposition is that the parents sound tentative and unsure about their leadership. If a child expresses distress, parental timidity is often further underscored by overexplanation: "But honey, look at the clock, it really is getting late. Getting a good night's sleep is very important. You know you get grumpy if you are tired, and then Mommy gets upset and we end up not having a good day." The more the child continues to protest, the more the parent apologizes and the lengthier the explanation becomes. Come on, Mom and Dad, stop talking and get moving. Get up, walk to your child, take his hand, and lead him to his room while talking about the fun you'll have tomorrow.

Remember that a large part of helping your kids get along well in life is getting them adjusted to the reality that life is generally not on their terms. It is a part of everyday life that children's requests must be denied and their pleasures interrupted. Children ask for and want a lot, and they don't like being redirected. It is just how kids are. They are curious, active, hungry, and the world is filled with tempting fun. *Parental regulation of children is a part of life, and children are well equipped to take the no's in stride if their parents take them in stride.*

Additionally, when parents fall over themselves and act as if their child has been hurt in a way that deserves an apology, the child becomes less likely to accept parental redirection. I am not suggesting that you shouldn't acknowledge disappointment periodically when something is a big deal to your child and you must say no, but when you make it a habit and apologize reflexively, you transfer power to your child and encourage his opposition and protest.

Misstep 3. Seeking a Child's Permission and Approval

If only I had a nickel for every time I heard a parent give her child a directive and at the end make it into a question by adding "Okay?" With that money, I could sell the house and follow the sun. Directives are not open for a child's consideration as to whether he would like to follow them or not. They are parental instructions for what a child needs to do next. When a parent says something like, "Honey, stay with the babysitter and do as she asks, okay? Will you do that for me, honey?" This phrasing conveys an overt deference to the child's power. When you give directives from a position of clarity and strength, your child will be much more likely to accept your authority without so much fuss and upset.

The second problem with parents asking "Okay?" is that they do not really intend to be asking; they are not posing a real option, and so the question is disingenuous. Furthermore, what happens when the child does answer and his answer is no? A power struggle is born.

PARENTING TIP

Drop the "Okay?"

The bad habit of transferring power to our children is often due to misguided parental attempts to be nice and to sugarcoat our authority. All experienced parents know this attempt is in vain. The only solution is to drop the *okay?* and focus on giving clear directives. This is easier said than done, but if you work together with your spouse, help to remind and reinforce each other, you can break the habit, no matter how entrenched it may be.

Misstep 4. Not Owning Parental Decisions and Directions

In the discussion of Pushover parents in chapter three, I pointed out a tendency we have to try to borrow the authority and influence of other people whom our children respect—teachers, friends, doctors, the police, and so on. A parent who believes her child won't listen to her tries to ride on the coattails of those the child might respect: "No, honey, I can't buy that cereal. Remember, the dentist told us cereal with too much sugar will hurt your teeth. The dentist said so; you heard him say that, remember?" "Sweetheart, you can't have a sleepover tonight; you have school tomorrow. Your teacher said all the children in her class have to get a good night's sleep so they can be well-rested and ready to learn."

With these statements, parents are inadvertently giving a very problematic message: It is not their judgment or direction being expressed; they are just following the rules and limits presented by someone with true authority. The most important point here is that in the context of power dynamics, a parent diminishes her own power by routinely referring to the authority of others as a way to coax cooperation. Children are empowered by their parent's lack of direct authority and, as a result, cooperate less, not more.

Not only does a parent undermine herself with this sort of communication, she also sets the stage for her child to learn that the best solution to getting around a no is simply to make sure the authority figure doesn't find out. In other words don't tell, just sneak around and don't get caught. The following exchange between a grandmother (who wants nothing more than to please) and her granddaughter (who is full of moxie) is a perfect example:

"Rosie, I am not allowed to drive until you buckle your seat belt because Grandma could get a ticket from the police. It is the law, you know. The police say you have to buckle up."

(Granddaughter, leaning over the front seat to reassure her):

> "Don't worry, Grandma, there aren't any cops around here. I'll keep a lookout."

See how this game can backfire? Grandma, and all you parents out there, are going to have to claim your authority and make it clear that it is *your* rule: "Everyone in my car buckles up for safety."

Misstep 5. Being Overly Focused on Parental Needs

Pushover parents win the award for overexercising this misstep, but Pleaser moms and dads are runners-up. It is simply not appropriate to ask your child to focus on taking care of your needs and your feelings. This includes trying to motivate your children into cooperating by telling them they have hurt your feelings, made you sad, caused you to have a headache or a muscle spasm, or left you feeling resentful, overwhelmed, stressed out, or about to go crazy.

Why not? First of all, you will not get very far leading from a position of weakness and woe. Second, the implication is that your child's behaviors are primarily a problem because they make you feel bad and you just can't take it. It is tantamount to saying that the real reason kids need to behave is to take care of the needs of their fragile parents.

Whatever your angst, your child will not be motivated to change their behavior because of it. What they *will* be is empowered by the knowledge that they can get you over a barrel easily. In your child's mind, the thought will be, "Wow, if I fuss and whine, check out what it does to Mom! Now, that's powerful." The child will continue to protest, and over time, even though she is provoking them, your complaints and ineffectiveness will lead her to regard you as weak and whiny, and she'll come to respect you less and less. The effective response to children's ordinary annoying behavior cannot be organized around how the parent feels about it. "I can't believe you just throw all the nice clothes I buy you on the floor. How do you think that makes me feel? It is like you are just slapping me in the face. I feel so disrespected." Laments like this hands over emotional power to the child.

While I can empathize with the parent's frustration, this tactic is not constructive or effective. If you always make it about you and your feelings, and expect that this will be effective in motivating your kids to become neater (or whatever you are angling for), you are just going to get more upset, because it won't work. The other setup here is that you are asking your child to change in order to take care of your feelings, and when she doesn't, what does this signify about her character? She must be the most selfish, uncaring, and inconsiderate kid, right? And you will probably end up telling her so. Eventually she will become defiant and there will be a new dimension to throwing her clothes on the floor—she will do it just to spite you. What a vicious cycle! Leave your feelings out of ordinary parenting leadership and corrections.

Misstep 6. Manipulating with Too Many Bribes and Threats

Bribes and threats are used all the time as motivators. You must be careful, however, not to overuse them, because they send the message to your child that manipulation is your best hope of getting him to cooperate. This places the power in your child's hands rather than in yours, and in so doing inflames his continued reliance on opposition. Besides that, no one likes, or responds well, to a heavy diet of bribery and threats.

Of the four parenting styles, Forcers use bribes and threats the most, and their threats can be quite harsh. Bribes and threats come with a higher cost than simply escalating opposition: Heavy-handed manipulation always stirs up resentment and anger and creates bad blood in the parent-child relationship. Threats are particularly problematic. Too often they tend to be rash, empty, and exaggerated because they are delivered in moments of exasperation and frustration: "If you don't stop it right now and cooperate, you are not going to go to Jimmy's birthday party tomorrow!" "If you don't stop being a brat and start listening, we are going to leave the zoo and that is it!" The parent is flailing here, grasping for something to get the child's attention. The reality of these two examples is that Jimmy is the little boy's best friend and the mom is close friends with his mother, so there is really no way they will miss the party. Similarly with the zoo—it is a planned trip, they are there with their cousins, and the zoo is an hour away from home, so they aren't leaving. The insincerity of such threats makes them particularly ineffective. They ring of impotent desperation, and the child knows he is really getting to you. This scenario simply further ignites and reinforces his power drive.

I am not suggesting that you make rash threats and actually follow through with them. What I am suggesting is leaving them out of your parenting altogether. Parents go too far too often, taking away trick-or-treating, the Easter egg hunt, or special outings in the belief that they are getting at the child's uncooperative behavior. The parental notion that if the child really has to pay a price it will result in a hard lesson learned once and for all is not only mean, but the punishment does not stem from an appreciation of what is really going wrong, and why self-control, respect, and cooperation are not more forthcoming from the child.

There are occasions, however, when motivating children to cooperate is necessary. This is where you have to distinguish threats and bribes from consequences and reasonable enticements. I like using consequences and enticements with children. Whereas threats are rash and harsh, consequences are delivered respectfully and matter-of-factly, leaving the threatening tone out of it and keeping the consequence relevant to the situation at hand. A Pleaser parent who is at her wit's end screams, "Okay, I am staying up all night to make sure that if the Easter bunny comes, he doesn't leave you any candy!" An effective parent would intervene with the Ladder:

> "You know I only say things two times, and this is the second reminder I am giving you. A third time means you're going to your room."

The effective parent follows through, climbing the Ladder as high as necessary, and then moves on, never bringing the holiday festivities or the special outings into the discipline mix at all.

Enticements differ from bribes in that they are used as motivators, not as a substitute for parental competence. Letting your child know something good will follow cooperation can be most helpful. But bribes are too blatant and often have a ring of desperation to them: "Honey, I really need you to behave in the store today. If you are a good girl for Mommy and let me get through the grocery shopping without making a fuss, then you can pick a piece of candy at the checkout." It is clear this parent has no confident power as the authority and leader in the relationship. In this scenario, the bribe is a vehicle for power transfer.

To distinguish threats and bribes from consequences and enticements, consider the phrasing. Bribes and threats are delivered in the context of "if–then" statements. For example, "*If* you are a good girl for

Mommy while we are running errands this morning, *then* I will take you to the ice cream parlor as a special treat." Threats are similar: "*If* you don't clean your room, *then* you will not go to Amy's sleepover party tomorrow night."

Shifting the language to positive motivational talk yields a much better response from your child:

> "Hey, let's get through our errands quickly! We'll do them together as a team, and then go get some ice cream afterwards!"

If your daughter acts up, you can handily say:

> "Stop and think, honey. This kind of fussing and carrying on means we'll have to go directly back home without our ice cream fun."

Here both the enticement and the consequence are kept without being manipulative, and as a result have a more positive effect on your child. Consider the effect of this approach on your child:

> "Honey, I know you have a sleepover party tomorrow. Don't forget, your chores will need to be done before you go. That includes cleaning your room. Did you get that clearly, hon? Room clean before you go."

Misstep 7. Repeating the Same Direction Over and Over

Okay, parents, this example is a classic and it should sound all too familiar:

> "Christopher, come here, stop splashing the water like that."

(Christopher continues his play.)

> "Christopher! Come here!"

(The father waits for a response, staying seated in his chair.)

"Christopher, I want you to listen to Daddy right now. Christopher, you are not listening. Stop playing with the water, and come over here now."

(Child continues to play. Father continues to sit.)

"Christopher, what did we talk about last night? What did Daddy say to you about listening? CHRISTOPHER JAMES! NOW!"

(Yelling from his chair even louder than before):

"CHRISTOPHER JAMES! YOU ARE ABOUT TO BE IN BIG TROUBLE!"

I can't go on anymore—but unfortunately this father could. He never once got out of his chair and shifted into action. He just kept repeating himself and increasing his threatening tone.

These kinds of scenes are common and futile. If only this dad knew about the Ladder, he would have given his directive only twice, and when he didn't get his child's cooperation, he would have gone over to his son, taken him by the hand, and escorted him away. If he still did not get his youngster's cooperation, he could pick his son up, saying, "If you do not cooperate, you will have to stay right by my side." Any action along these lines would get the job done, avoiding the father's threatening temper escalation.

The Real Million-Dollar Question

"How many times do I have to tell you?" is the million-dollar question parents ask their children. Well, I am of the opinion that the real million-dollar question is one you should be asking yourself: "How many times are you going to say the same thing?" If you climb the Ladder, you know the answer is only twice. Then the talking stops and the action begins.

Misstep 8. Blaming the Child and Looking to Him for Answers

Pleaser and Pushover parents have a terrible habit of trying to discipline and enlist cooperation from their children by asking them self-examining questions. For example, "Honey, didn't you know that that was wrong?" or "Why did you do that, sweetheart?" This is the fair-minded, considerate, feeling-based orientation of the current parenting culture, and it is such a mistake. I know it sounds gentle and respectful to address children this way, but the problem is that developmentally it goes completely over their heads. Young children are not self-reflective, and they have no idea why they do things.

Furthermore, what this means in the context of power dynamics is extremely problematic. Parents ask these questions with total sincerity, and so children get the message that it is they who are really the ones in the know and that parents are looking to them for answers. Asking questions of little children such as, "Honey, when will you want to start using the potty?" or "When are you going to be ready to sleep alone and not need me to stay with you?" is absurd and also constitutes a blatant transfer of power. The parent's leadership and better judgment in these exchanges is suspended by what is thought to be a considerate and gentle parenting style. To be effective, parents cannot look to their children for answers.

In order to enlist their children's cooperation, Forcers ask questions that tend to be less genuine and more rhetorical: "What is the matter with you? Why are you so impossible?" These questions constitute character attack and blaming. Pleasers and Pushovers, on the other hand, pursue their children as if they are really going to get an answer from questions such as: "What do I have to do? What will it take to get you to listen?" "How many times do I have to tell you? Do you want Daddy to get mad and yell?" "I can't be late for work, so you have to tell Mommy what to do to get you to keep your shoes on." These questions clearly say that your capacity for leadership is tapped out, and now you have to ask your child to step up and give you the answers.

In truth, the questions you have been asking of your child should be asked of yourself. "What is wrong with me? Why am I being so ineffective? What will it take to get me to stop talking and act to ensure my directions and requests are met?" "How many times will I keep asking my child the same thing before I get up and go into action and climb the Ladder?" When you do, your child will soon stop all the opposition and defiance that has been driving you so crazy.

Stop blaming the kids and asking them for knowledge and leadership they can't provide. You need to lead them, teach them, and extend to them your better judgment and authority. This is the key you have been looking for—but it resides in you and your abilities, not within your child.

Misstep 9. A Dismissive and Disrespectful Manner

"Hurry up! You're so slow." "Did I ask you a question? No. I told you to do something. Now do it!" "Fine, go find another family to live with. I don't know anyone who is going to put up with you."

While it's not unusual for most parents to express themselves disrespectfully to their children from time to time, Forcers make a habit of trying to exercise their authority and power by making their children feel cowed into cooperating. Consequently, the message these kids get is that their parents will readily sacrifice the respect and care they should have for their children in order to exercise their own power. Children who are treated this way may get in line sooner than those who are pandered to, but bad blood builds up and eventually they will challenge authority and power in ways that can create an even bigger problem.

Your child will never treat you with more respect than you give to him. You set the ceiling—however high or low. If you often lapse into a mean-spirited, dismissive, and disrespectful parenting style, it is wise to take heed. You are not gaining any real ground in imparting a cooperative spirit in your child, nor are you encouraging him to treat you with respect. In fact, you are working against establishing a healthy authority with your child, and he will consolidate anger and resentment that will fuel the oppositional behavior of acting out against you.

Very often the transgression that incites disrespectful and demeaning criticisms from parents is childish irresponsibility. For example, your child has forgotten to feed the dog, take care of his things, or put his clothes away. It is important to acknowledge and accept a developmental reality: children are irresponsible. That is part of what being a child is. Responsibility comes with maturity—gradually, and over time. Parents have to be realistic about kids taking care of their things, whether it is toys, clothes, sports equipment, or their pets, and have to be actively involved in overseeing all of these. Simply saying to your child, "It is your responsibility. Do you understand?" will not be sufficient. He will tell you he understands, but that does not mean he actually knows how to behave responsibly. Children need reminders and assistance.

Many parenting experts tout the benefits of what they call real-world consequences to teach children responsibility. The practice rests on the idea that tough lessons will help children to mature faster. For example, your daughter leaves her bike out in the rain repeatedly and as a real-world consequence, you stop bringing it in and let it rust. When she asks for a new bike you tell her she is not responsible enough to have one. Or, as one expert has recommended, if your child does not feed his hamster or clean the cage, you can give it to a neighbor's child, whom you believe will show more responsibility, and explain to your son that the hamster has to go to foster care where it will be well cared for.

The lesson these actions teach is that hurting is what it takes to learn, and that real gain comes with real pain. Maybe this is true on the athletic field, but in our relationships it is not that simple. What about acting in the following fashion instead? If your daughter's bike has been left outside again, go to her and tell her to put the bike in the garage right then and there. If she balks, climb the Ladder. The same action applies to the hungry hamster. Go to your child, and if your first request is ignored, take him respectfully by the hand and walk him to the food, telling him he cannot delay. Then move to the Ladder if necessary.

Effective parenting has to include a realistic acceptance of the childishness in children. Don't hold it against them and don't rub their noses in it. *Understand that shaping childishness into maturity is a developmental task that evolves over many years and that you are responsible for guiding the process.*

Misstep 10. Being Too Heavy-Handed and Using Corporal Punishment

Heavy-handedness and corporal punishment are other examples of bullying. Grabbing, yanking by the arm, slapping, hitting with a spoon, pointing a finger in a child's face or pushing it into his chest, and in general being scary and intimidating are all harmful to children and in the end, fuel their motivation to be oppositional. The use of demeaning sarcasm falls into this category as well: "Aren't you a real whiz kid?" or "Well, will you listen to Miss Princess." These parental tactics hardly exemplify self-control, respect, or the spirit of cooperation. Don't expect your child to rise above your behavior and give you better in return.

Children whose parents bully learn that this is how power is achieved. Being bullied hurts kids, it makes them angry, and they move farther away from self-control, respect, and cooperation, and more towards opposition and defiance. It is also common that kids who are yelled at, grabbed, poked, and intimidated will take it on the road to siblings, to the playground, and eventually to their own spouses and children. Bullies beget bullies.

To Spank, or Not to Spank?

A word about spanking—don't! First, you never have to because you can get your child to follow your directions without it, and second, and much more importantly, it violates the basic bond and fundamental contract of the parent-child relationship. Parents are meant to protect their children from pain—not to deliberately inflict it. You would never let someone else hit your child, and there is really no way to justify doing it yourself. This is a parental distortion at the most profound level. Don't tell me, or your children, that you are hitting them for their own good. Anyone who has ever been hit knows this isn't true.

What spanking teaches children is not self-control and respect, but fear and resentment. Spanking does not yield true cooperation, only compliance as a means to avoid punishment. Furthermore, spanking makes a mockery of telling your child not to hit.

There are experts who recommend corporal punishment and who even teach parents how to use it most effectively. In *The Strong-Willed Child*, for example, Dr. James C. Dobson instructs parents to always use an instrument of discipline when hitting their child, because hands are for loving, not hurting. I couldn't disagree more strongly. *Don't ever spank your child*—with your hands or anything else.

The good news is that if you use the Ladder, you will have an alternative that works. You will not only be spared the mounting frustration that so often leads to spankings and other angry and harmful reactions, but also spare your child, whom you love, the terribly confusing and hurtful experience of having a parent who sees hitting and hurting as a way to exercise authority.

Make no mistake, every time you hit your child, you scare him and you hurt him—if not physically, then emotionally. In turn, your child builds up fear as well as strong feelings of anger and resentment—all of which are fuel for anxiety, acting out, and defiant behavior. There are definitely times when children require parents to be physical with them—but keep it to picking them up, removing them, carrying them to their room, and holding on to them if they are out of control.

How Children Oppose and Defy, and What to Do About It

Children show opposition in two major ways: verbally and through physical acting out. All parents differ in terms of which of their children's specific tactics they are most susceptible to, or which they are most ineffective in handling. Kids catch on to this very quickly. They have not only an instinct to assert their power but a remarkable ability to pick up on their parent's vulnerabilities and play to them.

Verbal Opposition

REFUSALS

"No!" "You can't make me!" "I'm not going to." "You're not the boss of me!" There's nothing subtle here. These straightforward, direct refusals to a parent's authority are your child saying, "Oh, yeah? You think you have influence over me? Well, you don't. I'm the one with the power to say how things will go and what I will and won't do. So there!"

If parents cave in, collapsing into a position of accommodation by talking, reasoning, or failing to take effective action, then the child will be correct in his assertion that he is in charge. Any child who talks in such a brazen manner has already been given plenty of power and a wide berth for inappropriate self-assertion.

If your child is older than three or four and blatantly challenges your authority with such overt dominance, the diagnosis is IFP and you must get busy with a correction phase. Now. There is no time to waste. You and your child are missing out on fun and harmony, and your child is consolidating some very unlikable character habits. Below we explain what to do about that situation.

The Effective Parent in Action

When your child challenges you overtly with a blatant refusal, you can respond in one of two ways, depending on the situation. If your child has stepped too far over the line and is quite rude to you, then clear, decisive action is required. Start your response on Step Three of the Ladder (page 109). In a firm, disapproving (but not angry) voice, say:

> "Excuse me? What did I just hear you say? You may not refuse to cooperate, nor may you speak to me in such a disrespectful way. Come with me, you are going to spend some time in your room."

Parents, that's all the talking there should be. Now act quickly. Get your child to his room, and don't say anything further while you are escorting him there. You can expect your little one to say a lot to you as you steer him along, but hold your tongue and don't take the bait. If your child escalates his resistance to your authority by screaming, refusing to stay in his room, or becoming physical, you know what to do—keep climbing the Ladder to Steps Four and Five as needed.

If your child is just flirting with blatant refusal, and it has not yet become a part of his repertoire, you can moderate your response and start with Step Two. Put a little humor in your tone—something along the lines of exaggerated incredulity:

> "No? Did you just say no? What are you thinking, you silly-billy? You can't say no to me like that."

Then with a more serious tone, continue with the script of the Ladder:

> "Now, let me repeat my request . . . and remember, this is the second time I am saying it. If you need a third reminder, or if you are disrespectful again, you will have to go to your room."

The initial lighthearted tone is helpful in diffusing your child's defiance and opposition and lets him know that his behavior does not have the power to get you upset and excited. If he still does not cooperate, of course it is time to move and carry out Step Three, staying collected and unruffled as you climb the Ladder.

TALKING BACK AND BEING FRESH

"Stupid, stupid, stupid mommy." "Shut up!" "I hate you!" "Go away! Don't talk to me."

It makes my fingers itch just writing about such power-drenched language coming from a child. I have worked with many children who have spoken like this, and believe me I have fallen in love with every one of them. There wasn't a bad kid in the bunch; they were just children who were literally drunk on power and all messed up because of it. When their parents reclaimed their position of effective leadership and power with these kids, all of them settled down quickly, and their true, delightful nature and good-heartedness was free to shine through again.

If you can't see the wonderful nature of your child for all the back talk, keep a level head and start by acting, not talking. The correction for talking back and rudeness is very similar to the script and course of action outlined for refusals. Start your correction on Step Three of the Ladder. A key point here is to keep your emotions in check. A strong reaction will only tell your child he has gotten to you. For a child's power drive that means a direct hit, and it will fuel the back talk.

Before you say anything at all, walk to your child, put your hands on his shoulders and turn him towards his room. Only then begin speaking. Say to him:

> "Excuse me? Who do you think you are, speaking in such a fashion? Absolutely not. Now off to your room."

Follow the script and protocol for Step Three of the Ladder by directing him to his room and setting the terms for his staying there (page 109). Climb as high as you need to go. Be certain that your calm prevails.

Nothing can push a parent's buttons like back talk and a fresh mouth from his children. It makes us want to punish them. But don't. Showing your children adult self-control and respect here is the key to effectiveness. In the face of their outrageousness, you have to maintain your calm. Forcer parents, you will have to be on special alert because you will be tempted to really come down hard. Hold on tight to the Ladder instead. Stick to the script as if it were your job, and I promise you, you will be powerful and like the results.

NEGOTIATING AND WHINING

"Wait, wait, let me finish this." "Mom, I can't turn off the computer now; I will lose my level on this game. You don't understand." "If you let me eat it in the TV room, then okay." "But why doesn't he have to do it? That's not fair! I'm not doing it until Steven helps too." "Okay, but I want Daddy, not you!" "Ooh, I don't like these kinds of green beans. I want the skinny ones. Make me the skinny ones." "I want to stop at McDonald's. I will still eat my dinner, I promise. You know I need to eat before I go to practice. Come on, Mom."

These are the common whines and negotiations of younger children. As children get older they hone their skill of negotiation to an art. They can really wear parents down with their relentless bids to make sure things follow their agenda. When a parent tells me her child is a constant negotiator, she is actually giving me a lot of information about her parenting style, as well, because it takes at least two to negotiate. When kids are relentless whiners and negotiators, then you can be sure that more often than not the tactic is working for them and they are coming out on top. Otherwise they wouldn't put so much energy into the negotiation. These kids are eating in the TV room, or at the computer. They are dictating which parent puts them to bed, and they are eating at a lot of restaurants of their choice.

Parents, tread carefully here. Too many times your reasoned response falls into the category of, "Oh, what's the big deal? He just wants to finish his game, I guess that isn't asking for too much." Or, "She wants Daddy because she hasn't seen him all day, and right now she is in such a Daddy phase. I can understand that." If you focus on the specific content of the child's negotiation, you miss the larger dynamic. The salient issue is really about power, and who is in the lead. I am not saying you can never bend a bit and accommodate your child, but if the requests are frequent and becoming a burden or an annoyance, then you know you need to tighten up your responses and hold firm to your agenda.

The Effective Parent in Action

The best way to nip the negotiation habit is to engage as little as possible with your child—who has learned from his interactions with you that his words can derail your agenda. It is best to ignore his bid for a negotiation, and simply go right to Step Two of the Ladder:

> "Okay, stop right there; no negotiating, please. This is the second time I am giving you my answer. If you do not cooperate now, you will be heading off to your room."

If your child has been relying on negotiating, you can begin by saying:

> "David, rather than cooperating lately, you have been trying to make a lot of bargains or negotiate things on your terms. I am not looking to make a deal with you. I am expecting your cooperation. Now, I will give you a second reminder, and you need to stop talking and do as I say."

If your child keeps going on, it is time to take him to his room. While walking towards him you can say:

> "Oh my, still trying to tell me how you want things rather than cooperating. Come on then, it's off to your room for a bit."

This kind of focused intervention will clear up your child's opposition in no time. What a relief for everyone. Your child gets a headache from spinning his wheels, too.

DISMISSING WITH A SUPERIOR ATTITUDE

"Oh my God, Mom, no one cares what you think. You are such a jerk." "So what? I don't care." . . . "Go ahead, take it away. I don't like that old toy anymore anyway." "Fine, I'll go ask Mom and she'll let me." "You are so annoying! Don't even talk to me."

Children can also pretend not to hear your directions; they'll plug their ears with their fingers; or they'll acknowledge hearing you, but continue to ignore you and do whatever they want to do. Sometimes they even turn and walk (or run) away from you while you're talking to them.

Proceed with your response just as you would with any other dismissive behaviors that are rude, brazen, or over the top: with immediate action. Get up, or if you are already standing, walk directly over to your child. Your posture and focused look should convey, loud and clear, that you are in a business mode and that your child does not have a hope of prevailing this time. If your child is small enough, immediately pick her up and say:

> "Don't ignore me when I speak to you."

If she is too big to pick up, then with your hands under her arms, get her up and direct her to her room saying the same thing. Now you will have her attention and, most likely, an escalating protest as well. Stay the course, and climb the Ladder, as high as your child needs.

If your child dismisses you by saying "I don't care," or "Go ahead, your punishment doesn't bother me," the best response is to go right on as though she never said it. Give it no attention or power at all. Simply tell her it is time for her to go to her room. Keep your cool. Don't take her bait or escalate your response to try to get her to say "Uncle." That is not the point at all. Your clearheaded leadership is what your child desperately needs. Take the lead, not your child's bait.

I was in a shopping mall when I heard a mother ask her daughter, who looked to be about eleven, to please give her the cell phone so she could call home. Her daughter was clearly put out by this and said, "No. You don't need to. I am talking to Alicia." Her mother responded with a very agitated tone, "Nicole, I said give me the phone." Nicole rolled her eyes and, with a look of disgust, kept talking as she walked on ahead. Her mother raised her voice and said with exasperation, "Nicole, don't walk away. Come back here. I told you I need the phone!" Nicole increased her pace without even a glance back. Then, with disgust, the mother said to her young son who was also with her, "Oh, she is so impossible." They followed on, several feet behind, while Nicole chatted away on the cell phone.

Oh my. Yes, Nicole is a force to be reckoned with, and I can predict she isn't going to be improving anytime soon. When Nicole put out a power challenge, and in effect said," What are you going to do about it?" her mother's response was, unfortunately, not much of anything. If this mother doesn't do more than just get upset, if she fails to move to action, there is going to be a very rocky road ahead when Nicole hits adolescence.

The Effective Parent in Action

Clearly, Nicole's inflated sense of power and disrespect has been accumulating for years. Children just don't treat their parents like this out of the blue. I would have coached this mother to catch up to her daughter, take the package of new purchases out of Nicole's hand, and say:

> "Your incredible rudeness and disrespect certainly is not going to be rewarded with any more new clothes. For now, this shopping trip is over and we are going home."

The mother should then proceed to the car, escorting her by the elbow if need be. You see, because behavior like Nicole's has so much power of defiance and disrespect behind it, an equally strong counterforce is necessary to check it. Consequently, I would have advised the mother to continue her correction in the car by saying:

> "Your attitude has really gotten out of hand. There must be a change. So, once we get home, you will need to cancel whatever plans you have for the rest of the day and tonight. Before you will have access to privileges again, you need to show me a better attitude and more respect and cooperation for a full day. Remember, privileges include the phone and television as well."

This intervention is an example of the kind that will be needed for children who are older and whose power has never been adequately checked. Most likely, Nicole will not be able to extend respect and cooperation for an entire day because too much IFP has accumulated over time, and so her mother will have to hold her position and suspend her daughter's privileges until she can. Parental determination and fortitude are called for in order to realign the power imbalance. Continue to use the Ladder to manage any unruliness and disrespect as needed throughout the correction phase. Remember, the first interventions will provoke the biggest explosions in power-bloated children.

MAKING EXCUSES AND BLAMING OTHERS

"But I was just going to." "I'm too tired." "But he did it first." "I couldn't help it." "But I didn't hear you." Excuses and externalizations come in all shapes and sizes. It is human nature to try to buffer and cover our wrongdoings. Don't get too worked up about the fact that your child does not step up more readily to accountability; this is an acquisition of maturity that takes time to develop. It is better to pay little mind to his excuses and directly address his behavior instead.

The Effective Parent in Action

While she is in the kitchen, a mother sees her son push his sister off the couch. When she moves in to intervene, Johnny says, "But Mom, I was watching a show and Sara came in and changed it. She is the one who did a bad thing first."

Kids always try to redirect their parents' attention to what a brother or sister did. Don't take the bait. Your home is not a court of law. You are just a parent, and you can honestly say:

> "Well, I did not *see* that. I *did* see you push Sara onto the floor, and no matter what happened before that, pushing your sister is not okay. You're done watching TV for a while. Now go on and take a few minutes in your room."

Another response to these kinds of excuses is a general statement about how you have not asked for details or explanations:

> "I am not asking for an explanation, honey. What I have asked is for you to get moving and do as I have asked."

Then, if he starts to protest verbally, say:

> "Further talk without action will buy you a ticket to your room."

If you make a habit out of not being sidetracked and led astray by the craftiness of your child, you will hear far fewer annoying excuses from your children and there will be less blame-shifting.

RELENTLESSNESS

Requests, demands, conditions—our children can go on and on, refusing to stop until they get a response that satisfies them. Parents who can't take the aggravation another minute finally give in with "Okay, okay, I'll tell you what . . ." and proceed to offer an accommodation to avoid escalation into an all-out tantrum or an otherwise embarrassing scene. Each time a child succeeds in getting what he wants by using this tactic, he will be certain to use it again. Your ability to short-circuit relentless requests and curtail badgering is essential for peace and harmony in your family.

The Effective Parent in Action

Going up against a determined child with a one-track mind takes some fortitude. You must get into the mind-set of being equally unyielding in your redirection. If the answer you give to your child's relentless requests is not the one she's looking for, she will keep on asking. Interrupt the pleading with an attention-getting gesture. If your child's begging is a routine habit that escalates quickly, clap your hands once sharply and say:

> "Elizabeth, Stop. I have told you my answer. I am not going to talk about this with you any further. If you keep going on about

it, I am going to have you go to your room until you can get it out of your system."

Then, climb onto the Ladder if you need it.

For a child who does not push as relentlessly, try this lighter approach:

"Uh-oh! I can hear you revving up. You're like a train barreling down the tracks. Quick, put your brakes on. STOP the train. Don't keep asking the same question over and over."

Distraction and a supportive manner go a long way. If these just aren't doing the trick, then keep climbing the Ladder with:

"Oh shoot, honey, it seems you just couldn't get your brakes to work. That's okay. You can go to your room until you get hold of your self-control. It is important that when I give you an answer, even if you don't like it, you don't keep going on and on about it."

Then follow the instructions for Step Three of the Ladder (page 109).

Now that you have general guidelines for what to say and what to do in the face of various verbal oppositions, adapt your own words and actions to fit whatever circumstances arise with your children. The more often you assert your clear and firm leadership, the more comfortable you will feel about using it.

Physical Opposition
HITTING, KICKING, AND THROWING

Throughout my discussion of children's behaviors, I have stressed the importance of considering your child's developmental level. This is particularly relevant in approaching the management of physical opposition. There is a decided difference between a three- or four-year-old lashing out in anger with a swing at you or a swift kick and an eight-year-old who starts hitting. A younger child is still in the grips of a common aggressive impulse to strike out when provoked, whereas an older child should have pretty well mastered this impulse, and it should no longer be in his repertoire of behavioral options.

Still, when younger children act in accordance with the impulses of their age, do not be lulled into thinking, "Oh, it's just a stage" and respond passively to their displays of physical aggression. How you respond when your little one hits or kicks you will very much influence whether he will master those impulses or continue to hit and kick as he gets older.

The Effective Parent in Action

If your child is young and striking out with an age-driven impulse, it is best not to react with a strong emotion. As we know, big emotions signal to children that their behavior has been powerful—they've scored a hit, and they will be inclined to repeat the behavior. Even if your reaction is strongly negative, it still cranks up their power drive rather than turning it down. So for a three- or four-year-old, take his wrist or ankle and say:

> "Whoa there, big guy, keep your hands down. Being disappointed can't lead to hitting."

Keep holding his hand for a moment (or his ankle if he has kicked) and see if he seems to be settling down. Say:

> "I am going to let go of your hand now, and you must not hit again. If you do, you will have to stop playing and spend time in your room. You cannot be with other people if you hit or hurt them."

I take a somewhat different approach when a child is five years of age or older. For these children I refer to hitting, kicking, and throwing as the Big Three. The Big Three behaviors are set apart from other behaviors because they automatically signal to the parent a need to go right to Step Three of the Ladder (page 109). No talking, no reminders—ACTION first. Go right to your child if she has struck a sibling, peer, pet, or you and immediately direct her to her room.

"Oh, no. You may not hit. Ever. When you do, you go immediately to your room."

You will either walk with or carry her, depending on how much she's struggling. Once she is seated on her bed, say:

"Hitting, kicking, and throwing are The Big Three. You may not ever hurt other people or our things. When you do, you will always have to take time-out by yourself. I am very serious about this. You must use your self-control."

If your child is eight or older and is having repeated trouble, lashing out physically, I would follow the above script but also have her lose privileges for the rest of the day. Let her know that at her age, nothing is more important than exercising her self-control. She is simply too old for hitting or kicking to ever be tolerated. Take a hard line, but remember to keep your emotions in check. Use an "I mean business" tone rather than a threatening or exasperated tone. You will pollute the lesson of self-control that you are trying to impart if you do not exercise your own.

PARENTING TRAP

Making a Child Say "I'm Sorry"

Being an effective parent requires that you get smart about the power dynamics between you and your child. This means not only knowing how to assert your power, but also knowing where you have no direct power. One of the things a parent can't make a child do is to say something she doesn't want to say. Although it may sound obvious, parents fall victim to power transfers of this sort quite often. A classic example occurs when parents demand an apology from a child whose behavior has gone over the line in a situation where friends and family are gathered. Under these circumstances, a child with IFP is not likely to give over her power simply because her parents have demanded an apology. The scenes that unfold can be disturbing and mortifying for everyone—as well as surprising when a child displays an unexpectedly high level of stubbornness and defiance.

A story that exemplifies what an escalated mess this can become centers around a five-year-old girl who, after being uncooperative and having a fresh mouth, was given an ultimatum by her father: "You cannot get up from the couch until you say you're sorry." The child's grandparents, aunts, uncles, and cousins were visiting her home that afternoon, and they had plans to go out for dinner together. But to the dismay of the parents, the little girl sat in the corner of the couch and refused to apologize. As the time grew closer to their dinner reservation, first her grandmother, then her aunt and older cousin offered their best coaxing to convince her to say "sorry," but soon it became quite clear that she was not going to give up. Everyone just shook their heads and wondered what kind of willful and hard-hearted child they had on their hands, and the parents faced a real dilemma. Should they let their daughter off the hook in order to salvage the family outing? Should one of them stay home with her and have her remain on the couch for as long as it would take for her to give up and say she was sorry? What was the original transgression anyway? It had all turned into a big, dramatic mess, and the little five-year-old ultimately had the power. The adults couldn't *force* her to say she was sorry.

What if parents are successful in forcing an apology? What happens to the sincerity and real meaning of the sentiment? Telling someone you are sorry means you feel regret. But if you don't actually feel that emotion, the words are empty and the apology is false. Most children who have IFP are not inclined to extend an apology to anyone, unless it suits their own agenda.

Demanding an apology just doesn't work. It is better to stay focused on the behavior, have the child spend time in her room (Step Three of the Ladder), and after the time is up, sit with her for a minute and say something like:

> "I know this kind of behavior doesn't make you feel good. You know that kicking your cousin isn't a good way to behave. An apology would help your cousin feel better and actually make you feel a lot better too."

> It may be that your child still does not extend the apology, but your parental leadership has prevailed without a futile power struggle, you have enforced the priority of responding to the inappropriate behavior, and the seeds of a genuine apology, not a manipulated one, have been sown.

PHYSICAL TANTRUMS

Tantrums vary in intensity and duration. Some children just stomp their feet and scream. Others fall on the floor and flail both their arms and legs, try to hit and kick, throw things around their room, turn over furniture, swear, and threaten all the while. During intense tantrums kids will sometimes bang their heads on the floor, bite their hand, or scratch and pinch themselves. Parents understandably feel very frightened, uncertain, and insecure about how to respond to such dramatic and out-of-control behavior.

When tantrums are intimidating and shocking, the initial instinct is usually to move away. Indeed, many parents have told me that some of the parenting books they've read suggest that they should ignore tantrums in order not to provide fuel for the child's upset. When their child has collapsed on the kitchen floor in spasms of protest and rage, parents are told to simply step around him and go on cooking dinner. Or if their child has been put in his room and starts to throw things, they're instructed to stay out of it. The rationale behind such advice is twofold: Parental intervention in the face of a tantrum often temporarily heightens a child's anger, so it's better to avoid such escalation. Second is the perspective of natural consequences. If a raging child breaks things in his room, once he regains control, he will be sorry he hurt his things and learn from the consequence. I don't agree with these positions.

Children who throw these kinds of tantrums are beyond the pale. They have completely tapped out their internal resources, and that is a very disturbing place for anyone to be. Children need help when they have reached these states of internal disorganization. How can it make sense to ignore a child who is flailing and out of control? How can you pretend that it doesn't affect you at all or that there is nothing you can do to help? Parents who ignore their child's tantrums always tell me that it doesn't work. If anything, their child's tantrums become more intense and frequent over time. This is one parental misstep that has a most deleterious impact on our children.

The child who throws a tantrum is telling you that something is wrong and she needs your help. Ignoring such a plea will leave her in a terrible situation: She is becoming unglued under the weight of too much power. The absence of clear parental limits, boundaries, and effective lessons that help her exercise self-control, respect, and cooperation have left her feeling as if she is literally drowning. Her impotence in managing and regulating herself matches her parents' impotence in managing and regulating her. This child is suffering and is in need of a competent adult to step in and help her. This is why I ask parents to say to their children in Step Five of the Ladder, "It's okay, honey. I'm right here with you. I've got you, and I'm not going to let you go." The Ladder shows you how to move in and hold your child when she needs you most.

PARENTING TIP

Is It an Anger Problem or Is It IFP?

Parents often attribute the underlying motivation for intense tantrums to a fundamental anger problem within the child. They seek anger management strategies, relaxation, and coping mechanisms as solutions. What they fail to appreciate is the impact of IFP on their child's troubles with self-control and anger. Children with IFP are certainly angry, but they don't need to learn to count to three or to do deep breathing. They need parents to take the lead, in a respectful but effective way. The first step in helping a child who is stuck in a pattern of intense tantrums is to look at the dynamics of power in the parent-child relationship. Correct the IFP first, and then see where your child is.

The Effective Parent in Action

To manage a child's forceful physical tantrum, refer to Step Five of the Ladder, the Parent Hold (page 121). Don't walk away or just stand there and watch your child crumble in front of you. Move in close, because this is the time she needs your competence and containment more than ever. The Parent Hold is the most effective and appropriate way to provide the adult support and containment your child needs when she has veered out of control.

If your child's tantrum is on the milder side and does not reach out-of-control proportions, climb the Ladder to Step Three or Step Four as needed. It is important not to overrespond. It is fine and within reasonable limits for your child to cry and mutter a bit about how unfair you are and how you don't understand, or that you are not her best friend anymore. As long as she is in her room and you are not giving her an audience, going to Step Three or Step Four will serve as an adequate parental response to a mild tantrum. But if her carrying on does reach obnoxious proportions, remind her that:

> "The work of time-out is done quietly, and with all this carrying on, your time in your room hasn't even started yet."

Be certain to stay close by in case your firmness pushes her to the point of popping and her tantrum becomes physically out of control. Then, rather than moving away, move in and hold her close. Don't let her go until she has calmed down.

RUNNING AWAY AND HIDING

A lot of children run away from their parents now and then. The children of Pleasers and Pushovers tend to run away and hide almost as though they are flaunting their parent's ineffectiveness. It is often with a squeal and a giggle that they run, making a mockery of their parents' attempt at authority. These kids know what will happen. Pleaser and Pushover parents will keep on talking: "Why are you running away from

Mommy? Mommy needs you to listen now." Or they will keep on pleading: "Please, honey, Mommy does not like it when you hide like this. Mommy must be able to know where you are. Do you hear Mommy? This is not safe."

Children of Forcers, on the other hand, run for cover. They find their parents scary, and they are literally hiding to avoid their wrath. Where the children of Pleasers and Pushovers typically run under the dining room table or kneel by the side of the couch, children of Forcers find real hiding places: in the back of a cabinet in the basement or outside under the porch. These children are serious about not wanting to be found.

If you are a Forcer, you must correct your own behavior: Your child is running away from you because he is afraid of your temper. If you veer into harshness with your child, acknowledge your temper and apologize for it. Tell him that you are not going to scare him anymore with your anger but that you are going to help him to learn. Emphasize the importance of self-control, respect, and cooperation. Tell him that you know that when you lose your control and are not respectful, it does not help him learn to control himself.

The Effective Parent in Action
What to do when kids run and hide? If you are in the house, do not run after your child or go looking for him. Let him settle down wherever he is, and when he reappears you can take him to his room if need be. Using the Ladder will help you to be effective and yet remain respectful and supportive at the same time.

If you are a Pleaser or Pushover, and your child runs, don't run after him. You literally become a follower when you do this and will probably end up appearing rather foolish. Besides, odds are you won't catch him. Don't get coopted into playing his game. Simply go about what you were doing. Ignore the mischievous and rebellious antics; by refusing to take the bait, you remain in command of yourself and let him know he does not have the power to pull your strings. When he reappears and is close enough for you to take his hand, then quickly do so, and at that time direct him to his room. While escorting him there, tell him he owes you some time in his room for not cooperating with you and running away. You are on Step Three of the Ladder at this point. Proceed as your child's behavior indicates. If you are outside when your child runs, I would recommend a different course of action. Because there is more open space, parents have the ability to increase their speed when running and catch up to their young child. Act quickly and decisively so as to minimize escalation and avert any potential harm that could befall an impulsive and revved up child when outdoors. Once you have reached him, scoop him up, or take his hand and inform him that running away from you is not safe, and so he cannot be outside any longer. Either go to the car or go in the house, depending on where you are.

RUNNING AWAY FROM HOME

Many parents think it is normal for children to run away from home, or to angrily threaten to do so, but I don't see it that way at all. Packing a bag, running out the door to go live somewhere else, hiding in the woods—unfortunately, many children have said and done these things, but they are not part of normal acting out.

Running away, or threatening to, signals that something is definitely awry—much more than an in-the moment upset. I have noticed two primary motivators for kids who want to run away. One is the emotional manipulation of entitled children who won't tolerate their parents' limits. These are typically the little princes and princesses parented by Pleasers and Pushovers. The other is the frustration and anger of the children who feel they have no one to turn to. These are the children of Forcers, who parent with insensitivity and too heavy a hand, and of the Outliers, who leave their children too much on their own. Let's take a closer look at what's happening in these parent-child relationships that push a kid to such an extreme reaction.

The Entitled Children of Pleasers and Pushovers

Children in this group threaten to leave home when their usually over-solicitous mother or father finally reaches the boiling point and lays down the law. Their threats have a specific ring to them: "I am going to go far, far away to live, and you won't see me again" or "I don't love you anymore, and I am going somewhere else to live where you won't find me." These little guys don't have any intention of actually running away. They say the words or start to pack their bags to punish their parents and back them into a more subservient position. The threat to run away is used as an emotional hammer. Unfortunately, it often works. A common response from a Pleaser or Pushover in this situation might be, "Oh honey, why would you do that? Mommy would miss you so much and be sad every day. Please don't leave, Mommy loves you so much."

Although the behavior of these children is obnoxious, you have to scratch a little deeper to see what's really going on. They are in way over their heads with all their emotional power, and are confused and unhappy. To get to the point of saying you want a new family and would prefer to live elsewhere is pretty dramatic and is a signal that things have veered off course in the parent-child relationship.

The Overwhelmed Children of Forcers and Outliers

The children in this group threaten less but are more apt to actually run. Children of Forcers are usually caught in a power struggle with a harsh and at times volatile parent. The upsets can escalate quickly and can become quite ugly. Without the means to make sense of them or turn them around, these children are caught in a dynamic that feels so unfair, enraging, and scary that they reach the point where running away seems like the best option. They will often go and gather their things and secretly slip out the door without telling anyone. Other kids scream their resolve: "I hate you! I am running away and never coming back here." Off they go in a fit of tears and fury. They usually hide, with their hearts beating furiously, hoping to escape the Forcer, who often takes off after them in angry pursuit.

These kids are either dragged back in worse trouble than when they left or, if they haven't been pursued, try to sneak back home, hoping to slip in unnoticed and avoid punishment. Either way, the empathy and understanding they are so desperately trying to find remains elusive, and what they get is more criticism and disapproval.

Children of Outliers are overwhelmed by their own feelings and troubles and don't get adequate attention or help. These children are often prone to tantrums, as they flail around in fits of frustration and anger. In families with an Outlier parent, there is usually a lot of sibling discord and hostility. Taunting, hurtful tricks and mean-spirited competition can be common fare. The children are left without attention and empathy for their anger and hurt feelings. A continuing diet of this can be crazy-making and the kids become overwhelmed by their own feelings. Having had little help in developing emotional regulation and soothing, they fly off the handle and then out the door. The Outlier parent rarely takes this very seriously and probably doesn't go looking for the child. After a cooling-off period, the child slinks back home with no questions asked, right back where he started.

Regardless of the specific parenting style, it is not uncommon for parents to respond to their children's desperate intent to run away with a flippant and dismissive comment: "Good! I'll help you pack" or "Go right ahead, I will make you a lunch to take." Other responses can be even more cutting: "Go ahead. See if you can find another mom who can put up with you." "Better take a flashlight, because I am locking the door behind you and it is getting dark." "Don't plan on coming back, because I am going to rent out your room." I hear parents laugh with each other while sharing anecdotes about the times their kids threatened to run away. They seem to take pleasure in how clever and witty they are when they make these quips and seem oblivious to the pain they cause their children. I see nothing funny in their talk, only mean-spiritedness and a complete lack of understanding for what their child is trying to tell them.

The Effective Parent in Action

It is my contention that effective parents never have to hear such extreme reactions from their children. The relationship between them will never be so imbalanced as to lead to the kind of manipulation or desperation that leads to running away from home. For children with effective parents, home feels good, and they have an uncomplicated love and respect for their parents as leaders that makes threatening to leave something that just doesn't happen. However, if you are in a state of IFP with your child and bad blood does exist, below are the most effective ways to handle this situation.

For the entitled child, go to her and say:

> "No, of course you are not going to leave. No one is going anywhere, except you are going to your room for a bit. You're right that I am angry with you, and I know you aren't too pleased yourself. But you have a lesson to learn, so come on, off to your room you go."

A more conciliatory tone is needed for a child who is overwhelmed. Forcers, you must hear your child's announcement to run away as a signal that you need to be more empathic and sensitive. Outliers, you need to get interested and more involved with your child; he has a problem that requires your help.

This is the time for you to reach out to your child with empathy. For example, a Forcer might say:

> "Oh no. This has really gotten bad, hasn't it? You are so mad, and I am so mad, but you know what? No one is leaving. I would never let you go, honey. I am sorry I got so angry and was coming down on you so hard, but you know as well as I do your behavior has to change. Come to your room and settle down and we'll talk about it a little later when we are not so upset."

An Outlier might say:

> "Hey, honey what's wrong? I can see you're so upset. Why would you want to run away? Tell me what has happened. Let me see if I can help you."

In both of these situations, a child needs to be claimed and shown love and concern, rather than ignored, ridiculed, or viewed as bad and deserving more punishment.

Plenty of Room for Hope

If you develop a parent-child relationship where you are in the lead and are effectively shaping the development of self-control, respect, and cooperation (SRC) in your child, then the unpleasant and disruptive antics of opposition and defiance become limited to mere nuisances rather than organizing daily forces.

All children want very much to be good, and they thrive on earning their parents' positive regard. This is contradictory to their innate power drive. In the moment, children want their way, but in the second moment, and at a much deeper level, they want even more to be competently and effectively led by their parents. Children are happier and feel more secure and settled when they can count on your good judgment and authority.

When your children grow up mastering SRC, they will in turn feel good about themselves and be well regarded by others. This is the pathway to healthy, strong self-esteem. As they mature, your children with SRC come to prize how good it feels to be on good terms with you. They will prefer this to the momentary satisfaction that comes from dominating you and getting their own way. Life is good for these children and their families. My wish is that effective parents and their children (all of whom have mastered SRC, of course) will become the new epidemic that sweeps the nation—leaving IFP for social historians to ponder.

Chapter Eight

Anxiety

Few experiences are more powerful than holding your baby for the first time. The almost choking rush of love and devotion is a feeling familiar to most parents. It is this consuming parental love that compels us to do whatever we can to protect and care for our children and to make their well-being our priority. To spare them from pain and unhappiness whenever we can and to soothe them whenever we can't—this is the unspoken parent creed, and I share it with you in my love for my own children. I know firsthand just how compelling this feeling is. But if you want what is best for them, this creed must not become the guiding principle for your day-to-day reactions to your children's demands.

What should we do when our beloved little ones come to us with fear in their eyes, quivering lips, and tears running down their cheeks? What are we to do when they tell us they are afraid, that they will miss us, and that they can't do something we know they can do? Following the parent creed makes these times fertile for parental missteps. Parents instinctively want to scoop up a frightened child, hold him, reassure him, offer explanations, and do whatever they can to help him feel secure and settled again. Paradoxically, these instinctual acts of caring and compassion can often enflame a child's anxiety.

Not only does our parental love compel us to reach out to our children, but as adults we know how hard life can be, and how bad it can make us feel. We know the horrors, traumas, losses, and terrors that can befall us. Every adult knows what heartbreak feels like, or what it feels like to miss someone you love, to long for something or someone lost, or to be gripped by fear. Would you ever wish these feelings on your children? Of course not. Can you do anything to protect them from ever feeling them? Of course not. They are part of the human experience. Should we even try? Yes, of course we should! But here is where you have to be savvy about your parenting role. You have to be wise to the dangers of providing protection and too much reassurance from things your children don't actually need to be protected from.

Too often, parents calibrate their empathy and protectiveness for their children based on their own experiences of pain and fear, rather than on what their child is actually experiencing. When a three-year-old says, "Stay with me, Daddy; don't leave me until I am asleep," these childish trepidations and fears are not the result of a traumatic experience of abandonment and loss. Keeping the proper perspective is critical because most of the worries, fears, and trepidations you will be called upon to manage, as a parent, are inevitable features of the childhood terrain. When parents make a practice of overattending to their children's day-to-day fears, they are much more likely to end up with fearful, weepy kids than strong, confident ones.

PARENTING TIP

Anxiety, Fear, and Insecurity

Anxiety, fear, and insecurity are not the same experiences, but people often use the term "anxiety" to describe all three. *Anxiety* is not an actual emotion in and of itself but a state of distress when there is no specific, actual threat. Anxiety comprises feelings of alarm and dismay that lack an objective source. It can feed on itself. *Fear*, by contrast, is an emotion in which feelings of alarm and fright are caused by the realization of an actual danger, one that provides reasonable ground for dread and apprehension. *Insecurity* is generated by conditions of inadequate safety and certainty in one's life. In short, anxiety is not grounded in specific, present, reality-based dangers or threats, whereas fear and insecurity are. Children who have suffered some form of trauma, such as a car accident, a difficult medical procedure, separation from their parents, or having been temporarily lost, can have trouble keeping their fear circumscribed to the event, and it can evolve into a generalized anxiety. These children will certainly require careful reassurances and parental leadership so they don't get stuck and can find their confidence again.

IFP and Anxiety

Anxiety is one of the kingpins in an imbalance of family power (IFP) because, when mismanaged, it can lead so quickly to a state of imbalanced power in a child. Whether a child is more anxious because of IFP or because of her temperament, the way things are handled by the child's parents will largely determine if the anxiety escalates into a power struggle or not.

Kids who take the dominant position in a family do so because they can, not because it actually suits them. At some level, kids know when they are out of their depth. They feel burdened by their power, and it makes them nervous. When they are at the top of the family hierarchy, they have usurped power that by rights belongs to their parents, and any time you take something that isn't yours, it leaves you feeling unsettled. Plus, these kids are making a mess of their power, and while their parents try to help them with gentle reassurances, they wind up losing their empathy and become angry and critical when the child's anxieties continue to get worse and require even more accommodation and soothing. A vicious cycle of anxiety and anger gets set into motion.

This tangled state of affairs leads to a heightened state of insecurity and anxiety for some children, which is why so many of these roaring lions are also the ones who are afraid to go to their bedrooms by themselves after dark and worry that bad things will happen to them. Parents are often confused by the seeming contradiction of a headstrong child on the one hand and a timid, fretful child on the other. Yet this paradoxical behavior is actually rather typical of a child with more power than his parent.

Then there are those children who are temperamentally prone to being tentative and fretful, whose parents have a tendency to coddle them. Aware of their child's sensitivities, they go overboard with their protectiveness and accommodations. Just because a child is not necessarily assertive or outgoing doesn't mean she is without a power drive. Unfortunately for this child, the lesson she learns, in relationship to her parents, is that her own fragility, worries, and physical hurts exert a powerful influence in determining how things go.

The child whose IFP has stemmed from anxiety suffers a double whammy. On top of the childhood worries that she is temperamentally prone to, she soon develops another layer of generalized insecurity that comes from the realization that she has more power than her parents. When her anxiety becomes a force that shapes what her parents do and don't do, oftentimes at the expense of their better judgment, then it is powerful anxiety indeed. Eventually, a child in this position may suffer from a full-blown state of panic and look for reassurance and accommodations at every turn.

Lion or Lamb?

When parents understand the power of anxiety, it helps them control their tendency to overrespond when their children show distress. It is easy to see the power of a child who is protesting as loudly as a ferocious lion—the image cues parents to a serious and strong response. But where is the lion in a weepy and fearful child? The image that comes to mind is that of a little lamb, not a roaring beast. Anxious children, however, *do* have a lion's power, but it is veiled in tears. In fact, the power of their anxiety can lead their families into a whopping dose of IFP. How weak can your child be to have reached the top of your family hierarchy?

If you have any doubt that your anxious child has a reservoir of strength in him, just reflect on what happens when you challenge his anxious protests and resistances. If you insist that he go to sleep on his own, for example, or stay at the party without you, or take the bus to school—he freaks out and there's a huge scene. That's when your child's strength is in plain view. Unfortunately, though, his roar is not an expression of living life fully, freely, and with vigor; it is the sound of a child who is stuck and mired in parental accommodations. Remember, the more success your child has in getting you to view him as needy and fragile, and the more you accommodate him, the more he will show you his "weakness." But it is your child's inner strength that you really want to bring forward and empower.

The Five Phases of Powerful Anxiety: How One Thing Leads to Another

PHASE ONE. The seeds of powerful anxiety are found in the fear and upset a child expresses over something that is actually a harmless part of life. Parents' reassurances and accommodations (efforts to rewrap something scary into a friendly package) only make the anxious child more frightened. Instead of dispelling his fears, they cause him to clamor for more attention.

PHASE TWO. The parents have succumbed to their child's increasingly escalated demands to accommodate his anxiety—fear of sleeping in his own room, for example. Their accommodation only serves to reinforce their child's fears. In fact, he now becomes needier as his fears become bigger and more demanding.

PHASE THREE. Parents lose their cool and are completely frustrated and fed up as their child shows even more distress over his anxieties— despite all of their accommodations and reassurances. Frustrated by their own ineffectiveness, parents at this stage often blame and belittle their child for "being such a baby" and express their exasperation by saying things such as "I just can't take it anymore. You have to get over this! We simply don't know what else to do for you." When a child hears his parent throwing in the towel, he gets even more anxious. Now, the specific fear that first started the dynamic becomes more general and free-floating, and the child's fears and anxieties run wild.

PHASE FOUR. The child's anxiety becomes a fixture that shapes what parents and families do and don't do, often at the expense of the adults' better judgment. Now accommodations to a child's fears and worries are woven into the fabric of the day-to-day routine. For example, the improvised sleeping area next to Mom and Dad's bed is now permanently available for their frightened child. When visiting, even grandparents get pulled in and are given detailed instructions for all of the accommodations necessary to keep their child from becoming too distressed.

PHASE FIVE. This is when parents call me. Exhausted and feeling helpless in the face of their child's powerful anxiety, they are desperate to relieve their child's distress after suffering for months or even years. Finally, they want help. They want to be liberated from the confines of anxiety that has run wild.

The Top Four Missteps That Fuel Anxiety

Now that we've seen the progression of phases that get families into deep trouble when their children's anxieties are accommodated rather than managed effectively, it is very useful to understand the specific parental responses that fuel anxiety. These responses—or missteps—are not immediately damaging or problematic. The trouble comes when they are relied upon too frequently and over a long time, in effect cementing the anxiety and making it an organizing force in how a child sees himself and how his family functions. They are:

1. Too much emphasis on temperament
2. Supporting weakness rather than strength

3. Joining your child's magical thinking

4. Offering transitional objects.

Misstep 1. Too Much Emphasis on Temperament

"Andrew has always been extremely sensitive." "Julie is such a sweet little child. She just wears her heart on her sleeve." "Joey is a momma's boy; he always has been. He needs a lot of cuddling and reassurance because of his shyness and sensitivities."

Although a child's temperament is certainly a reality to be reckoned with, parents should not become beholden to it or be resigned followers of its dictates. Just as it is important to rein in a child who is temperamentally adventurous and a risk-taker, it is equally important to strengthen a child who is temperamentally reluctant and tentative. When parents place too much emphasis on "weak" temperament, their child is aware of it. They hear their parents describing their sensitivity and anxiousness to others as a way to account for the accommodations they make. Consequently, children become familiar with all the labels of weakness their parents use as they try to help their children understand why they are more afraid than other kids. "You are very sensitive, honey, we know that. You always have been." "Andrew's very shy." When a child also has sensitivities to medicines, fabrics, foods, and so on, the parents can really go overboard and create a whole persona for their child that emphasizes his fragility.

Whether your child's sensitivities are real or not, you will not serve him well by organizing your parenting and your child's sense of himself around them. It will only strengthen your child's weakness and convey the message to him that he just can't help himself; it is just the way he is. Doing this takes both you and your child out of the mind-set of being agents of strength and change.

Misstep 2. Supporting Weakness Rather Than Strength

If you see your child as highly sensitive and fragile, then the stage is set for you to do whatever you can to assist him. The trouble is that parental assistance too often supports weakness and suppresses a child's inner strength. All the unnecessary accommodations parents make—not flushing the toilet because Fiona doesn't like the noise, giving Danny earmuffs when there's thunder because the boom makes him afraid, picking up Brianna and holding her close whenever she sees a dog, and on and on—these are akin to giving your children crutches to get through ordinary life.

Parents have a terrible habit of engaging in what I call leading the witness when talking to their anxious child. They ask questions where they also suggest the answer. "Honey, are you afraid to ride your bike because you are worried about strangers? Is that why you want to always be able to see Mommy?" "Oh, sweetheart, since Grandma died, you have been missing her so much. Are you worried that Mommy or Daddy may die too?" "Honey, is the reason you don't want to ride the bus because you are afraid that the older kids might be too rough? Is that why you want Mommy to drive you?" You can count on the kids to shake their little heads yes to every one of these, leaving the parents certain that they have nailed the reason for their child's upset.

Misstep 3. Joining Your Child in Magical Thinking

It is a matter of course that children will engage in magical thinking. It is a fact of their cognitive development that they don't consistently adhere to reality principles until they are beyond ten years old. Prior to that, they are subject to the vagaries of fantasy, literalness, and illogical assumptions and associations. They have a real fear of monsters; think scary figures in a nightmare can really hurt them; they can be scared of toilets, bathtub drains, and having their face underwater. As adults, we know better. We understand the fears our children have, where they come from, and why they're scary. But what is the best way to help our children in the face of such childish fears?

I'll tell you what most parents do. They get spray bottles and tell their child it is a potion that keeps monsters away. They develop elaborate nighttime spraying rituals—under the bed, in the closets, and behind the chair so their child knows she is safe from monsters. They stock the bedroom with night-lights, put on music as background noise, give loads of reassurances that they will be right down the hall, and say they will be back to check on him soon. They buy decorations for the toilet to make it look more friendly and inviting. They put special rubber covers over the tub drain and tell their child that as long as the cover is on, she doesn't have to worry about going down the drain. Parents beware—you are joining your child in her magical thinking! In so doing, you send the message that her fears are in fact valid.

Some parents actually like ritual accommodations. It can feel nurturing and sweet to join your child in her world, and it always feels good to be her strong protector. Once again, however, this well-intended response results in fueling your child's anxiety, when what she really needs is a parent to provide her with a reality check. You may tell your child there are no such things as monsters, but what are you saying when you start spraying under the bed? Your behavior has to model that you know better, that there really is nothing to be afraid of. As a general rule, effective parents do not suspend their better judgment and knowledge to collude with the magical thinking and irrational assumptions of their children.

Misstep 4. Offering Transitional Objects

The idea is that giving a child something familiar to hold onto—a photo that is a tangible reminder of Mom or Dad or, as they get a bit older, a cell phone that gives them ready access to their parents—will make the "difficult challenge" of being apart easier to face. This common response actually does more to make the parents feel better than it helps the child.

I see a parade of anxious children in my office clutching stuffed animals as if their lives depended on them. Sometimes they come in squeezing small rubber balls. When I ask them why, they tell me their mom, or the nurse, or their guidance counselor told them that squeezing it will help them feel better. To the child who is anxious about going to school, parents often give a picture of the family to carry. This way the child can look at it anytime he feels upset. One little girl was given a yarn necklace with a laminated picture of her family hanging on it for ready viewing. She wore it every day, with quivering lips and teary eyes.

The fact that I see so many of these transitional objects in my office and hear about them is a clear indication that they don't work. These are classic examples of giving our children crutches rather than helping them to walk on their own. These kids become more frightened and insecure than ever. Left to clutch stuffed animals, squeeze balls, and cry over photos, they are far from discovering how to draw on their own inner strength.

What to Do About Anxiety

How do we fix our kids' anxieties? The short answer is, get effective. Be decisive, confident, and unwavering in your response! Parental effectiveness is the best way to counteract kids' having too much power, and parental confidence is a strong antidote to a child's emotional experience of anxiety. The major lessons of growing up are not imparted by talking but through action. Let's say a parent responds with: "Honey, I know you don't like the loud noise of the toilet, but really there is nothing to be afraid of. But don't be scared, calm down. You can wait outside and hold your ears. I promise I won't flush until you're ready. But will you be brave for Mommy next time? Okay, sweetie? Next time I don't want you to be afraid." With all this accommodation, what will make next time any different? If anything, this little girl will run out of the bathroom even faster.

The lesson this child, and all children, need to learn is that the noise, situation, or thing they fear is really quite harmless. Children must learn that the vast majority of the time, nothing bad comes from whatever it is they is trying to avoid. Words alone will not teach this lesson—it is the act of facing the fear, going toward it rather than away from it, that most effectively replaces anxiety with comfort. You may prefer the strategy of just letting age and maturity do the work in due time, avoiding having to put your child through the distress that comes with facing a fear. My experience is that far too often this plan doesn't work. Anxiety can get way out of hand, and its dictates can become far too interfering to tolerate. Besides, you can't be so reticent when it comes to distress in your children. It is the main cylinder in the engine that drives growth in our children, and handling it effectively leads to the development of inner strength and competence. Kids don't get strong if you rarely let them flex and use their own muscles.

Be Not Too Soft, Not Too Harsh

Complying with the pleadings of an anxious child who says "Stay with me," "Lie down with me," "Hold me," "Don't make me go," "Don't turn out the light," or "Don't go away so I can't see you" may succeed in reducing his distress for the moment, but in the long run it does not strengthen him. Parents who are quick to relieve distress are pushing their child's strength down, and chances are high that the child will keep experiencing the anxiety.

When a parent leads a child, gently and caringly, to stand firm and face his fear rather than retreat from it, she may provoke a sharp burst of distress in the short run, but in the long run she will be building her child's strength. Think of it this way: By tolerating your child's distress in the moment, you will spare him from having to keep re-experiencing it in the future. So by acting in this way, you are, in fact, being consistent with the parent creed—to spare your child from distress when and wherever you can. Here, though, it just doesn't come with immediate gratification.

I am in no way advocating that you plunk down your sensitive child in front of a horror movie to toughen him up or throw kids afraid of water into the deep end of the pool. There is a difference between not indulging a baseless fear and dismissing a fear as stupid, shameful, or a sign of weak character. My philosophy of parental power and the strategies in the Ladder are based on the developmental imperative that children feel cared for and respected. No child will ever want to follow leadership that is callous and mean-spirited.

Be Calm, Confident, and Trusting

Preparing your mind to attain and remain in a calm, confident state is an important step when correcting imbalances of power. You must find your inner strength and stay rooted in it. When IFP is anxiety-driven, staying calm is more essential than ever. Your child has become frantic inside, and you are going to have to lead her out of this tangled mess of fear. Keep in mind the notion of powerful anxiety—see the strength within your child. You have to know it is there and trust it. You have to help your perfectly able child to walk on her own. She is not the fragile, desperate little person her anxious protests would have you believe. Let her use her muscles to stand on her own.

To effectively block her anxiety from escalating, and to give it as little fuel to feed off of as possible, you will have to lend your child your strength and confidence in the beginning until she can find her own, within herself. You will be building a trusting relationship with her—one where she knows she can count on you never to lead her purposefully into danger or suffering. And when you do find yourselves facing turbulent seas, she will see you as a worthy captain who can sail her to safe harbor.

Using the Ladder to Control Anxiety

Obviously, you cannot discipline a child not to feel anxious. Parents have no actual power when they say "Don't be afraid" or "Don't be upset." Still, the Ladder deescalates anxiety by refusing to follow the anxious agenda of the child and by grounding him in leadership that is informed by confidence and good judgment. The Parent Hold is especially beneficial for the out-of-control, frightened child, as it provides safe, effective containment. When a parent who is facing his child's ungrounded anxiety responds with the Ladder, there will never be any confusion in the child about whether his fear is shared by his parent or whether his anxiety is valid.

Here's an example of how of this works. Sally is a worrier. In the morning she worries that she will be late for the school bus. She keeps worrying that she will run out of time to get ready. Sally's anxiety has so influenced her mother that her mom now wakes Sally up an hour earlier than necessary, hoping this will help her to worry less. Of course, the extra time doesn't reassure Sally. It just gives her more time to fret and pepper her mother with even more bids for reassurance.

In this situation, Sally's mother would be more effective if she told Sally the night before that the mornings seem to be getting worse, not better, and that there simply isn't any need to get up so early. Everyone would be better off with more time for sleeping and less time for worrying and waiting. She should state gently, but in a matter-of-fact tone, that while she knows Sally is worried about being late, she has never missed the bus, and there is no real reason for her to be worried. It is important to clearly tell her that it is time to let the worry go.

When children hear that the accommodations to their anxiety are being stopped, they understandably have a hard time. When Sally hears that her mother is bowing out of the anxiety dance, her distress will certainly increase for a time. In fact, she will likely bombard her mom with tears and pleadings: "No, no, Mommy, it does help. You have to wake me up early, please, Mommy, please. I won't have enough time and I will miss the bus!" Without getting caught up in explanations, reassurances, and the like, Sally's mom climbs the Ladder, using a script that is modified to specifically target powerful anxiety:

Step One

> "Honey, I know you have this worry, but it is a worry we have to fight rather than give in to. You will not miss the bus. Now, at this point, that is all there is to say about the matter."

Sally not only doesn't stop fussing, she ratchets up her pleas and protests.

Step Two

> "Sally, do you see how the worry builds when you keep talking about it? I am not going to say any more about it now. If you are having a hard time stopping yourself, and you just keep on, you will have to go up to your room for a bit until you can get it out of your system."

Well, Sally has been indulged so long in her worries, she just can't stop.

Step Three

> "Okay sweetie, come on, it's off to your room for a bit. You can have some time there to let the worry pass, and it will pass. I am confident of your strength."

Next, follow the directions for Step Three of the Ladder for getting your child to her room. Proceed with Step Four and Step Five of the Ladder if necessary. During the Parent Hold, instead of saying "You are very angry," say, "You are very worried and feeling frightened." Other than that, the basic script applies. The antidote to IFP is parental effectiveness, and the antidote to powerful anxiety is parental confidence. The Ladder is a simple, respectful way to help you as well as your child.

IFP and Separation Anxiety

Separation is one of the most common anxieties that children and their parents struggle with. There are two reasons that account for this. First, it is a normal anxiety that almost every child experiences to some degree. Second, because separation is such a loaded emotional issue for people, parents are particularly vulnerable to overresponding to it.

I have actually been surprised to learn from my work with parents over the years just what a negative and emotionally troublesome perspective they have about the concept of separation. For example, when I have given talks to parent groups about separation anxiety, I often begin by passing out index cards to the audience and ask them to write down their associations with the word. After collecting the cards, without prescreening them, I read the first nine or ten out loud. Inevitably the associations are dominated by words such as *alone, heart-wrenching, scary, hard,* and *overwhelming*. It is the rare exception when I get associations rooted in a perspective of healthy possibility, strength, or autonomy.

A Core Building Block of Healthy Development

Separations are, and have to be, an integral part of what propels our growth. Going away from mom and home base is where the bulk of important learning, socializing, and adventure occur. Visiting grandparents, staying with cousins, going to friends' houses, attending school, joining sports teams or camps, taking music lessons, going off to work or college—these are the basic, wonderful places that our children get to go and things that they get to do when they separate from us. There is nothing remotely lonely, heart-wrenching, scary, or hard about any of them. They are at the very core of a full life. Not to mention that, ultimately, leaving home and being able to live independently is the healthy culmination of growing up.

Parents sometimes resist this reframe of parent-child separations by saying, "Yes, but that is not how little children may feel about it." This may be true, but this is exactly why they need us. We must share our security and positive energy about leave-takings with our kids because, in fact, growing up is about having new experiences. Too many parents join in their child's emotional distress, loading them with reassurances and accommodations, not to mention laminated family photos for this "overwhelming" task they have to face as they grow up.

The Role of Attachment

Attachment is a central construct in the research and writings of developmental psychologists, but for our purposes let's focus on secure and insecure attachments. Children who enjoy a secure attachment with their parents are usually well equipped to handle separations. In fact, having a secure base is what allows children to venture out and explore. Children with powerful anxiety usually have a secure attachment—it is just that the misguided reassurances and accommodations of their parents have inflated their worries and blown power into them. The anxieties of these children are the easiest to dissolve, because the relationship distortion is born out of a power imbalance rather than out of insecurity. It is from the parents of such children that I am most likely to hear, "Dr. Grosshans, you are a miracle worker. The night after we left your office, Emma turned out her light and just went to sleep. No fuss or crying at all. We still can't believe it." There's no miracle here—a perfectly healthy, strong, and secure child was simply freed from the trap of her own powerful anxiety.

When Anxiety and Insecurity Make Separating Hard

In the past several years, I have begun to see a particular quality of separation anxiety in children that is a mixture of anxiety and insecurity. It is currently the most common form of separation anxiety in my practice. These children are scared to leave their mothers for any reason, including going to school. When I talk with them and help them to express what they are feeling so scared and worried about, they tell me they are afraid mommy might leave and never come back. Of course they don't usually express this fear directly. Instead, they complain about missing mommy too much, about not having fun when away from mommy, that the time away just feels too long, that their stomach hurts, and so on.

Why would they be afraid of that? With further support, they go on to tell me that at home mommy has a lot of work and gets frustrated and yells a lot. These children come to interpret their mother's ongoing irritability and annoyance to mean that she is not really happy in family life and might prefer life without them. They start to worry that mom won't come back when it is parent pickup time or that mom will get in the car and drive away or climb out the window and leave when no one is looking. They tell me they like being at school, sports practices, birthday parties, and sleepovers; it is just that their worry gets in the way and they start to feel scared. Once their fear gets bad enough, they feel better if they don't have to leave their moms in the first place.

When Kids Become Part of the Have-to List

When I talk more in depth with the mothers of these children, what is revealed is that life at home has indeed become one big chore—with not enough time or energy to get everything done. The phrase "have to" is the organizing theme of the day. It starts in the morning with "You have to get moving," "You have to get dressed, "You have to eat your breakfast," and "You have to catch the bus." There's also: "I have to help your sister," "I have to get to work," "I have to take this phone call." It isn't even eight o'clock in the morning yet, and already the day is a litany of harried dictates.

It is an anxiety born, as I see it, directly from the mayhem and "mommy madness" that is so characteristic of our current culture: Mothers who have gotten so caught up in the performance mode of mothering, taken on too many obligations, gotten compulsive about the house and the kids and the dog and the yard and the school volunteering, that they can't ever be in the moment. They have to get things done, they have places to be, calls to make, obligations to fulfill—and their children have become part of the have-to list. Truth be told, more often than not, the kids are treated as if they are interfering in getting the rest of the list done efficiently. "You have got to let Mommy finish this— can't you see I am busy? I have a million things to do, and you are driving me crazy. Go and find something to do. " Kids are sensitive. They get it. Life would be easier for mom without them. At some point they begin to worry that mom might choose that path.

The sad irony of course is that these mothers have no such intention. On the contrary, being a mother is their primary identity and commitment. In fact, most of the tasks and responsibilities they are bogged down with are on behalf of their children and families. Pleaser parents are vulnerable to falling into this trap. Up to their eyeballs in competition to be supermom, they ultimately fall victim to the harried, resentful feelings that go along with it. Outlier parents can get into trouble here too, since they tend to live outside the emotional experience of their children and are too focused on tasks and organization.

Moms, of course, have a hard time hearing this. But I offer it as a much-needed wake-up call. This is no way to live. Kids are tapping into the stress and frustration that pervades day-to-day life and saying, "Hey this feels awful, and I am not okay living like this." Good for them. I instruct their moms to take all of the *have to's* out of their lexicon. It's time to concentrate on putting some fun back into the routine, to be sure you are connecting with your child for at least twenty minutes a day in what I call a shared joy, where both of you are in the moment, together and feeling good. You can't fake this. It can't be contrived "special time." You can't pretend or just blow up some balloons and call it a party. You have to take real pleasure in the moment in whatever form that might come in—a walk in the park with your child, grabbing her and dancing to a song you love, throwing a ball around. Spontaneity is an important ingredient. Get rid of the clock and simply enjoy the time you spend with each other. This will quickly help your child to settle down.

I have another suggestion for overcommitted moms: The next time the phone rings, rather than reflexively turning your back on your child, or being irritated with her for interrupting, let her hear you tell the caller, "I only have two minutes to give you right now, I am with Maggie and can't talk longer. You can email me, or I could call you back later if we need more time than that." Let your child hear that you have chosen her over the task. Include her in some of the chores, and tell her you enjoy working with her. Spontaneously announce you are going to leave the dishes in the sink and go out for ice cream, or opt for a quick family game instead. Of course, chores must be done and schedules must be kept, but from time to time, try to whistle while you work. The main point here isn't just about having fun with your child. It is about securing the relationship, strengthening the connection, and deepening the intimacy with your child that has unfortunately and completely inadvertently gotten buried under the schedule and all your obligations.

It doesn't help much to keep reassuring your child that you won't leave, or promising you will be there at parent pickup, or telling her you love her if what she continues to feel is how burdened you are and that she only adds to your frustration. She has to feel that you actually enjoy being her mother. It has to be from your gut to her gut, it can't just be words she hears in her head. This is what will shore up your child's sense of security in the parent-child bond, and separations will become much easier for her to handle.

PARENTING TIP

Separation Anxiety Unveiled

Conventional wisdom has everyone focusing on making a child with separation anxiety feel more comfortable with where they are going. Considerable efforts are taken to ease the moments of transition or ensure that the destinations—school, a friend's house, a party—are friendly and supportive. These interventions often don't make children feel much better. What is not widely recognized is that the adult attention is in the wrong place. Separation anxiety actually has more to do with a child's relationship with his parent and the relationship environment he is *leaving* rather than with the place he is *going to*. The real payoff in treating separation anxiety comes from turning your attention back to the home front—the "from," not the "to."

Supporting Healthy School Separations

Going to school for the first time is a very common source of trepidation for children. When your child expresses apprehension about this separation, you know now that to prevent it from blowing up, you cannot overdo your reactions.

I recommend that a few days before school begins, you go to your child's school and do a run-through of how it will go on the first day. Have fun with this, but watch yourself to make sure you are not doing too much reassuring, asking your child if he thinks he will be okay, or in any way suggesting that distress is a part of going to school.

If your child expresses some worry or apprehension on his own, take his hand and in your best competent parent tone, say:

> "You are feeling a bit apprehensive because this is still new to you. I know, honey, it is only normal that you should feel that way, and lots of other kids are feeling it too, as the first day gets closer. That feeling will go away quickly once you are in your classroom and the fun of school begins. You will see! No worries; you will be fine."

Then change the subject, as you point out something interesting about the school.

Don't take an overly animated, cheerleading approach to sell your child on school. If you're too forced about it, he won't buy it or trust your heavy-handed sales job. Moderation is key. School really is appealing to children, so let that natural excitement and pride in taking a new step come to the forefront and counter any tentativeness your child may feel.

THE FIRST DAY OF SCHOOL

Do not get caught up in long good-byes or escort your child into the classroom. Separating at the main door of the school building is best; second best is the door to the classroom. The longer you stay around, the more it fuels anxiety.

Let the teacher know your child may need a bit of extra support in the first part of the day and ask her to call you should your child's distress be intense (he's too upset to focus on anything else) or prolonged (more than forty-five minutes). If your child tends to be anxious, refrain from putting notes in his knapsack or giving him transitional objects such as family photos to help him feel close to you. Don't go into long details about what you will be doing while you are separated either or stress that you will just be doing errands that your child would find boring anyway. This just draws more attention to the time apart and lets your child know you are focused on it as well. Whatever you do, don't stand within earshot of your child while giving directions to the teacher about how to reach you. There's nothing wrong with leaving these instructions, but if your child overhears you doing so, it sends the message that you're anxious about leaving him at school, too, and that you will be on pins and needles waiting to hear if he's okay or not.

If you are nervous, check yourself and remember the core strength your child has. Tap into your own strength, too, and let it emanate from you. A squeeze of the hand, a kiss, and then off you go. If your child is crying and trying to hold on to you, ask a teacher to be there so your child can transition immediately to her care. Then leave with a smile and wave and do not look back!

If you and your child have a bit of trouble with separation, keep your reunion low-key when you meet up again after school. It's best not to ask how he felt and if he cried for very long—focus on asking about the activities, the teacher, and new friends. If your child brings up distress, be gentle and understanding, just as you have been before, but again stress that the worried feelings will get better each day and will soon be gone altogether. Believe it, because it will be true.

YOUR STRENGTH IS YOUR CHILD'S STRENGTH

Remember, you can't follow your child's pleadings. As is always the case with anxiety, children act as if they know just what will settle them down and make them feel less afraid. But—you must believe me—they don't. The accommodations they cry out for—"Stay with me!" "Hold me!"—may mollify them for the moment but in the long run serve only to fuel your child's anxiety. Use your adult perspective and stay grounded in what you know is the reality of the situation: School is nothing to be afraid of. Your child's separation challenge is only for a few hours, and he is in an environment designed for children. Of course your child can manage this. Let his strength come forward by seeing your unequivocal certainty of this. Don't focus on his fear and prop up his vulnerabilities.

If Your Child Is a School Refuser

You may have a child who refuses to go to school out of defiant power rather than out of anxiety. He may even become ferocious and angry when challenged about going to school and say things such as "My stomach hurts really bad!" "You are so mean! You don't understand! You can't make me go! I won't go! Why are doing this to me?" "The other kids will all make fun of me, and my teacher doesn't understand why I get upset. I am not going back to school, EVER!" If your child refuses to go to school, you will probably need some professional help guiding you through the correction phase because it can escalate quite seriously. One thing you can be certain of is that the fight isn't just about going to school (you're child is more than up to it); it is the fight for the emotional throne of the family (will it be you or he that will sit there?) that is really driving his school defiance.

Help for Social Anxiety

Eight-year-old Robbie has always had a tendency to be shy and uncomfortable in groups, going to parties, and participating in sports. Within the last year his social distress has escalated significantly. His parents used to be able to coax him into starting a new sports season, and he would be okay after a few practices, but now he is just too anxious and keeps saying he can't, he doesn't feel good, and he doesn't want to go. When he was invited to a birthday party recently, he only agreed to go if his mother promised she would sit in the car in the driveway and wait for him. When he would go over to friends' houses to play, his mom would have to arrange to stay and talk while Robbie played. When he would get invitations to sleep over at a friend's house, he would want to go, but would then fret and worry about it so much he would make himself too distraught to go.

Robbie's parents went along accommodating his anxiety, but all the while they would say things like, "Oh my gosh, Robbie, this is so ridiculous. You are eight years old, for heaven's sake," or "Aren't you embarrassed? People are going to know I am waiting in the driveway. Do you want them to think you are a baby?" When he refused to walk into the gym to try out for basketball, their encouragements, reassurances, and support finally ran out. "Okay, that's it, we can't do this with you anymore. You are pathetic, you know that?" Then they hauled him, with no empathy left at all, into the car and drove home a little too fast. What started out as a partnership was now gone.

For parents of socially reticent children or shy children, it is always difficult to strike a balance—how much should you push, and what is the best way to do it? How can you help a child like Robbie, when his fear has already escalated to such a limiting degree? First—and I have to say it again—the best general change you can make is to increase your overall effectiveness as a parent who is firmly in the lead. When parents are able, strong, and confident (which means they do not get caught up in frustrated, exasperated, emotional outbursts), their children have the best foundation and model to find their own strength. Second, make sure you don't fall into the common missteps that fuel anxiety.

Show the Way

There is really no way a shy and reticent child will find his strength unless you show him he has it in him. Left to his own devices, he will most likely create what feels like a comfort zone, but in fact it will really be a constricted life defined by apprehension and nonparticipation. So it is best to go ahead and sign up your child for one or two activities in which he has shown some interest. Don't put him in the driver's seat too much in choosing though, and don't overtalk the topic. Avoid making him promise that he will participate and will not give you a hard time about going. No matter what he says, if he has had trouble in the past, he will likely have trouble again. It is up to you to be ready to handle it. It would be better to go ahead and straightforwardly say:

> "This is going to be really fun. But I expect you will be uncomfortable at first and might even tell me you don't want to go. We will be ready for those feelings, but we won't let them get in the way of your enjoying the activity."

This is a clear message to the anxiety that it will have no power—and your child will hear it clearly as well. Don't talk at length about the upcoming activity. Just casually mention it the night before, and if your child starts to protest, simply put a finger on his lips gently, and say:

> "Shhh, shhh, let's not to talk about it anymore. You're starting to get upset."

If your child can't seem to stop, climb the Ladder and have him go to his room until the upset has passed. Do not engage in reassurance or extended conversation; a simple statement that it is important not to let worry get in the way of doing fun things is enough. Also, avoid the temptation to offer bribes or rewards in return for his agreeing to go.

It can be helpful to arrange to have a friend or two sign up for the same activity so your shy child has a built-in source of familiarity. If you make such arrangements, make certain your child isn't aware of the plan.

You want to avoid letting him see that you are going out of your way to build supports for him. Do it when he is not around, and then just impart the comforting knowledge in a casual, matter-of-fact tone:

"Oh, guess what? Jimmy will be at the same basketball practice."

It can also be helpful for some children to be picked up by the friend's parent, so the separation from their own parent can happen at home rather than publicly. This can work well for birthday parties, too. Children usually fuss much less with non–family members and are more easily distracted from their anxiety by an interaction with a friend.

Mr. Bug

When working with socially anxious children, I often use the concept of "Mr. Bug" to help give them a concrete image against which to mobilize their strength. After listening to them tell me how they don't like going places and how they get really upset, and cry, I will say:

"Wow, you are really missing out on a lot of good stuff. How do you feel about that?"

I get them to take a side against their anxiety by saying they don't like it at all. Then I say:

"Well, we have to fight it then."

I tell them it can help to think of all the worry and upset they're experiencing as the work of Mr. Bug. He is a crafty little bug who gets kids worrying and fretting, and the more they worry, the happier he gets. Tears and upset make him just want to stick around longer, but when kids get mad at him, and fight against him, then he is the one that gets worried and upset and soon decides he wants to find somewhere else to hang out.

Mr. Bug feeds off of weakness but doesn't like strength at all. So I help children see that their weakness is shown through tears and worry, while their strength comes through when they get angry. I get them to talk back to Mr. Bug. For example, "Get out, Mr. Bug! Go away! You're not the boss of me! I am so going to this party!" Kids can get empowered by envisioning themselves karate-chopping Mr. Bug if he just isn't listening, or by giving him a good kick in the pants. Some kids even get up and act out stepping on Mr. Bug. When I ask them to look at how they feel afterwards, they say they now feel quite different from the teary, scared person they were before. Now they are in charge, and they tell Mr. Bug how things are going to go rather than the other way around. I reinforce the need for them to keep up their strength and not give Mr. Bug a foothold. This is an easy construct for parents to join and support, by saying things like "Sounds like Mr. Bug is here. Come on, get mad, tell him to get out!"

Storm Stories

Ross, a six-year-old boy, has become terrified of storms. It started out innocently enough when he would hold his ears whenever he heard thunder. Ross would ask his parents if the thunder could hurt his ears. They reassured him, and whenever there was a loud storm his mother had him sit with her on the couch with her arms around him until he said he felt okay. If the storm was still going on at bedtime, Ross would become really uncomfortable and scared. Since it was the thunder that bothered him the most, his father would go to the closet and find some earmuffs for him to wear so the noise wouldn't be so loud.

Soon, Ross was crying that he did not like the lightning—so his parents added an eye mask to the earmuffs. Still Ross could not settle down during storms. He was scared the windows would break. His parents taped up his windows to help him feel more secure. During a particularly busy storm season, Ross took to checking the weather station every day to see if any storms were forecast. Often he looked up to the sky for dark clouds and any sign of a brewing storm. By summertime, he was hesitant to go to the swim club or amusement park for fear he would get caught in an unexpected storm. By the time his parents came to see me, Ross had made a storm bed in his walk-in closet. He would go there when it was raining, to put on his eye mask and earmuffs. He wouldn't even go out to play if the day was slightly cloudy. His parents felt terrible for him and couldn't understand what was driving his continued distress. They had done everything they knew to reassure him and make him feel comfortable.

This is what I suggested that Ross's parents say to effectively handle his anxiety about thunderstorms:

> "All of these props are not helping. Actually, I see they are making things worse. Let's get back to basics, honey. Rain and thunder can be noisy, but they aren't dangerous. You have gotten afraid for no reason. It is time to put away the earmuffs and the eye mask and open the shades."

When a storm does come again, stay calm and lend your child your confidence, saying:

> "Wow, that was a loud thunderclap! That even startled me. Not to worry though, thunder can be loud, but it won't hurt us. Here, take your hands away from your ears. You have to learn to be comfortable with storms. They are a part of every spring and summer. Let's go to the window together and watch the rain and I will tell you about what thunder and lightning is."

If your child is still quite frightened, carry him to the window, and while holding him, or putting your hands on his shoulders, say:

> "Sweetheart, come on. You are fine. This is an ordinary thunderstorm and there is nothing to fear. Now, I want you to dry your eyes, take a deep breath, and tell your worry to get lost! Don't let that worry get the best of your strength. Come on, we are fine."

The effective parent is both understanding and yet not solicitous of the unwarranted anxiety. She appeals to her child's strength and lends him her own as a temporary support. After a few minutes at the window, she turns her attention to some other pursuit—perhaps a game or a project that will help her child stop focusing on his anxiety. No crutches, no special accommodations. Let it rain.

PARENTING TIP

Severe Anxiety

As with any group of problematic behaviors, there is always a subset that falls on the severe end of the continuum. For some children, anxieties reach such a fevered pitch that every day represents an anguished struggle. Five-year-old Douglas was terrified of separation, and when his mother didn't hear his calls one day, he bolted out the front door to bang on neighbors' doors, looking for his mother. Four-year-old Sophie would work herself into hysteria, sometimes even to the point of vomiting, when she had to separate from her mother. She was relentless in shadowing her everywhere—even to the bathroom. Ultimately she developed a fear of the wind, worrying that it would pick her up and blow her away. Ten-year-old Randy's sudden and severe fear about swallowing caused him to lose twelve pounds. He was afraid that food would get stuck in his throat and he would choke and die. If your child is struggling with severe difficulties such as these, seek professional help.

Move in Toward Opposition, Away from Anxiety

Opposition and anxiety—the kingpins of IFP—can take a terrible toll on both children and families. Much of what I have recommended may fly in the face of your instincts. As parents, we are typically repelled by opposition and want to move away from an obnoxious child, while we are touched by a child's distress and reflexively want to move in with soothing. What I am recommending is that you do exactly the opposite: *Move in toward opposition and move away from anxiety.*

The parental positions I'm advocating are about fixing, not fueling; about leading, not joining. Shifting to a new stance can be uncomfortable, and in the beginning you will likely be uncertain of yourself. This may be particularly true in the case of anxiety, where toning down your response to your child's distress will be going against your instincts. Let me give you one more dose of reassurance. Moving away from your anxious child in the form of minimizing your attention to and collusion with normal childish fears is all about putting out the fires of anxiety, not enflaming them. This is the best kind of parenting help because it works from the inside out. It strengthens your child's inner muscles of autonomy, independence, confidence, and ability to self-soothe and self-regulate. In turn, these strengths yield self-controlled children who are confident, well-grounded, well-behaved, and free to use their inner strength in service of living and enjoying a full life.

Sleeping, Toileting, and Eating

Sleeping, toileting, and eating behaviors often become a problem in families with IFP. In response to the overinvolvement of a Pleaser parent, the high anxiety of a Pushover parent, overcontrol by a Forcer, or lack of help from an Outlier, children can develop myriad problems that prevent their mastery of healthy, independent, and appropriate patterns for sleeping, using the bathroom, and eating.

Two distinct qualities characterize sleeping, toileting, and eating and set them apart from other behavioral functions. First, a distinct, potent physiologic drive underpins each of them: exhaustion, the need to go to the bathroom, and hunger. These behaviors are biological necessities. Life depends on them. The urges that lead us to these behaviors are strong; to ignore them is extremely difficult. When we are tired, our bodies crave sleep; when we have to urinate or have a bowel movement, there is an urgency that is extremely hard to deny; when we are hungry, we are compelled to eat. Despite how basic, instinctual, and strong these urges are, mismanaged power dynamics can result in children getting stuck in refusals and avoidances, which ultimately delay their developmental progress.

The second distinct feature is that *in each of these arenas, children have the ultimate control* because parents can't make them go to sleep, go to the bathroom, or eat. The dilemma we as parents face is that we have no direct control, yet we are required to be effective authorities and influence our children in mastering these developmental tasks. This dynamic turns these three arenas into a breeding ground for power struggles. Children quickly learn that parents are strongly invested in having them go to sleep, use the potty, and eat healthy food. They also quickly learn that when they don't or won't, they get a big rise out of us. Power, indeed!

With their power drive fueling them, and with parents who set the stage for a struggle, children can't help but play out the hand. Rather than using their power to move mastery forward in a constructive way, it works against them and keeps them stuck in the same place. Their power turns toward wanting to defy or outwit their parents, on the one hand, or keeping them engaged in overattending and overmanaging them on the other. So, instead of gaining mastery of their own bodies from this enterprise, it turns into a game of mastery over their parents.

The resulting struggles can escalate quickly and become extremely disruptive and anxiety-producing. What parent wouldn't be frightened and desperate when her child won't sleep, holds onto her bowel movements for days on end, or refuses to eat? Correction, while certainly possible, is not usually easy in these circumstances. Prevention is more important than ever.

A Caveat

As you read these chapters, keep in mind that IFP is not the only reason children have difficulty in the areas of sleeping, eating, and toileting. There are a host of developmental and medical conditions that result in trouble with these behaviors. Keep in mind the barometers of frequency, intensity, and duration, and seek consultation with a professional when your best parenting efforts just aren't helping.

Chapter Nine
Sleeping

"My kingdom for a good night's sleep!" The frazzled desperation of parents is no more frequently expressed than when it comes to seeking help for their children's sleep disturbances. Whether it is from a maddening struggle to get a child to stay in his bed and go to sleep, a child who refuses to sleep alone, or interrupted nights responding to a distressed child, parents have long been stymied by this parenting task. What parents endure (and therefore what their children endure) in the long hours of the night, when a tired body is desperate for rest, is always amazing to me. The yelling, tears, threats, pleading, pretzel contortions, and musical beds that go on take a major toll on everyone involved. How do you help children establish independent and peaceful sleep habits? Every parent needs to know, but more importantly their children need to master these skills because they are centrally important to a child's healthy development.

The Top Ten Bad Sleep Habits

When a body craves sleep, clear thinking and patience are rare commodities. The many bad sleep habits that parents and children develop together are a byproduct of exhaustion. Parents are willing to do just about anything to make the fussing stop so they can get some sleep. Here are the top ten bad sleep habits parents stumble into:

1. Bedtime routines that are too long and drawn out
2. Lying down with a child until he falls asleep

3. Sleeping with a child all night
4. Letting a child sleep in the parents' bed
5. Leaving lights and music on
6. Playing musical beds throughout the night
7. Allowing the child to sleep on the floor of the parents' bedroom
8. Bribing and threatening and ultimately exploding to get a child into bed
9. Letting a child dictate who puts him to bed
10. Parents clearing away shoes in their walk-in closet so they can have sex because children are in the parents' bed.

From my point of view, a bad sleep habit is any parental accommodation that interferes with your child's mastery of the important developmental task of independent and peaceful sleeping. While accommodations (such as those on the list above) may quiet a child in the short run, they only compound a family's stress and trouble in the long run. Not only have parents failed to impart the lessons of independent and peaceful sleep, they have led their children into behaviors that will have to be undone. Furthermore they have engaged in blatant transfers of power to their demanding or anxious child—resulting not only in exhaustion, but a heavy dose of IFP.

I routinely encounter parents who say they don't mind sleeping with their children or having them on the floor in their room. They say it keeps sleep interruptions to a minimum, so to their minds they have a solution that works. In other words, parents have rationalized that these aren't really such bad habits because they don't mind them.

Some parents take the position that they do not want their children to feel alone, abandoned, or frightened, so sleeping together is necessary for the child's well-being. Others recoil at the idea of having their distressed child "cry it out," feeling that is too cruel and rejecting a practice for them to follow. But who wants their sleep interrupted night after night for these reasons?

Whenever your child won't go to bed without a minimum of fuss and won't stay in her bed once you put her there, bad sleep habits have come into play. Okay, then. We have the definition of bad sleep habits. Now, what are you, as concerned and caring parents, going to do about it?

Why Is Peaceful Independent Sleep So Important?

Parents rate sleep problems as the difficulty they would most like to resolve. Certainly, people don't feel good when they are not adequately rested, and neither kids nor their parents are able to function at the highest level when they are tired. But few appreciate that, beyond exhaustion and nightly frustrations, there is a much deeper significance to mastering independent sleep. What has been given short shrift is that independent, peaceful sleeping is a critical developmental task for children. In fact, teaching children to sleep comfortably in their own beds sets the stage for three pivotal family dynamics. It helps the child:

- ❖ Achieve independence and autonomy
- ❖ Achieve a state of calm and repose
- ❖ Strengthen healthy boundaries.

Achieving Independence and Autonomy

Sleep is the arena in which the long process of psychological separation and independence is first grappled with. It is a state where each of us is, ultimately, alone. Going to sleep requires that we withdraw into ourselves and let go of our moorings to wakefulness and interactions with others. Will a child be comfortable and secure in his own skin, or anxious and distressed? Sleep is the first testing ground.

Most parents are familiar with the concept that for a child to be free to leave a parent and explore and strengthen his own muscles, he must have a secure attachment. This holds true for the separation required for healthy sleep as well. An assessment of a child's sleep behavior is a first measure of his security and orientation to separateness. Parents' core feelings about separation and autonomy are tapped here, and children, with their acutely sensitive antennae for their parents' emotional states, will most assuredly pick up on this. If you think being alone is hard or scary, then your children will too. If you are uncomfortable with the demands that being alone makes on a person, your children will know it and will internalize this discomfort themselves.

Achieving Calm and Repose

Going from wakefulness to sleep requires a transition period of quiet and calm. Achieving this state is a challenge for children. Always in forward motion, they have a hard time being still and withdrawing into themselves. To do this, one must use what I call the internal muscles of self-regulation. We have to use these muscles for self-control and self-soothing. When a parent is always with a child, taking leave only when the child is finally asleep, these muscles are never really exercised properly and therefore are not strengthened. The child who is not asked to use these muscles, who does not know how to reach a relaxed state on his own, or who is anxious and uncomfortable doing so suffers a significant developmental shortcoming.

Strengthening Healthy Boundaries

Independent, peaceful sleep helps establish appropriate and healthy boundaries within a family—boundaries that distinguish parents from children and underscore the union of mother and father. Young children need considerably more sleep than adults. Therefore, they go to sleep earlier. Parents and children should not have the same bedtime. The time after 8:30 or 9:00 p.m. is considered adult time—even television networks know this. The kids are asleep (or supposed to be), and the parents are winding down and enjoying some time to themselves. Lying down with your child until she falls asleep, routinely going to sleep with her, or letting her fall asleep in your bed with you collapses this boundary. On top of this, it means you are accommodating your child and putting the whole family on the path to IFP.

An even more significant boundary violation occurs when children sleep in their parent's bed, which I consider a very important symbol in a family. The parental bed signifies the head of the ship—it is the captain's quarters, if you will. In addition to this leadership symbolism, an important adult relationship plays out in the parental bed. It is the primary stage for the intimacies of a marriage—heartfelt discussions, arguing, relaxing, and sex.

An interesting observation I have made through years of clinical work is that the majority of parents who come into my office with children who have difficulties stemming from IFP are having little if any sex. An active sex life solidifies the connection between parents and leaves less room for kids to come between them. Strong parents tend to have strong marriages that they enjoy, protect, and prioritize. And nothing could be a better foundation for strong children. Kids love it when their parents love each other. If they are always trying to play one parent against the other, or literally try to come between you in the bed, this is a sure sign of IFP.

WHAT ABOUT THE FAMILY BED?

A discussion of children in the parental bed would not be complete if I did not touch on the topic of the family bed. Whenever I give talks to parent groups, there is always someone in the audience who wants to know my thoughts on the family bed. The family bed is the deliberate practice of welcoming children into the parental bed as their primary sleeping place. Sometimes the practice develops out of accommodation to a distressed or insistent child and becomes a family norm. Yet, on purpose or not, this invitation compromises separation, autonomy, self-regulation, and boundaries. Remember, the parental bed represents the top of the family hierarchy. Sharing it with children essentially up-ends this important parental position.

The motivation for a family bed usually has to do with an idealized sense that togetherness promotes attachment and well-being. Parents mistakenly believe that security will be strongest when there are no boundaries for a child to struggle against and no distress for them to tolerate. But it doesn't happen this way. All of the "inner muscles" a child needs to become comfortable with separation and autonomy get compromised. It becomes harder and harder to develop and strengthen these muscles the longer they are neglected. Children learn from their parents that being alone is too hard, and that being loved and nurtured is synonymous with togetherness that is experienced, literally, day and night.

FAMILY SLEEPOVERS AREN'T FAIR

It is not fair to set up the parental bed as a privileged, special place to be, a reward or special treat. It is not fair because it sets up children to want something that isn't healthy for them to have. It can be tempting for a parent to say, "Since Daddy is out or town, you can be Mommy's big boy and sleep in bed with her tonight." But this sets the stage for begging and pleading to be allowed to sleep there, because it has been established as the coveted place. Nor do I recommend that the parental bed be the routine place for children to get protected, reassured, or cared for when sick. In general, being in your bed should not be a reward or a special treat for your children, nor should it be the place where their needs are attended to.

I am not saying your bed should never have a child in it. Of course not! Snuggling together on weekend mornings, playful romps in the evening, and movie watching or reading books while under the covers are times to be cherished. But when it comes time to say good night and go to sleep, it is my strong recommendation that children do so in their own rooms, and in their own beds!

Who is in charge in a family? Check out who is sleeping in the parent's bed, and you will get a pretty good idea.

Setting the Stage for Peaceful Independent Sleep

Concerns about sleep start soon after you first bring your new baby home from the hospital. Since the focus of this book is children age three to ten, I won't address the specifics of helping infants and toddlers sleep. However, I will say that during the first few months of an infant's life, independent sleeping is not something to be too worried about. You want to begin to shape it, however, by having your baby nap in his crib and then move toward having him sleep in his own crib, in his own room, full-time at around five to six months.

Establish Healthy Sleep Habits Early On

The second half of the first year of life is when developing healthy sleep patterns should become a priority. A baby's development yields an explosion of new abilities. For one thing, she can now awaken, reposition herself, perhaps fuss a bit, and then settle back into sleep again. This is when a parent's responses really begin to make a difference in whether a baby is on the path to independent, peaceful sleep, or on the way to dependencies and middle-of-the-night waking for attention and feeding. As Tracy Hogg advises parents over and over again in *Secrets of the Baby Whisperer*, babies don't know anything about sleep habits or routines. They learn it all from us, so be mindful of what you are teaching them. Any bad habits you start will have to be undone, and this is always harder than preventing them in the first place. This becomes increasingly true the longer you let them go on and the older a child gets.

PARENTING TIP

Sleep Routines

Babies don't know anything about sleep habits. They learn it all from us, so be mindful of what you are teaching them.

PARENTING TIP

When Is a Child Ready to Sleep Alone?

Many parents tie their own hands by interpreting their child's sleep protests and anxieties to mean that the child is not "ready" for such a step towards independence. This is a common refrain of parents with IFP and signals a powerful parenting trap. The truth is that children acquire healthy, independent sleep habits over time, as a result of the shaping and leadership of effective parents. This process should start when your children are about six months old. Do you see your three-, four-, or five-year-old as not ready? Watch out! Children's protests may be intense, filled with tears and pleadings, and they may even tell you that they aren't ready themselves, but please don't do them the disservice of seeing this "unreadiness" as an actual weakness or fragility. Your children's protests are most likely byproducts of what they have learned from you, if you have coddled and accommodated them for some time now. Some parents even talk to their children about being ready and ask them straight out: "When do you think you will be ready?" The real translation of "not ready" is "don't want to," and the answer to the question "When will you want to?" will probably be, "I don't know, but not for a long time." Lead your kids. Help them to bring their strength forward. Teach them—they are always ready for effective parenting.

The Beauty of the Crib

I'd like to make one other point before focusing on children who are age three and older. Parents invite trouble when they put away the crib too soon. This is a big contributor to sleep troubles today. Kids still very much need the containment and safety that a crib offers them at night. I recommend that parents switch their child to a bed after the child is about three years old. When small children wake up in the night, which is very common, and find themselves in a big, wide, open bed, they are going to be much more inclined to get out of it. It is natural for them to get up and look for containment, something to make them feel more secure. If a child wakes up, however, and knows she is snugly contained by her crib and can't get out, she will be much more apt to roll over and go back to sleep. You can be sure it is much harder to correct sleep problems when you have a two-year-old who's wandering around the house at night. It can even be dangerous. Don't set yourself up for this kind of trouble.

Keep your child in her crib until she's about three years old. The containment will make her feel grounded and secure, and she'll be much more apt to roll over and go back to sleep if she wakes up in the middle of the night.

Here's another valuable tip to keep in mind as you head into peaceful night's sleep with your three-year-old and older children: A child's preparedness to sleep by himself, without distress, has a great deal to do with what goes on during the day. In fact, things going well at night are largely predicated upon things going well during the day. This is because sleep problems rarely occur in a vacuum. They are usually rooted within a larger picture of separation issues and, ultimately, of IFP.

When parents who are led by their children attempt to assert their authority, they become stymied and frustrated, resulting in arguments with their children, yelling, and temper flare-ups. Conflict only exacerbates an anxious and agitated child's feelings of distress. These children have a much harder time settling down and feeling secure and peaceful. Separations will feel a bit more difficult, too, as will being alone in their beds at night (another separation task). Competent parents who lead their children calmly and predictably through the day set the stage for calm, predictable, sleep-filled nights as well.

Setting the Stage for Bedtime

Most parents are a bit confused about what the prelude should be for their child actually getting into bed, especially if they have a child who resists settling down for the night. When working with families, I have found it most helpful to keep the bedtime routine to a limited number of activities. For many families, bedtime includes a bath or shower, getting into pajamas, having a snack, getting into bed, reading a story or two or three, and then having time to talk and share. This is a lot of activity, and consequently provides considerable opportunity for struggle and delay. For many children, bathing and hair washing are an ordeal; adding them to the bedtime routine sets the stage for a brouhaha that will only stir up a child. To avoid mayhem and insure a peaceful send-off to sleep, follow these three strategies:

1. Let activities such as bathing, having a snack, reading together, or watching television fall into what I refer to as end-of-day activities. This way, when it is actually bedtime and your child chooses to fix a peanut butter sandwich, you can clearly say:

   "Honey, having a sandwich would be fine, if only it hadn't gotten to be bedtime already. Always remember, anything you want to do has to be done before eight o'clock. As it is, you will have to wait for morning. Since I know you are hungry, I will be ready with a big breakfast. Now, off you go to brush your teeth and get into bed."

2. After your child takes a bath or shower, there should be at least a half hour buffer before he has to climb into bed, so he can start to relax and get ready for bed.

3. Limit your bedtime routine to four tasks: getting into pajamas, brushing teeth, getting into bed, and reading or telling one or two stories. For example: Let's say your son is five years old, and his bedtime is 8:00 p.m. At about 7:45 p.m., he should be preparing to get the bedtime tasks done. As a parent, you should be on hand to help him get ready for bed (if he needs help getting dressed, for example) or to read to him as soon as he is dressed and his teeth are brushed.

PARENTING TIP

How Long Does It Take to Get Ready for Bed?

Children can easily get washed, brushed, and changed in less than ten minutes. Bath or shower time should not be included in the earlier bedtime transition for children under the age of eight or nine. Once kids have climbed into bed, parents should be out of the room within ten to fifteen minutes at the most. As children get older, this time can even be shorter. If stories, reading, talking, singing, or prayers go on any longer than that, they work against healthy sleep habits. By age eight, nine, and ten, kids are fine with a quick kiss and a tuck-in to send them off to sleep.

The Three Phases of Peaceful Independent Sleep

Helping a child master independent and peaceful sleep requires effective management of their protests. It is helpful to break down the sleeping task into three phases:

- ❖ The bedtime routine
- ❖ The child says good-night and the parent leaves the room
- ❖ The child sleeps through the night in his own bed.

Almost without exception, no matter what the behavioral arena, children's protests are motivated by either opposition or anxiety. This holds true for sleep resistance as well. Parents are particularly vulnerable to their children's protests in this area, not only because they are exhausted at the end of a day and just don't have the energy to be clever and persistent anymore, but most saliently, because nighttime is laden with emotionally charged issues such as being afraid of the dark, monsters, being alone, scary nightmares, and so on. Understandably, when our children tug at our heartstrings, our best judgment can become clouded and our resolve can quickly dissolve.

Remember, all children, even the most power-balanced, will still struggle and protest. They will fight going to bed, have bad dreams, and want you to reassure them; they may try to get an invitation to sleep in your bed during thunderstorms or when Dad or Mom is traveling. This is perfectly normal fare for all children. Your response will determine if these remain occasional occurrences that are rather easily redirected or if they become regular issues with considerable energy attached to them. Keep the ratio of 70% to 30% as your barometer as to whether you have an entrenched IFP or not. If you and your child have established good sleep habits, this should translate into very few exceptions—the reality will probably be more like 5% of the time that you will have a nighttime disruption of any significance.

Before focusing on how to correct inappropriate behaviors, here is a reminder of the key points of any effective parental response. These apply to each phase and any protest your child will make.

- Whatever you say—keep it short
- Don't take your child's bait
- Don't accommodate
- Keep calm!

Phase One: Correction of the Bedtime Routine

Children display an array of behaviors that delay and disrupt getting into bed and ending story time. For example, they often try to assert where they want to sleep. The motivation fueling such delaying tactics usually has more to do with direct opposition and wanting one's own way than it does with anxiety. This section discusses ways to correct a bedtime routine gone awry.

EXPLAIN THE GROUND RULES

It is helpful to be clear and direct with your child about how bedtime works. If you have a child who has trouble staying in bed alone, or wants the lights to remain on, or keeps getting up after being tucked in, then you will need a correction period to get back on track. I recommend starting anew by setting the ground rules. In all fairness, your child does not know about good sleep habits, and it is your job as a parent to teach them to him. On the day you decide to begin setting the new rules, take a few moments at some point earlier in the day to let him know change is coming. For example, you may begin by saying:

> "You know, honey, our bedtime routine has gotten out of hand. You are five years old, and still you have not learned the habits of good sleeping. Starting tonight we are going to change that, because sleeping well is so important—it helps you to be healthy, strong, feel good, and learn at your best in school. It may be hard to get the hang of it the first few nights—changing habits always is—but your dad and I will help you, and you will get used to it in no time.
>
> "Do you know the habits of good sleep, honey? Let me tell you. First comes relaxing in your own bed, without anyone with you, where you must be still and quiet for sleep to come to you. Second, once you are tucked in bed, you never get out until morning unless you have to go to the bathroom. Third, after we have said our good-nights, you do not talk out loud again until morning. Lastly, you sleep without lights on, and you sleep the whole night through."

You can then identify with him the habits he needs to work on. Ask him to describe what his sleep habits are so that he has to take a look at his behavior without you being the one to point it out in an angry voice.

DON'T GET SIDETRACKED

Powerful children can take a bedtime routine that in actuality requires only ten to fifteen minutes and turn it into hours of pure indulgence or pure frustration. All that really needs to be accomplished in Phase One is for children to wash up a bit, brush their teeth, get into their pajamas, and settle in for a book or story (see Setting the Stage for Bedtime on page 240). Here is where they use a lot of delaying tactics and make a host of demands. Some children run and hide when bedtime is mentioned. Some suddenly begin organizing their book bag for school or decide they're overcome with starvation and have to have a snack. When they finally make it to the bedroom, there's more dallying, arguments over which pajamas to wear, balking over getting teeth brushed, and so on. When they are finally in bed, then comes the tug-of-war over which book, how many books, and which parent will be the reader. Sound familiar?

Whatever the maneuver—and remember it is a part of being a child to try to have things your own way—parents must not be deterred. As the parent, lead your children with the objective that once bedtime comes, there is no more time for any other activity. The bedtime routine is not open season for your kids to exercise their preferences and wish lists. You are not taking requests or making accommodations. There is no excess talking, bargaining, explaining, or deal making. Above all, keep moving! Your children's words should have no real power to stop you. They can move and protest at the same time, but as long as they are on track behaviorally, there is little need for you to pay any attention to their carrying on. There is, however, one generally helpful response to their protests:

> "For tonight, it is too late. It is now bedtime. So it will have to wait until tomorrow."

This general response can be adapted to a variety of protests. For scratchy pajamas, wrong-colored cups, or other disappointments about preferences, remain supportive and good-natured in your tone as you respond:

"Oh, you like the other color better, do you? Well, for tonight, the red cup is here, not the blue one. If you want a drink, you can have one. If not, then you can certainly wait until tomorrow to get one."

With a pajamas issue, if your child is only three or four years old, simply go about the business of taking his clothes off and putting pajamas on him while trying to keep an upbeat attitude as you distract him with an appealing story or topic. If he is old enough to dress himself, then go back to the formula above:

"Oh shoot, you hate these pajamas? Well, for tonight these are the ones that are clean, so you can either wear them or pick a T-shirt to sleep in."

PARENTING TRAP

Don't Confuse Asserting Your Authority with Being Dismissive

Don't confuse powerful, effective parenting with never giving your child any choices. Here is a mini example of how you can let your child know you are not dismissing her feelings all together: "Okay, you hate these pajamas. Since nothing else is clean, either wear a T-shirt or put up with these for one more night." This is striking a balance between not being dismissive and still not being suckered into an ordeal. This is where well-meaning parents can get trapped. Be considerate, but don't give your little ponies too much rein or they will run away with you, and return only when they want to. (Forcers: Remember the biggest error a Forcer parent makes is causing his child to feel bad too often, leaving the child to fight against and reject his leadership out of anger and spite.)

The emotional goal of Phase One is for children to begin to relax, to withdraw from the activity of the day as they lay quietly in their beds, and to soak in the comfort and security of their home and their family's love. It is the latter half of the equation that tends to get parents tripped up, particularly in our current parenting culture of indulging in feelings. More often than not, parents overdo the specialness and "love time" of the bedtime routine because they are trying to compensate for busy work lives, tumultuous days of struggle, or just are too exhausted at the end of the day to do anything but accommodate. Reading books, telling stories, saying prayers, snuggling, securing a favorite blanket or stuffed animal, singing lullabies, lying together and sharing personal feelings and experiences from the day—it all adds up to being too much. In most homes, it goes on way too long.

Children always learn where their parents are most susceptible to influence and then use it for their own gain. For children, a power gain at bedtime centers around three things:

- Delaying the actual "good-night"
- Being the one who determines where she sleeps
- Keeping you with her.

Unfortunately, parents who are invested in creating "specialness" for their adored child are vulnerable to getting caught up in each of these traps. Don't fall for it. Kids know if they are loved and if you care for them from the interactions you have with them throughout each and every day. There's no need to overdo it at night.

HOW MUCH SLEEP SHOULD YOUR CHILD BE GETTING?

Establishing an appropriate bedtime for your child is fundamental to healthy sleep habits; getting the right amount of sleep is important developmentally. Whatever bedtime you choose, make it a routine. This does not mean you can't be flexible on weekends or special outings, when you are on vacation, or in summertime. Kids can certainly adapt and do fine with these changes. Day to day during the school year, however, the less variation, the better. Every child, when asked, should know his bedtime. But he should not be the one to choose it. Mother knows best here. Once it is set, make it a given. As a general rule:

- Children ages three and four typically need at least twelve hours of sleep in a twenty-four hour period. Ten and a half hours' sleep at night and an hour-and-a-half nap during the day are common. However, if children sleep more in the daytime, they need less sleep in the nighttime. Parents should take note of this if their child is having trouble falling asleep at night. Maybe she has napped too long during the day.
- Children five to eight years of age typically need eleven hours of sleep.
- Children ages nine to eleven start to need a bit less sleep, but nine to ten hours is still standard for most.

DON'T OVERDO RELIANCE ON A LOVEY

Of course, there is nothing wrong with a child developing a preference for a favorite blankey or lovey. It is fine for children to hold them when they are relaxing or snuggling in for sleep. A problem can arise, however, when parents bend themselves into pretzels to ensure that their child is never without his lovey.

Here's an example I have heard countless times: After arriving home from a visit with his grandparents or friends, a child realizes his blanket was left behind and bursts into tears. What to do? Well, many, many parents make the decision that the father should get back in the car, even if it is an hour's ride back and it is already after 10:00 p.m., and retrieve the forgotten lovey. In the meantime the mother is busy placating her teary child, saying, "Don't worry, honey, Daddy is going back to get it. You will have your lovey in just a little while. Okay, honey? I have called Grandma; she is keeping it safe until Daddy gets there."

This kind of response represents the antithesis of strong parenting and will not produce a strong child. Too often, parents forgo their better judgment in order to keep their child from experiencing distress. When parents' heartstrings get pulled, their reasoning is deactivated. Yes, your child may be temporarily upset and is looking forward to getting his lovey back, but he will be absolutely fine without it. The next day, when it is convenient, you will go and get the blanket. Think carefully about the message you are communicating to your child through your frantic, irrational, inconvenient maneuvers to retrieve a forgotten lovey.

So many children today are holding onto their blankets and stuffed animals at much older ages—some even into their preteens and early teens. Where are the parents? The best way to help a child have a healthy connection to a cuddly toy is to establish, at age four or five, that the blanket or animal be used only when relaxing at home. It should not be taken in the car on errands or to social outings. When the child gets a bit older, it should remain in the children's rooms and should be used only at night. Parents, your children need you to show them the way to maturity. If you refuse to lead, they'll never get there.

PARENTING TRAP

Don't Say "We"

Pleaser and Pushover parents, in particular, use "we" when trying to lead their children into the bedtime routine. They include themselves in directives that in actuality pertain only to the child. For example, they say, "Okay, honey, we have to get ready for bed now" or "Come on, we have to brush our teeth" even when they, the parents, are not in fact getting ready for bed at that moment or planning to brush their teeth. Saying *we* when you mean *you* signals tentativeness and deference; it tells your children you are uncomfortable asserting your authority over them. Saying *you* makes the natural distinction between parent and child clear. Don't hide your authority—be simple, matter-of-fact, and straightforward: "Your bedtime is coming up. You will need to brush your teeth and get into your pajamas. When you have crawled into bed, we can read a story." In this last context, it is appropriate to say *we* because, in fact, you will be reading a story together.

USING THE LADDER TO CORRECT BEDTIME ROUTINES

To get children to get ready for bed, use a variation of the first three steps of the Ladder. As bedtime approaches, give your child a friendly ten- or fifteen-minute heads up that it is almost time for bed:

> "Hey, hon, it is coming up on your bedtime. You have about fifteen minutes before you will need to get ready for bed."

Direct your child to finish her end-of-day activity, or to be prepared at the end of her TV show to get ready for bed. Follow the steps described below.

Step One: "It's Time; Off You Go"

Step One is the clear directive that follows your heads-up. You state that it is time and say that it is bedtime now. Use pet names and keep your tone warm and upbeat.

> "Okay, honey, it's time now. Off you go."

Step Two: "This is the Second Reminder..."

If your child has not moved within a minute or so, the next step in the sequence is to give a simple and friendly reminder:

> "Okay, honey, it's time for you to get ready for bed. This is the second reminder. Please get moving now."

If your child makes a fuss or ignores you, move to Step Three of the Ladder.

Step Three: "Come On, Honey"

The key to Step Three is to MOVE first, talk second. Get up, go to your child, and escort her to her room.

"Come on, off you go, sweet pea. It's bedtime."

Place your hands behind her shoulders, point her towards her room, and keep moving her along if she isn't moving on her own. Don't get sidetracked by talking, pleading, explaining, or bargaining!

Above all, don't start barking or yelling at your child. This will only jangle her nerves and rev her up for battle. You don't want your manner or harsh words to ever be the reason your child cries when you are leading her. Should she cry in protest or disagreement to your direction, that goes with the territory and should be given no more than a passing empathetic comment such as:

"Oh my, sweet pea, such a fuss over bedtime. Nevertheless, off to bed you go."

Don't get suckered into losing your lead. Tears are common for children and they flow easily when a child doesn't like something. This is perfectly benign, ordinary childishness.

Don't be intimidated by her distress, worried that you are putting too much pressure on her, or concerned that her self-esteem is being damaged. You're asking your child to comply with going to bed—which is totally normal request for a parent to make and is completely manageable. Nor is your loving bond with your child being strained. This is not going to change her thinking that you are the "best, best, best!" Keeping with the program proves a long-term benefit. Her tears will pass quickly and get triggered much less frequently if you keep your response to them kind but minimal. Maintain your one-track mind and focus on starting the bedtime routine—and that's it. If you have fallen into really bad bedtime and sleep habits with your child, chances are good that your one-track mind will be enough to ignite your child's protests now. If you are met with a big struggle, pick her up sooner rather than later in order to avoid things spiraling out of control and carry her to her bedroom. (For a reminder on how to handle Step Three protests, see page 110.)

When you reach the bedroom, leave her with a calm but unwavering direction to change into her pajamas. As you leave, remind her that:

> "It is, after all, only bedtime—something that comes every single day and always will. No need to fuss or fight it. The sooner you settle down and get your business done, the sooner we can enjoy a story together."

You may leave her for a few minutes (of course, remain close to the door in case she runs out) to see if she can get on with things herself. If not, after five minutes or so, go back into the room and proceed to calmly help her remove her clothes and put on her pajamas. Take her hand and walk her to the bathroom for teeth brushing and potty. If she can't settle down, tell her that story time and tears do not go together. Only if she is able to calm down and dry her eyes will you be able to read together. Tell her you understand if she just can't stop crying and that there will always be tomorrow night. Say:

> "I was looking forward to reading with you, but that's okay. Sometimes kids just need to fuss; I understand."

Step Four: Stay Close to the Door

Once you have left your child's bedroom with instructions to her to get her pajamas on, don't forget to stay close to the door in case she tries to run out. See page 114 for more detailed instructions on Step Four.

Step Five: When Fussing Gets Out of Control

If your child's fussing gets out of control and her protest becomes physical to the point of hitting or kicking, throwing things, or refusing to stay in her room, proceed up the Ladder and help her with a containing Parent Hold (see page 127).

After she has calmed down in the hold, proceed without delay or detour to finish the bedtime routine. If it has been a doozy of a fight, and both of you are pretty spent, feel free to skip teeth brushing altogether, letting her know that in the morning she can brush double time, but for tonight, settling directly into bed will be best. And of course, there will be no story time now: All the fussing has taken up the reading time for tonight.

Your child's protests may have drained you somewhat, but be upbeat with your child about the fact that while some lessons are harder than others for kids to learn, few are as important to being healthy as learning how to be a good sleeper. Tell her you trust tomorrow will be easier, and you will have plenty of time for a story then.

Most parents can predict the severity of resistance their child is likely to express. So if you think you will be in for a rocky time of it in the beginning, then be realistic and start the bedtime process thirty minutes earlier than usual. The key to being effective with any behavior is that you must prevail in the end. What you have said needs to happen on your terms, not your child's. Once you have started a bedtime routine, you are not finished until your child is alone in her own bed and drifting off to sleep on her own.

Phase Two: How to Say Good Night and Take Leave

Phase Two is where children can get really worked up and when anxiety and fear reach a peak. Children will often refuse to stay in bed after being tucked in and may beg and plead for a parent to stay with them until they fall asleep. You are so close to your goal, but for some families, still so far. Take heart. This is where you will make your mark and help shape your child into an independent, peaceful sleeper.

All of your child's protests and delaying tactics in this phase are focused on keeping you engaged with him. So what you have to do in this phase is quite simple:

1. Get up from where you've been lying down for storytelling.

2. Turn out the lights

3. Bend over and give a kiss or two

4. Say, "Good night and sweet dreams!"

5. Walk out of the room.

That's it! Well, just that and managing all the protests and signs of distress your little one will kick up when you do.

For the first step, after you have finished reading and have closed the book, or come to the end of the story you were telling, get up. Don't give your hugs and kisses, or say your nighty-nights while still lying down. By standing up, you signal that you will not be staying. The longer you lie there, the more of a tease it is for your child, and the more it whets his appetite to see if he can get you to stay. Remember, don't overdo your reassurances, as this will actually inflame whatever anxiety he may have.

He may try to beg and plead his way into your bed, but the same formula applies here. A calm, unruffled reminder is best:

> "No, honey, Daddy and I sleep in our bed. This is your bed and this is where you sleep."

Some children will protest that it isn't fair that they have to be alone while you get to be with Daddy. Remember to keep your response short:

> "It is not a matter of fairness, honey. It is the way families are. Mommies and daddies sleep together in the parents' bed, and their children have their own cozy beds. Now, snuggle in."

If your child is used to having you lie down with him, he will of course try everything he can to keep you with him when it's time for you to get up from storytelling and give kisses and say good night. At this point, remind him of your earlier conversation and let him know that he will be learning from now on how to enjoy relaxing and waiting for sleep on his own. Without getting yourself caught up in explanations, reassurances, and so forth, just say:

> "I know you aren't used to it yet, but that's okay. You will settle into it soon enough. Love you, good night!"

Having said this, leave his bedroom promptly.

SLEEP WILL COME TO YOU

When most children are put to bed, they are instructed by their parents to "GO to sleep." Parents often give this direction repeatedly, and of course their frustration and irritation level rises with each repetition. Soon parents are barking and adding a threatening tone to their voice when they command, "GO TO SLEEP!" As I have said before, escalation and harshness are not helpful in shaping children's self-control and cooperation. We can never expect them to be more self-controlled and respectful than we ourselves are, and this is especially true at bedtime. Getting riled up will only serve to take your child further from the calm that precedes sleep. Besides, what do we mean when we instruct our children to go to sleep? "Go" is an active verb that suggests the child should be doing something. Children have no clue how to go to sleep. In fact, they routinely cry out, "But I can't! I can't go to sleep!"

Years ago, I started teaching parents a new phrase to use instead of *go to sleep*. It has worked quite well. You can use it, too. When your child is balking and saying that he can't go to sleep, say in a soothing and understanding tone:

> "Oh honey, you don't have to go to sleep, sleep will come to you. All you have to do is lie still and be quiet."

Point out that when he is noisy and moving around, sleep won't come. He has to be still and quiet; then, sleep will come. Sometimes it comes very soon, and sometimes it takes longer, but sleep always comes. Parents find this phrase soothing to say, and children find it soothing to hear. It is also a concrete, clear direction they can grasp. Soothe your child with the reassuring words:

"Sleep will come to you."

WHEN YOUR CHILD DOESN'T WANT TO BE LEFT ALONE

After you have left your child's room, continue to follow the guidelines for Step Three of the Ladder (page 109). Your child may mutter and whimper a bit but not get too wound up, and eventually may drift off to sleep. If this is the case, your parenting work is done for the day. But if he lies in bed and cries or yells pleas or protests, you must continue to provide more support and containment.

In response to fussing, after waiting a few minutes, go in to your child and without sitting down, just lean over and rub his back a minute, saying:

"Honey, what do you have to do for sleep to come? Be still and quiet, remember? You are fine, and there really is no need to fuss. I am not going to lie down with you anymore, because that isn't helpful to you. The sooner you settle down, the sooner sleep will be here. Also, since it is time for there to be quiet in the house now, I am going to close your bedroom door so all your carrying on stays in here."

Give another kiss and go out, closing the door if the fussing continues. Then, after a few more minutes, if the protest is in full force, go back in, this time with a tissue, a warm, moist washcloth, and a glass of water. Sit down next to him on the bed and with a very sympathetic, soft voice say:

"Wow, such a big fuss and upset. It is a really good thing we are working on these good sleep habits; you really need them! Here, blow your nose, wipe your eyes, and take a drink of water."

Still following the structure of the Ladder, the next step is to say something along these lines:

"Now, why it is that you are still making such a big fuss, I don't know. Sleeping is a wonderful thing that comes to us at the end of each day, and gets us rested and ready for more fun tomorrow. But, I guess sometimes you just need to get the fuss out. If you need to cry, so be it. I will leave the tissue, washcloth, and water. Cry until you're finished, and then you will be able to be still and quiet, and sleep will come to you."

As you leave, close the door once more.

For some children the very thought of a closed door sends them into a panic. Some will start to quiet down immediately and say, "I will be quiet, I will! Just don't close the door." If your child does show some sign of settling, then you can say:

"Okay, honey, you do seem to be quieting, so it will be fine for me to leave the door open. I will only close it when your yelling or crying gets too loud."

For children who are going crazy with distress, go ahead and close the door, as long as they remain in bed. I know this is going to be hard! After all, it is your child's anxiety and protest that have led you into accommodations in the first place. So when it sounds like your child is coming unglued, stay focused and grounded in the reality of what is going on: You are helping your child to learn to relax and go to sleep in his own bed. That is it. His protest may sound like he is being tortured by you, but he is not being tortured. Going to sleep is normal, daily behavior that in truth isn't scary or dangerous. Nor does it hurt in the least.

If your child is provoked to get out of bed and tries to run out of the room, or if he comes to the closed door and struggles to open it, go to him, scoop him up, and carry him directly back to bed. Tell him with gentle support in your voice that as hard a time as he is having with sleep habits, the only way for him to learn them is to stick with it. He is going to sleep in his own bed, lying still and quiet so sleep will come to him. If his out-of-control behavior escalates, then move to Step Five of the Ladder (page 127), holding him close and soothing him until he calms down. Then, after blowing his nose, wiping his face, and giving him a quick and calm reassurance that he is fine, say:

> "I know that you are having a hard time, but that's okay; I am going to help you. Don't worry, sweet pea. In no time at all you will be feeling so proud of yourself and the good sleep habits you have."

After tucking him in again, leave the room and wait and to see what happens. If he keeps on crying and pleading, repeat Step Four and Step Five as needed until he finally falls asleep. Remember, though, you must *not* bail out or collapse until your agenda has prevailed. Don't give in and lie down with him; don't offer bribes or make threats; don't plead with him. If you do so, you will only be saying to your child that ultimately you cannot handle his distress, and this will become a certain pathway to power he will continue to use. Stay strong, supportive, and very confident and deliberate about what you are doing and why. Your parenting work on this evening can end in this way only: Your child has fallen asleep in his own bed without you lying down with him or reading more than one or two books or stories, and you have not yelled, pleaded, or gotten angry. Instead, you have been steady as a rock and led him with strength and confidence. And that means you have now set the stage for both sweet dreams and a strong child.

PARENTING TRAP

"You're a Big Boy Now"

Parents very commonly say, "You're a big boy now" when trying to find a way to talk their child into sleeping independently. "You're a big boy now. Big boys don't sleep with their mommies and daddies. What would your friends say if they knew?" Forcer parents may crank it up a notch and say, "You are being a baby. What is the matter with you?" But remember—a child wants to sleep with you because you have not adequately helped him to feel comfortable sleeping alone. Both during the day and at night you have not been providing the competent and respectful leadership he needs to master the task. Just getting older is not going to get him there; he needs to be guided and shaped by you. Trying to talk him into it won't be sufficient, and making him feel bad will only undermine his security and confidence even more. So don't get so desperate or provoked that you tell him he's a crybaby or threaten to embarrass him. You want to soothe, reassure, and encourage him with the security he needs to become independent, not cause anxiety and hurt feelings by belittling and threatening him.

Phase Three: Children Sleep Through the Night in Their Own Bed

Some children experience middle-of-the-night or early-morning waking, perhaps out of habit or because of a nightmare, and call out to a parent to come in, or they clamor to get into their parents' bed for the remainder of the night. Anxiety plays a central role in this familiar scenario.

What do you do when you hear the pitter-patter of little feet coming into your bedroom in the night? Or the little voice calling out and waking you up, asking you to come to her? As with every corrective measure, action is required. You won't make any progress unless you get up. I know it may seem easier just to talk, plead, or sound angry, but none of these responses will get the job done. It is hard, but you just have to get up, sometimes in the middle of the night, when it's cold or your body is pulling you back to sleep. And if your child is expressing distress, you undoubtedly will feel for her and will not want to deny her your comfort if she is so afraid.

What I ask you to keep in mind, however, is that there really is nothing for your child to be afraid of. Darkness and sleep are part of everyday life, and there will never be an exception to this. Many people are in fact plagued by anxiety, worry, and fear at night—and it is a terrible burden. This is certainly not the foundation you want to be laying for your child, and countering his fears with calm, confidence, and an air of security is the very best antidote.

It is so important to pay close attention and not to let your good-hearted intentions inadvertently reinforce and encourage your children's unnecessary fears. Remember that your child is fine—he's safe in his cozy bed and secure in your home. That is the truth, and the basis from which you should respond. Don't make the mistake of validating his fear.

GETTING YOUR CHILD BACK TO SLEEP

Here's the advice that will return your child to the coziness, security, and comfort of sleep. In short, here's how to get him back into his own bed. At the beginning of this correction, your child will have had little experience with independence and peacefulness, so he may kick up a real fuss. Take a deep breath, stay calm, don't forget to keep your voice down to a whisper, and stay firm in your guidance. You cannot permit him to leave his bed under any circumstances. If you have to, go to Step Three of the Ladder, and proceed to Step Four and Step Five as needed (see pages 115-136). As always, do not get caught up in conversation or explanations. Tell him that no matter how much he fusses or cries, he must learn to be comfortable in his own bed. There's simply no other way around it, and it is up to you to hold the line.

When Your Child Calls Out

If your child awakens you by calling out to you but has not actually come into your bedroom, simply call back to him (assuming he's within earshot), keeping your voice as quiet and reassuring as possible:

> "Honey, it is not morning yet, you have woken up by accident. Snuggle in, and sleep will come back to you."

If your child's room is too far away for him to hear you, you will have to get up and go to his door to deliver this correction. The key is to respond minimally to his waking up. There's no need for lights or conversation. It is the middle of the night.

When Your Child Comes Into Your Room

If your child has gotten up and come into your room, get up quickly, and without turning on any lights, take his hand and walk him back to his bed. Keeping your voice down to a whisper, say:

> "You woke up by accident. Sshh, it isn't morning yet, so it's not time to be up and talking. Snuggle back into bed, sweetie, and let sleep come back to you."

This is basically the same advice and language that you used in the previous scenario.

When Your Child Has a Bad Dream

If your child has had a bad dream and is frightened, give him gentle and soothing reassurance, such as:

> "Oh yes, bad dreams really cause you to feel scared for a few minutes. But it was just a dream. You are awake now and can see that you are fine. Let me tuck you back in, and you can get all snuggled up in your cozy bed."

If you like, sit with him for a minute or two and/or rub his back a few times. Then give him a kiss and return to your bed. If he wants to tell you about his dream during this time, it is okay to listen, but help him to keep it short. You can say:

> "Oh, a bad monster dream, indeed! Stupid monster, get out of my son's dream. He wants good dreams."

Then remind your child it is best not to think about it any more, now, and if he wants, you can talk about it in the morning. You can help him think of something he would like to dream about, to get positive images in his head. Then go back to bed. Beware of the ubiquitous parent trap of too much reassurance, too much talking, and too much time spent staying by his side. Again, keep all conversation to a minimum and remember: Your child really is fine.

PARENTING TRAP

Making Up Excuses and Hiding Behind Irrelevant Reasons

Parents who are uncomfortable and uncertain about their authority and leadership very commonly make up excuses or try to influence their child to be an independent sleeper for manufactured reasons. For example, after she tucks her child in bed and he begs her to stay with him, a kindhearted mother might say, "But honey, I have to go and do the dishes" or "Sweetie, Mommy needs to have her grown-up time now." Or, after a long day at work she may feel compelled to say, "I have important phone calls to make and I have to pay the bills. If I don't pay the bills, we will have big trouble, you know." While all of these circumstances may be true, the point is that these are the wrong reasons for not staying with your child. By saying these things, you are implying that if you didn't have dishes, weren't working, or didn't have business to attend to, you would gladly stay with your child. The real message needs to be that good sleep habits are extremely important for children to develop, and sleeping independently is a primary one. So when your child says, "Stay with me," simply say:

> "No, honey, you are fine. We will have more fun together tomorrow. Nighty-night."

Similarly, don't manufacture reasons why your child can't sleep in bed with you. You might be tempted to say, "You kick and squirm in the night and I can't sleep," or "The bed is just too small, and there isn't enough room." But these are not at the heart of the matter, and they introduce the notion that sleeping together would be fine if only the bed were larger. In fact, many parents feel an adequate solution to a crowded bed is to buy a bigger one.

Other parents, desperate to have their own bed to themselves again, manufacture excuses to try to convince their children to stay in their own beds. In fact, one parent I spoke with, who had succeeded in getting his children out of his bed, proudly told me how he had done it. He said that he had had a minor surgical procedure and that when he got home from the hospital, he showed his two kids his bandage. He then told them his doctor said that if he was kicked where the incision was, he could die, so there was no way the kids could sleep in bed with him. They didn't want to accidentally kill Daddy, did they? This ploy worked, and the father was so pleased with himself. Fortunately, most parents can quickly see the manipulation and dishonesty in this excuse.

Excuses, manufactured reasons, and threats: these are the tactics of parents who don't know how to harness their true authority and competence or how to give their children the leadership they need. Don't fall into this trap. Be a strong parent. Lead with straightforwardness, kindness, and care, but hold the line!

NIGHTTIME PLEAS FOR SNACKS, DRINKS, OR TOYS

If you are bombarded with requests for water, juice, or something to eat because your child says his stomach is so hungry or if your child wants a certain stuffed animal that is downstairs in the playroom or in the basement, your answer should be *no, no, no,* and *no.* Keeping your voice down to a whisper, and using a friendly matter-of-fact tone, let him know that there are no food or drinks in the night, but in the morning you will be happy to give him a big glass of juice or prepare an extra-big breakfast.

If he wakes up in the night and wants a toy or stuffed animal, tell him that for sleep to come back, he does not need toys, he only has to be still and quiet. Remind him that he should have anything he wants for the night with him before the lights are out, since there is no getting up and roaming around the house again until morning. Then give him a quick kiss and leave the room. If he protests and says, "No, Mom, wait, wait! Mom!" stay at the door for a moment and whisper, "No more talking; it is still nighttime. If you are going to cry and make a fuss, that is okay, but I will close the door so that your noise won't disturb the quiet of the house." Then keep going. If need be, climb the Ladder with him until he can settle down once more.

As with any corrective effort, your child's resistance and protest will be the worst the first time around. It might be helpful for you to keep a log of the amount of time your child fusses each night, so that you can chart his progress. By the third and fourth nights, you should see a dramatic reduction in your child's fussiness. Yes, it really does shift that quickly! But you have to be determined, deliberate, and at the same time remain very comfortable, confident, and calm about what you are doing.

This is the kind of leadership that characterizes strong parents and creates strong children. And strong children are peaceful and independent sleepers.

AT THE HEART OF IT ALL

Normalizing sleep is at the heart of the effective parenting strategy that you are getting across to your child in a matter-of-fact way. You are letting your child know that his upset is something for which you have compassion, but that since going to bed and sleeping are no big deal, it does not distress you or cause you to doubt your judgment. Your demeanor lets him know, as you hand him a tissue and calmly help him blow his nose, that all his tears and shouts haven't sent you into a fretful, out-of-control tailspin. It is not your issue, and his tears and yelling have no power over you. They don't perturb you in the least. Instead, you are extending yourself with compassion and understanding, but you are not overdoing it, not veering off course. A strong parent leads. By setting an example of calm, the strong parent demonstrates that there is really no big deal here—even though the child may be freaking out. Strong parents completely sidestep the power struggle that can so easily swallow them like quicksand.

When you achieve success, continue to keep things matter of fact. When morning comes, if you have had a successful night, don't overdo your praise. Just as you are teaching your child to be matter-of-fact about sleep, you must remember to do the same as the adult and to stay calm when your child actually sleeps in his own bed without any fuss. There should be no trips to the toy store, no exclamations about what a big boy he is and how proud you are of him, no phone calls to Grandma saying, "Guess who slept in his own bed last night!" It is just sleep; everybody does it, and they do it every night. It's an activity for which prizes or fanfare are unnecessary. All that's needed is a simple:

> "Good morning to you! Doesn't it feel good to start the day after a good night's sleep? So much better without the fuss too, don't you think?"

Chapter Ten

Toileting

Have you ever wondered why the toilet is sometimes referred to as "the throne"? Well, for kids with IFP, it can indeed become a mighty seat of power. "Mommy, I have to go potty!" is an announcement that can, and does, send parents into hyperreaction mode, with an urgency that matches having to put out a fire. Everything becomes secondary in importance to getting Cindy Sue on the potty.

One father described to me how he was using the first floor bathroom when his daughter, who was three and a half, knocked on the door and said six magical words: "Daddy, I have to go potty." He immediately went into action, frantically hurrying to finish up his own business as he called out, "Okay, sweetie, just hold on one minute, I will be right out. Just hang on. Daddy is finishing as fast as he can so that you can get in here in one second." It never dawned on him to just say, "Okay, honey, run on upstairs and use the potty up there." Parents literally fall all over themselves to respond to their children's toileting needs. Although I have stressed the importance of moving quickly into action to ensure effectiveness in other parenting contexts, when it comes to toileting, jumping into action can actually backfire. Parents can appear anxious, not to mention deferential, when they are so quick to respond to any sign or comment their child makes about needing to go to the bathroom. Play it cool, parents—feeling the urge to go is not a national emergency.

Another misstep many parents make is taking on their child's toileting as too much of their own issue. They are way too involved in it as a major parenting task, thinking it is something *they* have to do. It's true, parents have to lead children and do some teaching, but ultimately it is not the parent's task to accomplish, it is the child's. The truth is, if you lead them a bit, offer some instruction and support, and don't get overinvolved or give them props and crutches that derail their progress, the process will unfold naturally, as a matter of course.

The transition from using diapers to using the toilet occurs naturally as children mature. The discomfort and the nuisance of diapers and diaper changes gets old for kids. They become aware that diapers are for babies, and seeing siblings and other big kids using the potty spurs them on. Most children develop a natural interest and motivation to use the toilet.

Just like sleeping and eating, going to the bathroom is universal to all people, a daily occurrence driven by physiology. Neither peeing nor pooping is hard to do. Our bodies do them naturally and no real effort is required. Most troubles that occur in the toileting arena crop up when parents inadvertently get too involved or focus too much attention on the task. Too much parental anxiety and personal involvement will surely register on your child's radar, since children are always on the alert for areas where they can mine power and finagle control.

Parental Missteps That Lead to Toileting Trouble

If you find yourself struggling with your child over a toileting problem, the first thing to do is take stock of what is happening between you. In contrast to eating, where the power issues center on rejecting versus taking in, here it has to do with withholding versus giving it up. As with sleep, the psychological dynamics of toileting have to do with independence, autonomy, and separation. To correct trouble in the toileting area, begin with a quick assessment of what you are doing and saying to your child and listen carefully to how she is responding to you. Here are three of the most common mistakes parents make:

✢ Overcontrol and use of force

✢ Overattention and overinvolvement

✢ Overanxiousness and overaccommodation.

Notice what's going on here: There's a lot of excess, with too many *overs*. What is in short supply is a realistic parental perspective about the ordinariness of this daily and universal activity. The pressure parents put on themselves to be perfect, the pressures schools put on parents to have their children out of diapers before they begin school, and the pressure of competition and comparison that is so hard to avoid among parents all contribute to overdoing in this department. When a child who is invested in autonomy and separateness feels overly managed and overly controlled, it can trigger a withholding and countercontrol response. Parents, what are your *overs*? Take a look at the following list and give yourself an honest assessment. Do you:

✢ Talk about, explain, or ask a lot of questions about peeing, pooping, and how to use the toilet? (This includes asking your child if and when he will be ready to stop using diapers, and when he answers that he just wants to wait until Saturday, accepting the answer as if it were a real plan.)

✢ Spend a lot of time in the bathroom with your child: reading, telling stories, and playing music while he sits on the toilet?

✢ Offer incentives and/or rewards such as toys or candy to encourage peeing and pooping in the toilet?

✢ Talk a lot about your child's toileting struggles with friends and family? Does your child at times overhear you?

✢ Set up too many contingencies around peeing and pooping?

✢ Blow up over peeing and pooping? Criticize your child for his toileting delay?

❖ Rush to get your child to a potty the minute your child says he has to go? If you are in the car, a store, or on the road, do you snap to with a rather frantic and overdone urgency to get him to a toilet ASAP?

❖ Prowl the potty section at Babies "R" Us, hoping to find the product that will be the answer to your child's dilemma and deliver you from the frustration of it all?

Parents, does your child:

❖ Say "I don't want to!" "I don't have to!" "I can't!" or "I'm trying!" too often?

❖ Hold it in and wait to go when the moment is the most inopportune for you?

❖ Refuse to poop in the toilet, insisting on a pair of disposable training pants?

❖ Have "accidents" that actually seem purposeful?

❖ Put his poop in places other than the toilet, such as the bathtub or the floor?

❖ Wait too long to go to the bathroom and then have it be a matter of urgency that doesn't always end well?

If you recognize yourself or your child in any of these scenarios, an imbalance of family power (IFP) is likely clogging your toilet works. You have, without even knowing it, joined your child in a dance for power that you cannot win with force. In fact, these tactics ignite and fuel resistance in your child, rather than encourage him to embrace his own motivation to take this step towards growing up.

What gives the dynamic even more energy is your willingness to accommodate your child's ploys, game-playing, and refusals. After all, children are looking to assert themselves and thwart you at the same time. Playing games or refusing outright to use the toilet according to cultural standards pretty much gets that job done. Before long, their struggle to assert themselves against you derails their natural motivation to get out of their diapers and onto the toilet seat. If you climb the ladder of accommodation and give in to your child's agenda of thwarting yours, you will have a little toileting gremlin in your midst before you know it.

PARENTING TRAP

Excessive Fanfare over Peeing and Pooping

A parent's reaction to pee and poop is the first emotional measure of the process that your child internalizes. It doesn't come from within him. This is certainly true of parents who exclaim over their child's natural functions and often ignore their child's right to privacy and respect: "Oh, that's a big one!" "This one is a real stinker!" "Does someone smell in this room? Uh-oh, I think it's Sammy! Yep, smells like he did a poopoo!" "P.U.! I have to change that diaper? I am going to need a clothespin for my nose!" Reactions like these communicate volumes to children. Be mindful of the stage you are setting and be especially careful not to convey the message that what your child's body has produced is disgusting. When parents giggle too much or call in family and friends to take a look, children almost certainly feel self-conscious and humiliated.

Lilly, a three-year-old girl, was visiting her grandparents for Christmas. On the evening of their arrival, while the family was gathered in the living room, the Christmas tree began to fall forward. There, behind the tree, Lilly was squatting and making a bowel movement in her training pants. When she was discovered and saw that all eyes were on her, she pleaded, "Don't smell me! Go away!" On hearing this, everyone burst out laughing and there was great hilarity over the event for the rest of the holiday visit. Everyone was amused—except for Lilly. She didn't think there was anything funny about it at all. In fact, it was her self-consciousness about her parent's exclaiming and making such a big deal over her poop that motivated her to go behind the Christmas tree in the first place.

Promoting Independent Toilet Use

There are many different approaches to toilet training, ranging from the traditional "wait until they are ready" method, to intensive two-day immersion programs, to the current fad of holding eight-month-old infants over the potty. Since I believe toileting troubles arise primarily from relational problems, I'm less interested in the particular program parents choose to follow than I am in their attitude and the style of communication they adopt when following a program. My focus in this chapter is on preventing and correcting the distortions of IFP that can derail kids and parents in the process of toilet training. For those parents who are imminently facing toilet training and who are looking for general toileting information, I encourage you to read Dr. Spock's advice in his classic *Baby and Child Care*, which after these many years is as relevant and on target today as it was sixty years ago.

Toilet Learning versus Toilet Training

Dr. Spock makes a wonderful distinction between toilet learning, all the exposure and teaching children get before they ever begin to try to use the toilet, and toilet training, which involves getting a child to actually sit on the potty and use it (an activity that doesn't usually occur until after the child's second birthday). The difference is all about learning versus doing. Parents today are too caught up in the doing and often do not pay enough attention to the long-term process of readying their child. Here are some suggestions for imparting toilet learning to your child.

BODY AWARENESS

When you are teaching babies and toddlers the name for each part of their bodies, don't skip over their private parts. Familiarizing young children with their bodies and how they work is a very important preliminary step to toilet learning. I can't help thinking of the many times I've watched parents playfully ask their young children to point to their ears and noses, elbows and belly buttons, and then down to their knees and toes. What happened? There are some very important parts in between!

For boys, learning about where their pee comes out is more straightforward because their genitals are external and readily visible. Their penises get erect and stand up, making it impossible to overlook them. There's no such luck for our little girls. The truth is, most girls never see their own genitals, leaving a central part of their bodies foreign to them. An easy way to remedy this is to use a hand mirror, so they can see for themselves what their genitals look like. You can talk about how girls have three holes—one for pee to come out, one for poop, and one for when they are grown-ups, for babies to come out. Girls like it when they find out boys don't have that one and have only two holes. This can also be the launching point of an ongoing conversation about sex and reproduction with your children that unfolds gradually over the years.

A PRACTICE POTTY

My second recommendation is to introduce a little portable potty around the child's second birthday to let your child play with and build mastery. Just as you would give your child a toy vacuum cleaner or a toy oven with which to play house, offering a potty to sit on allows kids to pretend they are toilet users before taking the real step. Children invariably love this and will pretend to sit on the potty with their clothes on. Or they may undress completely and sit on it, or use it for their dolls or even a pet kitten.

Whatever your child's fancy, introducing her to a little potty is a valuable step in preparing her for actually using the toilet. You can tell her that she will be learning to use the real toilet when she is about three years old. Make it sound as if this is a matter of course. Don't dwell on it or oversell the idea by saying, "Won't that be neat? Will you like that, honey?" And don't turn the training over to her: "I want you to tell Mommy when you are ready, okay, honey?" Don't confuse a young toddler's curiosity about a potty with a signal for training readiness. This doesn't usually happen until closer to age three.

In fact, as you move your child into actual toilet training, it is not helpful to use a plastic potty. Putting the child on the toilet from the beginning of training means you won't have to train your child twice. Let the child know that little potties are good for learning and getting used to, but toilets are best for putting our pee and poop in. You can make toilets more user-friendly with a small step stool and a child's seat on the commode. The child will be able to use the toilet with considerable independence.

PARENTING TIP

In the Diaper or in the Toilet

A simple and clear statement I also find helpful to say to children throughout the learning phase is:

> "There are two places for pee and poop. One is diapers. Those are used by babies and little children, and the other is toilets, which are used by older kids and grown-ups."

Diapers or toilets—in our culture, these are the only two places. If your children get this basic fact, it will be easier to remind them that underpants are not one of those places when it is time for them to transition from diapers to being a full-time toilet user.

Knowing When the Time Is Right

Knowing when to transition from toilet learning to toilet training boils down to a consideration of developmental factors. Children need to be able to go into the bathroom and take care of business without you. Just as in the arena of sleep, the psychological dynamics of toileting have to do with independence, autonomy, and separation. Problems arise when parents impose training too soon and encounter a child whose body is too immature or who has little motivation of his own. The child is ready when he can:

❖ Recognize his body's signals that he has to pee and to poop

❖ Use his muscles to delay voiding until he can get to a toilet

❖ Respond to his own internal motivation and be willing to stop what he is doing and take the time to go to the bathroom.

Cognitively, physiologically, and emotionally, your child should be ready for this task when he is about three years old. Therefore, my recommendation is to make the transition, the training phase, from diapers to toilet sometime around the third birthday.

If you feel compelled, because of your child's age, or because of your own issues with anxiety or control, to micromanage your child's bowel and bladder urges throughout the day, this will translate into an impediment to your child's sense of self-sufficiency and competence. While it is true that you will need to be available to assist in helping your child with wiping after a bowel movement until he gets a bit more coordinated and efficient at doing it on his own, your goal is to train your child to be an independent, full-time toilet user.

One last developmental consideration I want to mention: Children are able to master dry pants and use the toilet during the day about six months to a year before they are able to master nighttime dryness. Sometime after age three, children are usually mature enough for daytime toilet use. Nighttime dryness is achieved closer to age four or four-and-a-half. During this in-between period, simply put your child in a diaper for the nighttime, when he changes into his pajamas. After he has woken up dry for a week or two in a row, you can phase out the diaper altogether.

Nighttime wetting can be a source of terrible frustration and embarrassment, particularly if it persists into kindergarten and the elementary school years. The most common reason for this is physiological, not psychological. If your child is struggling with this well after age four or five, it is best to consult with your pediatrician and set up a consultation with a pediatric urologist.

Props, Crutches, and Gimmicks

There is so much on the market these days for parents to buy that promises to make parenting tasks easier. The majority of these products are intended to minimize the distress a child will experience while transitioning to greater independence. Unfortunately, the whole premise is a setup. All these crutches and props, gizmos and gimmicks suggest that the tasks of growing up are really hard, and that you need to cushion your children from the process as much as possible. This is nonsense. When was the last time the sight of a white toilet was distasteful to anyone? Marketers want you to load up the shopping cart with props—animal faces that disguise the toilet seat, for example. But children don't really need them. Nor do you, if you believe in and have confidence in yourself as a parent and in the natural abilities of your child.

Marketers also tap into parents' good intentions and their misguided belief that buying all the props and aids signifies genuine parental commitment. But of course they don't. Your love and concern for your child are just as strong without all the gimmicks. Peeing and pooping are natural body functions that have a very powerful drive behind them. Going to the bathroom isn't scary or hard; it's simply a common facet of everyday life. If you are tempted to build a shrine to the behavior or an amusement park in your bathroom, you will lead your child into thinking the job really does require distraction and decoys, and you will only be prolonging and complicating the process.

Disposable training pants such as Pull-Ups® are, in my opinion, the number one toileting crutch; they confuse more children and prolong more toilet training than all the other props combined. Think about it: Disposable training pants are really just diapers shaped to look like underwear. Not having to lie down for diaper changes might make kids temporarily feel as if they've taken a giant developmental step forward, but in fact they have not learned anything new by wearing them. The advance is only one of design, not of accomplishment. The intended advance is for your child to break his dependency on diapers, not prolong it with a design change.

Children will learn to use the toilet in a much more straightforward way if they are taken out of diapers and put directly into cotton underwear. It is also helpful to have children sit on the toilet between diaper changes, before and after baths, and so forth. Many children will pee in the toilet during these trials, which is a good sign that it will soon be time to phase out diapers. The inevitable pants-wetting that kids do when they are toilet training is all part of the process. They learn that having wet underwear and pants is unpleasant and gets in the way of their playing comfortably, which in turn motivates them to get to the toilet. Poop in the pants is even more of a nuisance to them.

The Opposition Path: Gamers and Refusers

In my experience, children commonly experience two kinds of toileting troubles: either they play games and refuse to use the toilet or they avoid it out of anxiety. Children who travel the path of opposition are resistant game-players, which can be maddening. These children often develop procrastination games, won't go to the bathroom when it is convenient, and won't comply with parental prompting, preferring to wait to go until it is an emergency. For such children, it is routine to answer "no" reflexively every time a parent asks, "Do you have to go potty?" If the parent pursues the point, "Are you sure, honey? I bet you could go if you tried," the child just gets more emphatic: "No, I really don't have to go. I am sure." These children also resist using the toilet at their parent's request before leaving the house or before they climb into bed. They wait until they are buckled into the car seat, or all tucked under the covers, before calling out, "Mommy, I have to go potty! I have to go really bad!"

They also have "accidents" that seem to be more on purpose than by mistake. In another frustrating ploy, they sit on the toilet with seeming compliance and bemoan that they are "trying" and "pushing," but nothing is coming out. They may also flat out reject the toilet, demand disposable training pants for bowel movements, or go to the bathroom in the bathtub or on the kitchen floor!

PARENTING TRAP

Overusing the Word "Accident"

It seems to be built into parents' vernacular to refer to the times their children pee in their pants as "accidents," even when children are learning to be toilet users. In my work with families, I have learned to pay very close attention to language and what our children are hearing from us. Since our words and how we say them carry so much power, we want them to work for us and our children, rather than against us.

When parents use the word *accident*, they are trying to make certain that the child who is standing in a puddle of his own making does not feel bad or ashamed. "Oh, honey, that's okay. Don't worry about it. You couldn't help it. It was just an accident." Comments such as this, while reassuring, also imply that the incident somehow just "happened," that the child "couldn't help it," and that it is not his fault. Fault is not a concept that is warranted here—there is no fault in toileting, so there is not need to absolve children of it. There is, however, the need for increased control, awareness, and responsibility. Emphasizing the accidental side of things suggests that these skills are not in play in the toileting task. Rather than the reliance on the concept of accidents, I suggest you say something like:

> "Whoops, you put your pee in your pants rather than in the toilet. Now you have wet pants and a puddle. See, that is why the toilet is easier, and you will love using it. No big deal, this is bound to happen while you are learning to use the toilet full-time. What do you think happened?"

What to Do: Stop All the *Overs!*

The first order of business with any toileting correction is to stop all the *overs*—your *over*control, *over*involvement, and *over*accommodation. Stop talking about, asking about, and attending to your child's pee and poop. Take your emotions out of it. Relax. Your goal is to strike an attitude of "no big deal." This is the best approach because it is so realistic—going to the bathroom really is no big deal! By shifting your attention and investment away from toileting, you will no longer be infusing your child's behaviors with so much power.

Toilet mastery will happen, I promise. So to regain the lead with a child who is demanding and opposing, give it up, let it go for now, and concentrate your efforts instead on remedying the IFP that is running your relationship. You have to turn down your emotional desire to succeed at toileting now in order to encourage your child's own motivation to kick in. By doing this, you neutralize whatever power your child has harnessed around toileting and free him to get on with being a powerful toilet user rather than a powerful toilet resister.

If your child baits you (and she probably will), don't take the bait. For example, if you have given her a routine direction to use the bathroom before leaving the house and she says, "No, I don't have to. I can't go!" then say, with no irritation or anxiousness at all:

> "Oh, okay, honey, you know your body best. That's fine. Just thought I'd give you a reminder in case you did have to go."

Not much fodder for struggle there, right? Your little one will have a hard time figuring out how to further resist or escalate her resistance, because you just aren't giving her anything to react to.

What if your resisting child really does have to go and once you are underway in the car says urgently that she has to go "really bad?" Well, so be it. After all, the worst that can happen is that she will wet her pants and get her car seat wet—a nuisance, but hardly a big deal. It's a rather common situation for kids, actually. So if you are driving and she starts urgently demanding action on your part, keep your cool. Don't join her in developing a frantic state and try to find the fastest place to pull over. Stay pleasant and unruffled and say:

> "Well, we're still about ten minutes away from the store. So this is a time when you will get some practice holding it in. Every now and then a bathroom is not convenient, and what you have to do then is squeeze your inside muscles to keep your pee from coming out."

"But I can't! I have to go now!"

> "It's okay, sweetie, you actually do have a few minutes available to you for holding it in. But fussing makes it harder to do. So settle down. You will be fine. And remember for the next time, it is easier to use the bathroom before we leave the house."

Don't have lengthy conversations, and don't turn yourself into a motivational speaker or be repetitious. Keep your emotions and encouragements tempered as you are guiding her along. Don't overdo reassurances about wet pants or overhype successes. Steady as you go. Keep in mind that the actual toilet use is up to your child and learning to use the toilet isn't a hard thing at all. If you keep this perspective, it will be easy to remain matter-of-fact in your teaching and training efforts. This attitude conveys confidence and leadership, and your child will respond to it.

If you have gotten yourself into a real state of *overs*, and for weeks or even months you have been in a pattern of paying too much attention to your child's toilet behavior, then take this time to deliberately back off for a week or so. Take a complete holiday from any toilet program, conversations, rewards, and consequences for toileting for a week or so, and let your child know why you're doing that too. Tell her straightforwardly:

> "You know, honey, I have been thinking. We have been focusing a lot on the potty and your going on it. I ask you about it all the time, and I even get upset feelings over it! That is silly, isn't it?

Getting upset over the potty—it is just pee and poop, for heaven's sake. I know you will get to be a full-time toilet user soon enough; everyone gets there, and you will too. So let's not worry about it, and let's definitely stop talking about it! I know I am going to!"

Eliminate Rewards and Bribes

If you are using a reward system to motivate your child to use the toilet, back out of this too. Tell him that no one needs candy, toys, or treats to pee and poop—it is just something people do every day. Tell him you are putting the M&M's away and that you can go toy shopping sometime soon, but it won't be connected to using the bathroom. A little humor and perspective is helpful here, so you can say:

"I mean, gee, honey, I don't get candy or toys when I poop!"

Tailor your withdrawal to fit whatever dynamic you may be embroiled in, and then don't be tempted to retread old ground. Bite your tongue, walk away, do deep breathing—whatever you need to do to ensure you do not give any further power to your child's toileting, whether it is in the form of treats, your attention, or your strong feelings.

Using the Ladder

As you lower the volume on your attention and emotional involvement, turn your focus on the game playing and oppositional behaviors your child is engaging in. Obviously, you cannot use the Ladder to put your child on the toilet and make him go. If you try to have direct power where in fact you have none, you will surely activate your child's power drive. *The Ladder is not to be used directly for toilet training but for correcting the relationship troubles between you that are leading to the games and opposition that are blocking successful training.*

When parents first shift their gears and begin a correction phase, their children are sometimes stymied by the fact that their power plays aren't working anymore. They figure they must have to crank it up a notch to get the responses they have become accustomed to. If this happens, use the Ladder to target the inappropriate whining, demanding, and crying that they might employ. If your child insists you meet his demands, and won't let up, stay calm and say:

> "Oh my, honey, such a fuss over the potty. Come on, I am going to have you go upstairs to your room for a bit until you stop fussing."

Start the Ladder at Step Three (page 109). If he cries, "But I have to go to pee!" say:

> "That is fine. You can pee, but right now it is more important that you settle down and find your self-control. The bathroom can wait."

This is a particularly helpful correction tactic because it conveys that your child's peeing is no longer the most important, urgent, and compelling event for you. You are saying that peeing can wait, but calming down and having appropriate self-control cannot.

A Child with IFP in Action

Sydney, at four years, is only a part-time toilet user—she uses it when it suits her. Mornings are the worst. Her mother very much wants her to go to the bathroom before she gets dressed, but Sydney often resists and has accidents in the kitchen after coming down for breakfast. When her mother asks her to go, Sydney whines and says, "You have to pull down my pants, I can't do it by myself." When her mother responds with, "Oh Sydney, Mommy doesn't have to help you with your pants. You can do it; I know you can. Your teacher tells me you do it at preschool." With this, Sydney's whines increase: "No, I can't do it. It's too hard. You have to do it!" Her mother sighs and gives in because she doesn't want to have to deal with a full-blown tantrum.

But Sydney's demands are not over yet. In the bathroom, Sydney insists her mother stay with her. "Be in the bathroom with me! You have to stay with me or I can't go!" Again her mother goes along, albeit with increasing annoyance (which Sydney is well aware of). Once on the toilet, Sydney just sits there. Her mother urges her to hurry up, and Sydney responds, "I'm trying, I'm trying." Her mother runs the water from the faucet, and tells her to really concentrate on peeing. "But I need a book," Sydney demands. Her mother weighs whether it would take more time to just get the book, or to say no and provoke a fight. She opts for the book. Still Sydney does not pee. Mom finally says, "That's it. You are going to be late for school; just get dressed." When Sydney comes downstairs she complains about hating the cereal her mother has poured out for her and says she wants a waffle. While her mother is explaining that there is no time to make a waffle right now, Sydney wets her pants.

How to handle this? Here's what it takes to effectively redirect your child's resistance from start to finish.

The Effective Parent in Action

> "Honey, I was thinking about this morning and the whole scene with me pulling your pants down, sitting with you in the bathroom, turning on water, and reading a book. I actually had to giggle thinking about it—what a silly bunch of girls we are, huh? There is no reason for all this! We are acting like peeing is a big deal. Oh, my gosh. I think this has been making it so much harder for you. You know your body and can tell when you have to go to the bathroom. If you are having trouble and it is best for you to wear diapers again, then we can certainly do that. But no more fusses over peeing! Okay, I just wanted to let you know this. Now we will have more time for a fun morning, not a headache morning."

If your child whines and responds, "No, Mommy, I really do need you to help me," then say casually as you are getting up:

> "Oh, my goodness, honey, no one needs help to pee. It is something your body does all by itself."

Then be certain to disengage from the conversation; don't respond to any of her attempts to keep you focused on her toileting. You are leading the way, redirecting the responsibility back to the your child, underscoring your faith in her, and clearing up the misconception that successful toileting has something to do with you.

In the morning have a pleasant wake-up, and don't mention anything about going to the bathroom at all. Not a word, not a question! Let her go off to school without going to the bathroom if need be. She will have to figure it out. If Sydney kicks up a fuss and tries to get you to join her in the bathroom, or somehow get involved in toileting, just pay little mind to her, and say:

> "Sydney, I have already said that you can take care of going to the bathroom yourself, and that I don't want to talk about it any more. If you want to keep talking about toilet stuff, then I will have you go into your room for a while until you are finished. This is the second time I have said it, honey. If you need a third reminder, you will have to go to your room."

Then keep climbing the Ladder if need be. If she is prone to having accidents at school, give her a change of clothes. If she wets her pants at home, stay unfazed:

> "Using your pants again and not the toilet, Sydney? Hmm. You know pee only goes in the toilet or in diapers. Since you are not choosing the toilet, then you can get back into diapers. Come on, let's get you changed real quick."

Keep moving, and if she baits you for more, change the subject and say:

> "You know, sweet pea, I don't really want to keep talking about bathroom business. You will get the hang of it. Don't worry. So, let's see, today is Tuesday. Oh good, after school you have ballet. That is your favorite."

If she really fights the diaper (I mean diaper here, not training pants) use the Ladder to manage her protests. Have her stay in her room until she has put the diaper on, reminding her that wearing underwear just isn't an option right now because she has been not been using the toilet. Tell her when she stays dry for a full day and uses the bathroom appropriately she can go back to underwear again. She has to be active in initiating the toilet use, though. Don't hover and micromanage by peppering her with questions about whether she has to go.

PARENTING TRAP

Buying into "I'm Trying"

One day, after a few years of working with different children who were stuck on potty issues, it clicked that they all said the same thing at some point. When pushed a bit by their parents to poop on the toilet, they would respond with "I'm trying! I'm really trying!" accompanied with big puppy dog eyes, a tear or two, or an indignant, accusing tone. At this point most parents pull back from their pushing and offer understanding and support: "I know you are, honey, and I am really proud of you for trying. You just have to keep trying for Daddy, okay, big guy? Mommy and I need you to keep trying."

I finally wised up and made the obvious realization that pooping is one thing that takes no trying. The natural physiological urge of a bowel movement pushing to be released is quite a force. The truth is, the only trying that comes into play here would be that of trying to keep it from coming out! Holding back is where the "trying" is. So when children play the "I'm trying" card, keep the pressure on:

"You're trying? What do you mean, 'You're trying?'"

When they say they are trying to poop, but they just can't, respond by saying:

> "There is no 'trying' with pooping. Poop just comes out; all you ever need to do is a little pushing. The only 'trying' is to hold it back. If you say you are 'trying,' either you aren't really or you are trying not to poop. So no more backward trying, please. Your job is to let your poop come out. Wipe your eyes, please; there is no crying while pooping."

The Anxiety Path: Avoiders

The second pathway to toileting trouble is paved by anxiety. A child struggling with a bit of anxiety sets off a chain reaction of anxiety in her parents. Parental anxiety leads quickly to unhealthy accommodations. Unable to deal with their child's distress, parents move in quickly to try to reduce any discomfort. They provide lots of reassurance, explanation, and crutches, and in the end don't have any staying power to help their child punch through her anxiety and get the job done.

Anxious toileters are afraid to be alone in the bathroom, afraid to sit on the toilet, or afraid to put their poop in the toilet. They may insist on a diaper or disposable training pants. Lots of tears, begging, pleading, and expressions of panic and dread are children's means of power here. Parents who hate to see their children in distress, and who fear making matters worse by pushing them, soon become trapped in a cycle of anxiety with their children.

It always seems to start innocently enough: A young child expresses fear or distress about toilets because she doesn't like the sound they make when they flush or doesn't like the idea of her poop being flushed away. Perhaps she worries that she will fall in and be flushed away, too. Parents offer thoughtful reassurances and explanations, and when these don't work and their child continues to show distress, they go further by accommodating or offering a crutch. Even though there is no real danger, parents allow their child's anxiety to lead the way. This is the beginning phase of how anxiety escalates until the child does the directing instead of the parents. Before they realize it, their child is wedded to her avoidance tactics.

Concerned and empathic parents try everything they can think of to help make it easier, but in so doing inadvertently reinforce the mistaken concept that going to the toilet is in fact hard to do.

Many parents have described to me their selfless efforts to assist their anxious child in being more comfortable in the bathroom. They move into the bathroom with their child for extended sitting periods. Thirty or forty-five minute sessions are not unusual. During this time books are read, dolls and stuffed animals use the potty, songs are sung, and lots of encouragements and reassurances are given.

As parents describe their efforts to me in my office, it becomes clear that many of them have become completely obsessed with the whole dynamic. They think about getting their child to poop on the potty all the time and build up their own anxiety about it. For them, a natural, effortless biological function has taken on dimensions more appropriate to a major event.

What's Going On?

Children usually become hesitant and anxious about using the toilet for one of two reasons. The first (and most common) reason is that it is natural for them to be hesitant. Sitting on a toilet is unfamiliar, the flushing noise can be frightening, and the idea of something dropping out of the body and getting whooshed away can be a worry. The second reason is that they may have had an unpleasant or painful experience with toileting that they aren't keen on repeating.

Both are perfectly understandable and legitimate reasons for distress. Since your child's feelings of apprehension are real, they should not be minimized. The question is what are you, the parent, going to do about it? Are you going to lead your child with calm and reason, grounded in the reality that toilets and pooping are really nothing to fear?

Or are you going to get anxious yourself and get sucked into a circus of reassurances and accommodations? Children may balk at toileting at some point, but whether their feelings become entrenched as a full-fledged fear and panic depends on your response.

What to Do about It

Once again, you have to regain your perspective. Move away and get your anxiety under control. Ground yourself in the reality of the matter. Do people routinely have others in the bathroom with them providing support and encouragement? What about being read to, or offered prizes or promises of special outings? Think about how it would feel if you did. Most likely, you'd see it as an invasion of your privacy, leaving you annoyed and wanting to shoo them out of your way. I think our children experience overattention in the same way.

If you have been spending considerable time in the bathroom with your child, repeating lots of explanations about how bodies work, explaining why poop has to go in the toilet, offering reassurances, and so on, it is important to put an end to all of it. At a time that has nothing to do with your child using the bathroom, sit down with her and let her know you have seen the light. For example, you might say:

> "Jane, you know what? I was driving home today, and I found myself thinking about you and your poop! I thought of myself sitting in the bathroom with you for forty-five minutes last night and all the talking and upset that was going on. You know what? Are we ever nuts! I mean, I started laughing out loud. What are we doing? I certainly haven't been helping you by engaging in all this bathroom hoopla. I actually think I have been getting in your way and making it harder for you. The truth is, peeing and pooping are one of the easiest things your body does. It just comes out! I know you have become afraid and you think it is hard and something you don't want to do, but the reality is, there

is nothing to be afraid of, and going to the bathroom isn't hard in the least. You are going to get over your worries and be a toilet user like all the rest of the people in the world. So from now on, let's not have any more marathon sessions in the bathroom."

ELIMINATE CRUTCHES

Brian, well past his third birthday, is getting frantic and pleads with his mother for disposable training pants. "No, I don't want to go on the potty! Hurry! Give me a Pull-Ups! Please, Mommy." He has become dependent on them. Dana won't go unless she has one of her parents in the bathroom with her. Libby will only go on the portable plastic potty, but she is getting too big for it, and her parents are really tired of the cleanup. What to do? Don't get started with these crutches and routines in the first place, or if you have used them, eliminate them. You may have to tolerate some distress in the short run, but it will be much less painful than what you'll have to undo down the road.

What you need to do is stop your own emotional overinvestment. For instance, you could respond to an urgent plea for training pants with these words:

> "Brian, since this has turned into such a big deal these last few weeks, it will be good to just let it go. Don't even worry about using the toilet at all. Everyone learns to be a full-time toilet user, and you will too. You can use a diaper if that is your choice, and soon enough you will be ready to use the toilet. But we're done with the training pants."

That is it. You have made it clear that you are stepping out, that you are seeing things clearly, and that you have let go of all your overdone focus and feeling on the matter. You are turning toileting back over to him with full confidence and peace of mind that he can handle it, with only one caveat: No training pants, only diapers.

MAKING IT WORK

For the first week, be certain not to initiate one discussion about pooping. Don't ask if he has to go or wants to try the potty. Don't make any reference to toileting, being a big boy, or anything of the sort. Speak about the subject only if your child approaches you and asks for help. If he shows interest in using the toilet, keep your response supportive but low-key.

After a week or so, you can start to offer more direct leadership. If your child is past his third birthday and is resistant to being an independent full-time toilet user, it is time for him to get the job done, and you should not shy away from telling him so. Explain that once a fear has started, you can't just wait for it to go away by itself. Fear doesn't work like that. You can say:

> "You have to use your strength, push past it, and do the very thing you have been afraid to do. This is what makes fear go away. Only by doing it will you learn not to be afraid and prove to yourself that you can do it."

Challenge him by saying:

> "You are three years old now (or four, or five, whatever the case) and going to the bathroom has gotten to be a big deal for you. Crying, screaming, running away—what a commotion! Over poop, no less! Do you want to keep going on like this? Taking this upset into your next year, and the next? I am sure you don't. This is something you will have to master."

Notice how the brand of leadership I am suggesting stresses that whatever the task, it is the child's to do. It is his body, his experience, his well-being, and his accomplishment. It is not about you, it is about him. With this emphasis, you communicate healthy separateness, encourage autonomy, and support the innate drive in all children for growth and mastery.

The First Push

Most children who have become stuck need a push to get going. So after taking a week off, reapproach the task feeling confident and ready to move your child along with strong leadership. You are going to help him to go into his fear and get through it, rather than helping him to buffer or avoid it. Start by taking away your child's toilet alternative. If he is well past his third birthday, throw away all of the disposable training pants! Don't leave yourself a hidden supply, because in a weak moment you may be tempted to give him one. Throw them out, and don't buy any more.

If your child is using you as a crutch in the bathroom, discipline yourself not to join him there—no matter what. When your dependent or anxious child freaks out, screams, pleads, begs for his crutch, offer him your calm, certainty, and fortitude instead:

> "Come on, honey, we talked about this. You have become frightened over something when there is absolutely nothing to fear. You must find your strength inside and bring it forward. Tears and screaming will not help you; they will only make it worse. Using the toilet is not a big deal. You can do it, and you are going to do it. When you feel your poop pushing to come out, you will sit on the toilet and let it come out, and that is that. You will have done it, and you will like it. You will be proud of yourself."

Since most parents know their child's bowel rhythms, it is helpful to watch for signs around the time that he needs to go. You can lead him into the bathroom and say:

> "Now is the time."

Stay extremely calm, absorb his fear with your steadiness, and show him you are not fazed. If he protests about sitting on the toilet, then tell him it will be the easy way or the hard way. He can sit on the toilet by himself, or you can pick him up and sit him on it. Since you are being firm and really employing your power, be extra certain you remain upbeat and friendly and that there is no trace of harshness in your voice.

If he won't stay on the potty and tries to get off, pick him up and put him back. Kneel in front of him and hold him there for a while saying:

> "Hey, you are fine. If you settle down for a second, you will see that. If you keep getting up and running away, you will not get past your fear. Look, I am here, and I am helping you."

You will probably need to hold him on the toilet to help him get past this sticking point. If his anxiety escalates into a full panic, then it will be best to pick him up and take him to his room. Tell him he will never be able to get the job done when he is so worked up, so instruct him to take a few minutes to find his self-control and calm down. Here you are on Step Three of the Ladder. Continue to follow the script of the Ladder. Do not let him leave his room until he has calmed down. If he needs a Parent Hold, by all means offer it with loving arms.

Once the storm has passed and you have wiped his tears away, take him back to the toilet. If it seems as though his urge has passed, don't worry. Simply tell him his poop will be ready again in a little while, and then he can let it out in the toilet.

Repeat the scenario as often as needed. Tell your child he is always welcome to just go in and use the toilet himself if he prefers that. Keep your eye on him so he does not disappear behind a chair or climb into the bathtub.

If he screams that he just wants training pants and implores you to stay with him or give him back his potty, keep a supportive tone but say:

> "No, honey. You are fine, and it is time for you to learn to use the toilet."

When he accuses you of not loving him, being mean, or the like, smile understandingly and gently correct him:

"No, honey, I am not being mean. I am helping you get over being stuck."

What you are telling him is exactly true—helping your child to get over fear is not at all mean or unloving. He just has to use the toilet a couple of times, and then he too will see it is no big deal. If you keep neutralizing the anxiety he expresses, he will engage his own strength before long and assert himself. Happily enough, he will feel terrific when he does.

Anxiety and Constipation

Constipation can create a vicious cycle, both physically as well as behaviorally, between parent and child. Passing large, hard stools can indeed be very painful for children. The pain is visible and parents need to offer help and reassurances in this instance. First, however, you must be proactive about dealing with the physical aspect of your child's constipation, so consult a pediatrician for directions first. You also must be certain not to fan the flames of anxiety and avoidance by overdoing the emotional attention on your child's situation.

If he keeps bringing up his worry, fight the temptation to engage in long discussions, explanations, and reassurances. You can say:

"Honey, you need to put those worries out of your mind. Poop is nothing to worry about. The medicine you are taking will do the trick."

Then change the subject!

If your child is already stuck in fear, and you have overresponded with attention and accommodation, you will need to follow a cease-and-desist plan similar to the one described on page 286. Let your child know you have had your eyes opened, and you can't believe all the time and upset that has been spent on pooping; this has been a real mistake! Nobody needs company in the bathroom, or endless anatomy lessons on the large intestine and colorectal function. Poop will happen without any of this attention and effort. Ground yourselves in the no-big-deal reality of bathroom business, and get on with more interesting and enjoyable pursuits.

Remember too, that being physically active is a natural enhancer for healthy bowel movements. Put down the books, stop the overtalking, get out of the bathroom, and see that your child starts enjoying some fun physical activity.

WHEN THE TIME IS RIGHT

When your child actually has the urge to pass a bowel movement, you will probably notice him sitting, squatting, clenching, or the like. His bowels should be able to move pretty readily with the help of a stool softener. Remaining totally relaxed, and without making it into a big deal, lead him to the bathroom. Your strength, your clear thinking, and your confidence will help to counter his fear. Doing it the easy way or the hard way, help him to stay on the toilet and get past this difficult moment. Do not get upset or nervous yourself. Don't plead, bribe, or threaten. Just offer calm parental competence as you cheerily tell him:

> "Get that poop in the toilet where it belongs!"

A bit of humor and playfulness helps such moments, counters your child's tension, and distracts him from any lingering discomfort. Try saying:

> "Bombs away, honey!"

Or

> "Whew, you're gonna love getting rid of this poop! You're going to feel like a new man!"

Use the Ladder to manage any inappropriate or escalated reactions your child may have that make staying on the toilet unproductive.

WHEN YOU'RE REALLY STUCK

If your child is really stuck and keeps fighting his urges, give him some added incentives to help him along. This is an example of exercising indirect power in an arena where you do not have direct power. Tell him in a friendly, supportive tone that since that poop wants to come out, it will be a good idea for him to not go outside and play with friends until it does. That way his poop won't get in the way of his having fun. You can use any anticipated outing or event to keep him focused in this way.

When he protests and cries, "No, it won't get in the way. I just want to go play now!" stay very supportive, but convey that you know better:

> "Sweetie, I am not saying you can't go; you just need to get rid of that poop inside before you do. That's all. No big deal. It won't take any time at all once you feel it pushing on your bottom. Just hop on the toilet and let it come out, and then you'll be on your way."

Again, use the Ladder to manage any noisy and unpleasant reactions. Do not hover, repeatedly ask him if he has to go, or continue to talk about it. Get on with your tasks, or whatever you were doing, but do not let him go out to play until he has gone to the bathroom. If the day ends and he still has not pooped, be kind to him. Say:

> "I know you are disappointed that you have not been able to go outside and play, but tomorrow is sure to be the day. That means you can look forward to getting past this and having fun."

If constipation has been an ongoing problem, be certain to use some form of stool softener or stimulant (following your pediatrician's advice) to ensure that your child's bowels are moving well enough. Then steadily hold to your position. Your child needs to feel that you have the situation well in hand on his behalf, and that he will be better off for because of it.

Prolonged Withholding and Soiling

For a small percentage of children, troubles with withholding can become very entrenched and can develop into a host of complications. Some build up such a resistance to moving their bowels that they will not poop for days and days on end. This degree of withholding can snowball into serious secondary complications, such as bowel impaction, reduced colon motility, and involuntary soiling.

Entrenched withholding and soiling are behavioral difficulties that require the help of professionals. When I work with families who have these issues, I always insist on teaming up with an experienced pediatrician or a pediatric gastroenterologist in order to thoroughly manage both the physical and psychological aspects of the problem.

Treatment for a child with a long-standing problem of withholding requires an involved and individually tailored approach. As you might imagine, the earlier you seek guidance, the easier the correction will be. The longer and more entrenched the problem, the more complicated and difficult it is to reverse.

When You Get It Right

"Mommy, I went potty all by myself!"

> "Hey, good job, honey. You're on your way to being a full-time toilet user. That sure must feel good!"

I know it will feel good for both of you. There is no better feeling than basking in your child's pride of accomplishment as you watch him take steps towards independence and a stronger sense of self. Don't let IFP rob you or your child of these priceless moments.

Chapter Eleven

Eating

We have come a long way together. Your children are not having tantrums or whining. Your daughter is not afraid to go outside because it looks like a storm is coming. You're finally getting a good night's sleep. You are not spending an undue amount of time in the bathroom. Now it is time to enjoy a relaxing meal with your family. A relaxing meal . . . when was the last time you had one of those with your kids?

Eating is the last of the three behaviors in which physiology plays a prominent role in parent-child head-butting. The potential for a power struggle looms large, because it is your child, not you, who has ultimate control over her body. But there is a lot you can do to take IFP off the menu. Just as with toileting and sleeping, you should not get in the way of your child's natural physiological urges by being overattentive or over-controlling. Children learn quickly that their parents can't make them eat, so you must take care not to fuel your child's appetite for control in this area. The potential is there for kids to become more invested in their power plays with you than in their physiological urges. In a serious state of IFP, children will limit what they eat.

Food Is a Big Deal

The many layers of importance and meaning connected to food and eating set it apart from other behaviors and add to a parent's vulnerability in making missteps with their children.

First and foremost is the fact that we must eat to live and maintain our health. What parent wouldn't be concerned when her child limits or refuses food? Yet if your concern and attention becomes overtly focused on poor eating habits, your child's antennae would quickly pick up your anxiety. She would conclude that she has power to wield and will be driven to maximize it.

In addition to being essential for sustaining life, food also has a strong connection to nurturance. Feeding her baby is a primary organizing task for mothers, and the bonding facilitated by having a baby at your breast can be profound. Feeding our children is fundamental to caring for them; when our kids block us from meeting this primary responsibility, we understandably get very anxious. We also get very frustrated. Striking the right balance between being concerned and being matter-of-fact is a tough balancing act, making this a ripe area for children to harness power.

A Caveat

This chapter addresses food issues and mealtime antics that result from IFP. However, IFP is not the only pathway to eating troubles. A host of medical problems such as food allergies, anatomical problems, metabolic disorders, and gastrointestinal disturbances can interfere with a child's appetite and weight gain. If your child is struggling with eating issues or there are weight gain concerns, work closely with your pediatrician and possibly a pediatric gastroenterologist to ensure that there are no underlying developmental or medical reasons that might account for the trouble.

A third aspect also distinguishes eating from other behaviors: Food customs and menus are wedded to social, cultural, and religious traditions. Entertainment, celebrations, holidays, and gatherings of all sorts focus on our coming together over food. Every family has favorite recipes and cherished memories of the food they have shared. Even nightly family dinners have an enormous significance. The expression "families who eat together, stay together" carries weight in the popular culture, and many social critics point to the unraveling of family dinnertime as a major contributor to the ills facing families today. When children act up during meals, it is certainly a hot button for many parents.

Have Some Carrots and Put Your Napkin in Your Lap

No child will embrace nutrition and good manners without a parent's guidance and, at times, insistence. Our primary job is to shape and direct our children so that they learn how to satisfy their natural hunger drive in a healthy and mannerly way. Nutritionists tell us that adult eating patterns take shape when we are young, and this is certainly true. Children will not eat well if they are not taught or if good eating habits aren't enforced. Nor will they develop table etiquette on their own. Frankly, it is my experience that far too many children are entering adulthood with bad eating habits and poor manners. Parents who do not effectively lead their children to eat well or mind their manners place them at a distinct disadvantage. Their health and civility suffer.

There's no gray area here: What, when, and where your children eat is determined by you. As obvious a point as this may be, parents need to be reminded of it. I have listened to so many of you complain that your child is "addicted to junk food," "has the worst manners," or "always eats in front of the TV." Such a perspective unfairly lays the trouble at the feet of your child. Take note: If your child is eating poorly while sitting in front of the television or computer and has bad manners, it is because you are allowing it.

Children do not have any real independence or autonomy with regard to food. They do not have any money to buy it, they do not have independent transportation to go get food on their own, and for the most part, they do not have the ability to prepare their own meals. They are dependent upon adults for all of this. Your child cannot sabotage himself without your help. The truth is, most children who habitually eat in front of the television or computer have a parent who has carried their plate to them and served them there. If a child's napkin is not in his lap, if his mouth is open when he chews, or his elbows are consistently on the table, it is because a parent has not insisted otherwise.

As far as healthy choices go, don't expect your child to make them without guidance. Left to decide for themselves, almost all children will pick fat, sugar, and salt over fruit, vegetables, and whole grains. Don't buy packages of cookies, ice cream, soda, and chips and then expect your kids to choose yogurt, carrot sticks, and strawberries. Good eating habits start with the choices parents make in the grocery store or supermarket. If you do not like what your child is eating, load the grocery cart differently.

When children are given the balance of power in the food and eating department, it will turn into a problem, just as it does in every other domain.

Dinnertime Has Changed

A lot of lifestyle changes have affected dinnertime for families today. Dual-career parents have made a significant impact. When both parents work long hours, putting together traditional meals is virtually impossible. At the end of a long day, exhausted parents simply want to relax and spend some enjoyable time with their children. But more often than not, evenings morph into another long program that involves overseeing homework and school projects, piano practice, and baths. Under such a time crunch, families easily fall prey to suppertime accommodations. And it's just as easy to cave under similar pressure in the morning, when breakfast can become another battleground between you and your children.

Since workdays are much longer than they used to be, it is not uncommon for at least one parent to get home after 7:00 or 7:30 p.m. This leaves the other parent to prepare and serve dinner alone. I've noticed that without the structure of two parents, it is easier to take short-cuts and relax expectations and standards around meals. A single parent putting together a meal is more susceptible to children's persuasions and protests. He is more likely to agree to a kid-friendly but less nutritious meal and more apt to say yes to eating in front of the television. As the accommodations stack up, so does the transfer of power from parent to child.

Another challenge families face is the commitment to afternoon and evening sports and other activities, including lessons and other activities for kids. Parents dash out of work so they can pick up their children and get them to hockey or basketball or soccer practice on time. Typically, they have a narrow window in which to do this, and somehow dinner has to fit into the schedule, too. When their children come home, tired and hungry from a long day of school and activities and press for fast food, it is easy to understand why so many parents say yes so often, against their better judgment. The more children learn that pressure works under these circumstances, the more they will apply it. Soon, kids who want a Happy Meal are throwing hearty fits if their parents tell them no.

While there's no turning back the clock to a less hurried time, parents do need to structure a set of expectations for nutrition and manners that is manageable for them and to stick with it most of the time. Well-defined standards, consistently applied, are important for children's well-being.

Common Parental Missteps That Fuel Food Trouble

While parents do have to oversee what, where, and when their children are eating, it is important that they not go overboard. Here are some of the most common missteps parents make:

- ✛ Taking on the role of food police
- ✛ Becoming bite counters
- ✛ Starting a catering and personal chef service
- ✛ Reasoning, enticing, pleading, threatening, or yelling.

Food and eating are areas of particular vulnerability for parents with control issues and anxieties about weight. They get into all manner of food police surveillance. They hide snacks and candy, count the number of cookies in the cookie jar to tell if any are missing, dole out portions, and train an eagle eye on who is eating what at mealtimes. Over and beyond this type of vigilance, they are also overly judgmental in their views on eating habits and have a lot of opinions on eating in general that they don't hesitate to share.

What about bite-counters? These parents say things like, "You can't leave the table until you eat two more bites of broccoli and two more bites of chicken." "There will be no dessert unless I see you take at least three more bites of dinner." Parents will also insist that no one can leave the table until everyone is finished, so if Billy balks, the whole family sits there, focused on counting his bites.

Here are some things I have never been able to figure out: What determines how many more bites should be taken? Should it be two more? Three more? How much time do you allow a child to take the bites? You can see how quickly this situation can escalate into an arbitrary and ugly power struggle when your child refuses to take three more bites.

Parents can also unwittingly find themselves in the role of caterer and personal chef. With electronics dominating much of daily life, many children are hooked on their video or computer games. Heaven forbid they should have to leave the game for dinner: "Mom, there is no way I can turn it off now, I can't lose my level! Okay, okay, I will eat, but bring me my food in here." Parents, if you agree to these demands rather than face the fight, you have some serious work to do.

Kids also demand to eat in front of the television. This often starts when a parent has made an exception one evening, allowing a relaxed family-room dinner, but then makes the mistake of allowing the exception to become the rule out of sheer exhaustion because it is easier not to enforce it, especially under the considerable pressure of one's children. Thus begins a bad habit in which your children have set the standard instead of you.

Preparing special meals for picky eaters, being certain to use your child's favorite utensils and dishes (even if it means washing them before every meal), routinely asking your child what he wants to eat and following all of his idiosyncratic demands regarding preparation and serving—these are the tasks of a personal chef. I know all of this catering and accommodating is done because parents are tired of fighting and they just want to make sure their child eats, but you will be cooking yourself up a stew of IFP if you keep this up. You may not like the heat your child will kick up when you refuse, but you'll never be able to get out of the kitchen if you keep caving in to his demands.

If you're worried that your child isn't eating enough, it is easy to slip into the role of a meal coach, too, as you sit beside your child, long after everyone else has left the table, and find yourself talking and talking and talking. Usually this pattern starts when you try to sell your child on the virtues of a specific food. "Carrots give you good eyesight, spinach builds big muscles, milk makes strong bones and white teeth." When that doesn't work, you move into coaxing and bribing. "But honey, I made you your favorite barbecue chicken. You love Mommy's chicken. Remember? Just eat a little bit and then you can pick your dessert. Okay?" From there, it's a brief detour into guilt. "Think of all the children who are starving and just wish they could have such a delicious dinner to eat." Next stop, threats: "If you don't eat, you aren't going to grow and you're going to get sick too. Really, honey, this is serious. You have to eat more. If you don't eat at least half of that small portion I gave you, you can't watch *American Idol* tonight, and I am not kidding." At this point your child usually starts crying and you start yelling.

The Opposition Path

How do kids do it? How do they always find a way to dominate every situation so deftly? The answer, of course, resides in the stealth of their innate power drive. Where there is an inch to be gained, they will squeeze in and take a yard, and if they gain that, then they'll press ahead and try for a mile. Poor darlings, they know not what they do. But then again, most parents don't know what they're doing, either, when it comes to these fraught family scenarios. Take a look at this list of the four most common child mealtime misbehaviors:

❖ Making unreasonable demands
❖ Engaging in antics, interruptions, and silliness
❖ Being finicky, picky, or whiny about what they will eat
❖ Hoarding and sneaking.

Each of these childhood behaviors causes distress for parents, not to mention how annoying they are when they happen every day. While the basic correction for each of these mealtime disruptions is to withdraw your emotions from the scene, there are specific suggestions and directions for managing the unique challenges presented by each one. Remember, corrections target upsets and unpleasant behaviors, not your child's actual eating. You can't start climbing the Ladder with the directive "Eat your broccoli," because ultimately you can't make your child eat. Rather, use the Ladder to target the annoying or unpleasant behaviors your child uses to try to keep the upper hand. You can certainly be effective in managing those.

What to Do about Mealtime Demands

Children who learn that being pushy and insistent is successful in getting their parents to give them what they want will bring this bossiness to mealtimes sooner or later. Here are two examples:

❖ Six-year-old Tessa makes her morning entrance in the kitchen in an angry mood. If Mom offers oatmeal or a muffin for breakfast, Tessa demands pancakes. If the next day Mom has pancakes, Tessa wants a Pop-Tart. Almost every morning is a battle and a headache.

Tessa's mom says she often gives in because if Tessa has a complete meltdown, she will likely be late and miss her bus.

❖ Four-year-old Jacob makes a series of mealtime demands, which include eating only with his Batman fork and spoon and eating only in front of the television. Food can't be too hot, bread can't have crust, and no foods can be touching. He has even more directions about how his food should be prepared, served, and cut up. He demands chocolate milk at every meal, and if Mom has run out, Jacob is none too forgiving.

MAKING THE CHANGE

These behaviors are maddening, to be sure, but they won't take long to correct if you follow the steps shown below. You have to make up your mind that enough is enough and that your lack of fortitude in the past must be replaced with a commitment to giving your child the foundation for peaceful mealtimes and appropriate eating habits. You may have to endure a full-blown tantrum the first few times you hold to your agenda, but your child will follow along cooperatively sooner than you might think.

After you've made up your mind to reverse mealtime madness, you need to have a brief conversation with your power-laden darling to let him know "the times they are a-changin'." In a tone that conveys assuredness, but that is good-natured, review the mealtime problems that you've been having. Try using this framework:

"You know, honey, I was thinking about dinnertime last night and all the fussing and demanding you were doing over things like which spoon to use and where you want to sit, and so forth. It seems that I end up yelling and you end up crying at most meals. What a mess! Well, today is the day we are going to change things. Mealtimes and tears just don't go together. From now on, Mommy and Daddy will be helping you get past all your whining and move on to having more pleasant meals."

Tell him these changes will begin at the next meal. Then, at breakfast, when you offer cereal, and your child wails that he wants a bagel, remain calm and tell him that cereal is being served for breakfast this morning, but you will remember he has a taste for bagels, and maybe you will serve them another day this week. Consider this Step One of the Ladder. When he continues to fuss, use the phrasing of Step Two by saying:

> "Honey, this is now the second time I am saying this: We are having cereal for breakfast this morning. If you continue to fuss and make demands in this way, I will have you leave the kitchen. You can take a breakfast bar on your way out."

Keep climbing the Ladder to effectively manage his protests. Your mission is to stick to offering cereal, with no exceptions. It is highly likely that the first few times you go through this correction, your child will get so angry and upset that he won't eat the cereal at all. I recommend having a box of breakfast bars on hand so you can give him one for the bus or car ride to school. If breakfast bars are his preference for a while, so be it. To win this struggle and take back your power, you have to withdraw your investment in what he eats for breakfast. Don't worry about short-term losses—missing a few hot morning meals (or whatever it is you are offering) will result in a long-term payoff.

PARENTING TRAP

Offering Too Many Food Choices

In general, children are better off with fewer choices when they are young. This is particularly true when it comes to the three main meals of the day. If meal offerings are rejected, they can be wrapped up and saved for later, or your child can wait until the next meal to get filled up.

Take care not to get caught in the snack trap, though—a child who has passed up a meal because of his demands and protests should not be given free access to the snacks he wants as a meal replacement. As children get older, their ability to participate in meal selections and dinner planning becomes more possible and appropriate. If IFP dominates a family's organization, however, age will not matter, and even older children will make a mess of their power to choose.

Once you have corrected the IFP in your family, you can be more flexible with offering choices and making a few accommodations to suit your child's tastes and preferences. But as soon as your child veers towards being inappropriate, inflexible, or rude and makes demands instead of asking for options, you must tighten your reins and stop making accommodations.

If your children are participating in meal planning, it is appropriate to do it on Sundays or whenever you make your plans for the week ahead. Avoid asking your kids what they want to eat every night—it's too much like placing orders!

If your child's demands center around a certain dish, cup, utensil, or drink, here is how I would address such inflexibility:

"Sweetie, we don't use the same fork to eat all the time, and you can't have a special drink every night. Your Batman silverware (or chocolate milk) is your favorite, but it has actually become a problem because your throw a fit when you don't have it. Favorite things are to be enjoyed; they are not meant to be the source of upset and problems. So, I am going to put your Batman silverware away for a few days (I am not going to buy chocolate milk for a few days), until you can get unstuck from always wanting to have it."

This will most assuredly provoke a storm of upset, so be prepared. Don't join in the escalation or anger. Remain calm and understanding. Offer your incensed child reassurance that it will be disappointing at first, but he will soon see he does not have to get stuck on just one thing. When he has learned this, you can get the Batman silverware down again.

If his protests continue, use the Ladder to help him until he has regained control in his room. If he is quite strong-willed and refuses to eat or drink because his terms have not been met, stay calm. Offer an empathic tone and a reassurance such as:

> "I know it can be hard, honey, to get used to different things, but it is much better for you this way. Don't worry; soon you won't find it to be so bad. If you're so mad now, however, that you don't want to eat, you can just sit with us at the table until we have finished."

Don't get caught up in his attempt to wield power by refusing to eat. Stay neutral and above his power play.

Again, you cannot be shortsighted in this correction. A few uneaten meals, a few hours of hunger will not hurt your child at all. But if you collapse your terms and give in to his inappropriate demands, you will cause lasting problems. Hunger is a powerful drive and eventually your child will eat. Even if he just picks, or doesn't eat as much as he usually would, he won't let himself starve. Relax. Your child's healthy hunger drive will prevail, allowing you to stick to your correction efforts.

THE KITCHEN CLOSES AT 7:00

Anytime your child refuses to eat because her agenda has not been accommodated, she will most likely try to eat later on because she's hungry. Wanting to eat as it gets close to bedtime is common childishness. To combat this habit without creating a direct power struggle, establish a matter-of-fact kitchen schedule. When your child refuses to eat, simply say:

> "Oh, you're not hungry right now? Which spoon you use is more important than eating right now? Okay, that is fine. What I will do is wrap up your food, and if you want to eat later, let me know. Just remember, the kitchen closes at seven o'clock, so if you don't want to be hungry overnight, be certain to eat before then."

About twenty minutes before seven, give your child a friendly reminder:

> "The kitchen will be closing soon; just wanted to give you a heads
> up! Remember, I have your dinner wrapped up in the fridge."

After seven o'clock, your child cannot eat again until morning. She may really carry on and accuse you of being mean, threaten that she will starve, or heaven forbid—say she won't be your best friend anymore—but remain firm. The kitchen closes at seven o'clock.

Because I have learned to be so mindful of power and how it operates in the parent-child relationship, I am always careful about the words I use, and how I say things. In the example of "The kitchen closes—" you can see that the language is matter-of-fact and not driven by any personal feelings. I'm not saying "I said no!" or "I have had it with your games. You are not getting your way this time." Too often parents put themselves and their feelings front and center and advertise how they feel about the matter. By doing so, you inadvertently set up a more potent stage for power struggles. Just be straightforward about telling it like it is, and leave your feelings out of it.

When your child complains that her stomach hurts because she is so hungry, be supportive and sympathetic.

> "Oh, darn, honey, you didn't eat before the kitchen closed. I am
> sure you are hungry. Okay, well I'll be ready to make you a big
> breakfast tomorrow, and I trust you will remember from now on
> to eat before seven o'clock."

If she continues to carry on, climb the Ladder. Your Step Two reminder can go something like this:

> "Look, you are well aware that the kitchen rule is no more food
> after 7:00. I know you're hungry, but you will have to wait until
> morning to eat again. There is nothing more to say about it. If
> you cannot stop your complaints and upset, you will have go to
> your room until they have passed."

What to Do about Mealtime Antics, Interruptions, or Silliness

Up and down and out of the chair; relentless requests for Mom to get more juice, ketchup, or another napkin; kicking the closest sibling under the table; burping the alphabet—any childish mealtime behavior can easily be addressed with a cool head and the Ladder. None of these behaviors have anything directly to do with eating, they simply occur at mealtime. Parents often endure these antics longer than they should because they are reluctant to ask their child to leave the dinner table. The truth is, you want your child to eat and you have a keen investment in having a meal where everyone is together at the table. For correction purposes, you have to put both of these objectives on the back burner for a bit. Since parents have different parenting styles and different ways of tethering themselves to ineffectiveness, the manner in which you approach this correction can vary, depending on how patient and accommodating—or harsh and rigid—you might be.

WHEN YOU NEED TO REMAIN FIRM

For those of you who err on the side of Pleasers and Pushovers, remember, your best payoffs will come when you stop talking and start acting. Follow the Ladder closely with one short and clear directive such as:

> "Hey, kiddo, please remember your manners at the table."

Your Step Two reminder is:

> "Jonathan, you may not continue these antics at the table. They are interrupting our enjoyment of the meal. This is the second time I am reminding you, so the next time I will have you leave the table and spend time in your room."

Then return to the conversation, shifting the focus from your child's antics.

If your child continues to act up, simply say to your tablemates, without any display of emotion:

"Excuse me for one moment,"

and go into action. Don't say anything else until you have gotten up and are standing behind your child, pulling back his chair (remember, Step Three of the Ladder always starts with action before talking). Then direct him to get up and move towards his room, saying:

"Okay, honey, let's go now. You may not remain at the table if you continue to carry on (with rudeness, silliness, interruptions, or whatever the case may be).

Keep climbing the Ladder as needed. The first two times you climb the Ladder for mealtime interruptions, do not have your child return to the table with the family. He may finish his meal at the table after everyone else has left. However, once you have reestablished the commitment to the corrections, and you know he knows you mean business, he may be able to successfully rejoin the family after a brief time spent in his room. After all, the idea is not to banish children from dinner, but to get rid of unruly behavior. If he is able to return to the table, tell him supportively that you know he has good manners and trust he will use them from now on. If he fails to rise to the occasion and becomes disruptive again, bite your tongue to keep from lashing out and go directly to Step Three. Without giving him a second reminder, remove him from the table and direct him back to his room.

WHEN YOU NEED A LIGHT TOUCH

For those of you whose style is more strict and rule-bound, approach your child's silliness with a more relaxed attitude and a softer touch. Remember, if you are conveying a strong emotional response to your child, it means he has power. By giving his antics power, you reinforce them and ensure they will continue. So less is more: Let's say your son has been quite the clown at the table and for weeks you have been sternly redirecting him. You have barked at him, you have lectured him, you have told him his behavior is inappropriate a dozen times, and you have gotten really frustrated and smacked his hands and pushed his elbows off the table. Nonetheless, his antics continue. The next time he acts up at a meal, simply and quietly reach under the table and put your hand on his knee. Look at him, and without saying anything offer him a redirection just by using a pointed facial expression. He will get the message, and in this way you will have stayed totally neutral and not put the spotlight on him.

If he continues to act up, lean over towards him, and quietly, with a soft voice and tone, remind him of his manners. Tell him this is his second reminder, and you are hoping he will not have to leave the table. If he pushes it and keeps up his silliness, of course you must escort him to his room. After you have gotten up and are at his chair, say,

> "Darn, honey, I was hoping to hear more about your day and have you with us during this mealtime, but your antics don't belong at the table, so you will need a few minutes in your room."

Another strategy that can be very helpful for parents who have been repeatedly and sternly reprimanding their child for silliness at the table is to loosen up and be a bit silly themselves. Sometimes when you take things too seriously and sound like a drill sergeant, a little bit of humor can go a long way. For example, if your child insists on burping or sneaking in an "arm fart" at the table, hold your tongue and don't let him see that you are bothered in the least. You might say:

> "Man, you really are a master burper! We are going to have to have a burp contest—but we can't do it at the table. Hold your burps, and we will do some burping after dinner."

You could suggest that he go to another room for a few quick burps or some arm farts to get it out of his system and then come back to the table. The idea is to diffuse the tension and irritability that has built up around the silly behavior. Regain the power you had turned over to your child earlier by responding to his silliness with rigidity and strong reactions.

He's a kid, after all, and overblown, angry reactions can spoil a meal faster and leave more damage in their wake than any amount of childish burping.

If your child just can't shift gears, then say supportively:

> "Hey now, big guy, I know arm farts are fun, but they really don't belong at the table. Get your self-control working now, or you will be heading to your room for a few minutes until it can kick in."

Force and rigidity are no longer part of your style, but now you are in the lead and taking care of business.

Another playful suggestion to lighten things up is to institute a monthly bad manners night. Set aside one night a month where everyone can indulge in a few of their favorite bad manners—elbows on the table, smacking lips, or using a finger to put peas on a fork—to show your children you have perspective and don't take yourself too seriously. In this way, when the kids slip up on other nights, you can remind them to chew with their mouth closed and save it for bad manners night. It is a fun way to teach what good manners are by periodically shining a spotlight on bad ones.

PARENTING TRAP

Using Food as a Reward or Punishment

Parents make trouble for themselves and their children when they promise to give special foods for a reward or threaten to take away food as a punishment. The old days of "That's it! You are going to bed without dinner!" need to be left behind for good—such tactics invite more trouble than they correct. Yes, there are times when kids act up at the table and you have to excuse them before they have finished their meal. Wrap up the uneaten dinner and offer it later, when your child's behavior is more appropriate. Keep your focus on his behavior, use the Ladder for correction, and don't make the trouble about food.

Tasty foods are rewarding in and of themselves. It is fine to tell your child about plans for a fun day with friends that will culminate with a meal at a favorite restaurant or to promise that the two of you can stop for ice cream while running errands. Building in pleasure around food in this way is healthy. Problems arise when you promise the reward of food for one of your child's accomplishments or behaviors: "Okay, honey, if you're a good helper for Mommy in the store, I'll take you to McDonald's on the way home" or "Since you helped me clean the house today, you can have an extra brownie for dessert." Avoid linking food with performance and reward.

The more your children make the connection between food and hunger, food and nutrition, and food and health, the better off everyone will be.

What to Do about Finicky, Picky, Whiny Eaters

The best approach is not to make an issue of your child's picky eating. Many children have a limited palate; not many tastes or textures appeal to them. Eventually their palate will mature along with the rest of their body. I have seen many families where this is the case, and the parents have taken it in stride without undue attention or fanfare.

I have also seen families where moms and dads feel the need to label their child as "picky," roll their eyes, and make his food preferences a public issue. They try to cajole and entice their picky eater to just try a bite of something else, or they attempt to motivate him to eat by comparing him to his cousins or friends. "See, Johnny is eating his vegetables. He is going to be stronger than you." These parents also tend to go overboard with their accommodations, for example, calling friends and relatives ahead of time to make sure they'll have something on hand for their picky eater or packing special foods for their child "just in case." All this attention is a sure way to blow your child's limited tastes out of proportion and create a distorted self-image that goes well beyond the developmental state of his taste buds. Just let it be: If your child seems to like ten foods, then so be it. Prepare meals as you would ordinarily and serve them family-style, always making sure that there is at least one thing your picky eater will like. Don't have any conversation about the food or point out that you have made one dish especially for your finicky one. Simply serve the dinner, call everyone to the table, and proceed with a conversation that has nothing to do with the food. If your child whines, "I don't like this kind of chicken," put the ball right back in her court without any irritability whatsoever:

> "I know, honey. It's your taste buds. But don't worry. They change as you grow."

Then direct her to eat what she does like. Don't take the bait and get ensnared in a struggle over what she will or won't eat.

If your finicky eater lets out a loud "Yuck!" or makes some other nasty comment, then your focus needs to be on his rudeness. Say quietly to him:

> "Excuse me, but that is really rude. You may not make nasty comments at our table."

If he continues, then so must your correction. Climb to the next rung of the Ladder:

> "I know you have good manners, and you must start using them, or you will be excused to go to your room."

In this correction, remember you are targeting his overt disrespect, not his picky eating.

When I was addressing a group of parents some months ago, a mother was describing her daughter as a very finicky eater and said the family had tried to employ the "just-one-bite-and-then-you-can-say-no, thank you" practice. But employing a "no, thank you" bite is akin to the misstep of being a bite counter (and you know where that can lead!).

What about the concern that a child's exclusive diet of chicken fingers, hot dogs, and macaroni and cheese just isn't healthy? I would agree. But the way around this is not to keep focusing attention on the food. Micromanaging meals, letting your child see how upset you are, letting your child hear the concern in your voice as you coax, warn, and threaten will only lock you into the struggle even more. You are going to have to pull completely out of this issue. It is time for a holiday, where you stop all your *overs*. After not speaking about food or trying to get your child to eat something healthy for at least two weeks, start loading up your refrigerator and cupboards with delicious, enticing food that you'll feel good about giving to your child. (Leave the chicken fingers, hot dogs, and frozen macaroni and cheese at the store.)

Remember, hunger is motivating, as long as you are not clouding it with all your emotional energy. Stay neutral, matter-of-fact, and supportive when your child starts lobbying for junk food:

> "You are a pizza lover, aren't you! Sorry, sweet pea, no pizza in the freezer today."

Don't give a lecture on nutrition or the need to eat healthy food. When she continues to protest, say:

> "Honey, there is no need to get upset. There are plenty of other things you can eat."

If she doesn't accept any of your suggestions, say:

> "Oh well, I'll put some apples and peanut butter on the table. If you change your mind, you can help yourself."

If your child's tears and protest continue, or you provoke her into a tantrum, it's not a problem at all. Simply climb the Ladder. Just remember the correction must target your child's continued upset, not the food!

If you have made food into a battlefield, you must lay down your weapons and give up the fight. You are losing anyway, I would bet. Parents never win when they engage in these battles. Why go on losing and having strife at every meal? Instead of trying to coax your child to take just one more bite, redirect your energy toward the broader effort of correcting any power imbalances that are affecting your relationship both in and out of the food arena. When limited palates dominate mealtimes, it is very often symptomatic of a more general state of IFP.

PARENTING TIP

An Alternative to Dinnertime Battles

Set up a rule that applies to everyone in the family. For example, at meals where a child or even your spouse does not want to eat what's being served, a yogurt or a peanut butter sandwich with milk can be an alternative. I wouldn't go any further than this in offering optional meals. When the menu is chicken, don't end up making a bowl of pasta for your complainer. If you know in advance that your picky eater will turn up his nose at your chicken main dish, I would suggest serving a bowl of pasta as a side dish the whole family can share. Avoid special accommodations. If your finicky child chooses the alternative meal option four nights a week for a while, this is fine.

The long and short of it is, let your kids be picky. There isn't much you can do about it, anyway, except stop fighting it and focusing on it. Stop letting them know you care about it, and put your mind at ease. Picky eating is usually a benign part of many children's early years.

"GOOD FOOD FIRST!"

"Can I have dessert now?" This is a question every parent has to field. The potential to get caught up in *overs*, bite counting, and power struggles can be great if you strive to make sure your child's nutritional needs are being met. When your child asks, "Can I be done? Can I have dessert?" simply remind her in a friendly tone that good food comes first. This parenting nugget allows you to respond to your child's question while avoiding many common IFP missteps.

If she presses you ("But Mom, I did eat some; is it enough?"), don't get pulled into micromanaging what she eats. You can say:

"Honey, you still have quite a bit of food on your plate. There is no problem with having dessert, but your dinner isn't finished yet."

If she persists in baiting you—"How much more? Are two more bites enough?"—you can reply:

"I am not interested in counting bites. That's silly. The point is that the nutritious foods of the meal are eaten before the sweets; that's all. Good food first."

Busy yourself in other conversation, or if you and others at the table are finished eating, then say:

"Honey, we're done, so I am going to start clearing, but feel free to take the time you need to finish."

"But I don't like this and I can't eat anymore!"

"Oh, OK. I didn't realize you were finished too."

"Can I have dessert?"

"You don't have to ask me that question, honey; just look at your plate. What do you think?"

If your child gets all worked up over not eating her meal and still wants dessert, be supportive of her. You can say:

"Hey, I'll tell you what. If you don't want to eat any more now, I am happy to wrap up your plate, and if you change your mind later, we can heat it up in the microwave. I know you were looking forward to the pudding I made, but you know good food always comes first."

If she just can't handle things on your terms and starts to crank up her protests, then it is time to climb the Ladder.

"Honey, that's enough now. If you can't move on and settle down, you'll have to go to your room until you can."

If she decides to put off eating, be sure to set the additional limitation: "the kitchen closes at seven o'clock."

Remember, you want to take a supportive, understanding, and matter-of-fact stance with your child. This is not you against her; this is just the way it is. As the parent, you are providing the guidelines for nutrition and healthy eating, and you are not emotional, anxious, or frustrated by it. Do not get pressured into exasperation; stay good-natured:

"Sure, you can have dessert, honey. That is no problem, but what comes first?"

Stay rooted in this position. State it with a supportive tone and you will remain effectively in the lead.

What to Do about Hoarding and Sneaking

I have noticed over the years that children who have a particularly strong power drive often have an equally strong taste for junk food and sweets. They will climb on a chair to reach the sweets basket; get up extra-early in the morning to get an ice cream bar out of the freezer before their parents are up to say no; beg for candy at the grocery store checkout and then clutch the bag for hours. Other kids have food stashes under their beds or in the back of their closets. If you don't effectively manage their power drive and IFP takes hold, things will go from bad to worse for both of you. Keep the Ladder handy and be certain you are effectively countering their bids to do everything on their own terms. Remember, though, that what you want to target is their lack of cooperation, not what they are eating.

As a general rule, don't buy food you don't want your kids to eat. Find tasty foods that your children will enjoy and that you won't have to police. If your child persists in sneaking and hoarding, and you feel it is getting out of hand, or if your child is putting on weight due to unregulated eating, it is time to seek professional help.

Other children who dabble in sneaking and hoarding food are driven by a reaction to overregulation by the food police more than they are by a strong, intrinsic power drive. A dynamic of trying to get one over on the parent can take hold, and a bad game of subterfuge can ensue. If you have a tendency toward food policing, my best advice is to retire your uniform; you are not leading your child effectively. You are setting up a relationship characterized by defiance and distortions of power, and you may be setting up your child to carry a lifelong burden of emotional eating issues.

Parents do not have to teach their children to regulate their eating; children do this naturally. With no teaching at all, babies turn their heads away when they are full. Their body-based feeling of satiation regulates this response automatically. This control is already in place in children too. The trouble starts when kids develop such strong feelings about food and eating that they ignore what their bodies are telling them. Once food and eating become loaded with strong emotions, it is hard to separate them.

The Anxiety Path

While oppositions, food demands, and game playing around mealtimes are rooted in normal childishness, eating anxieties are typically symptomatic of more complicated and entrenched problems. Children usually don't have any natural fears about food. Unlike thunder, dogs with sharp teeth, flushing toilets, or the dark, there just isn't anything scary about Cheerios, chicken fingers, or apple slices. When fear does consolidate around food, it is usually a displacement of feelings from some other source. Food anxieties are generally not fueled by mere parental missteps.

Specific Eating Anxieties

In my work with children over the years, I have encountered three specific eating anxieties, each of which results in a child being afraid to eat. One anxiety centers around a child's fear that when he swallows, he will choke and die. Another stems from a fear of being poisoned or sickened by food. Somewhat similar is the terror of vomiting, which causes children to seriously restrict their eating. They are afraid that what they eat will make them sick to their stomach.

The corrections and repair needed to help a child with eating anxieties such as these will most likely require the help of a professional, particularly if your child has begun to lose weight as a result of his food restrictions. In my experience, IFP is certainly a factor in these families, but there are other layers of trouble that need to be sorted out first. Of course, when this kind of trouble arises, parents look for a reason—what could have caused it? For some children the cause might be a specific event, such as a mild choking episode or a stomach virus that caused vomiting, which they haven't gotten over. Consequently, they develop a fear of swallowing, thinking they will choke again, or become fearful of eating solid food because they're worried that it will cause them to vomit.

Others may have experienced the loss of a grandparent or a family pet, or may have had some other event happen that triggers a full-blown anxiety. Understandably, the event is perceived by the parents and child to be the cause, but usually it is the straw that broke the camel's back. Anxious fears are the culmination of troubles that may have been brewing for a while, and in my experience they are rooted in an IFP difficulty.

Eating Disorders

While the onset of eating disorders such as anorexia and bulimia is typically between late adolescence and early adulthood, these problems are now emerging in much younger children. These insidious and dangerous conditions should be treated quickly and aggressively. Eating disorders are notoriously difficult to treat effectively, so do not take a wait-and-see approach, if you are concerned about your child. The longer an eating disorder goes on, the harder it is to correct.

Stick with the Program

Yes, eating is an arena that can lead to serious problems when things go awry. The best defense is to keep a cool head when teaching your children when, where, what, and how to eat. Don't worry that they'll starve if they don't eat much at a certain meal, don't think that saying no to food demands will cost you your child's affection, and don't link food to rewards and consequences. Do insist on good nutrition and appropriate manners and behavior at mealtimes. Your children shouldn't get a pass excusing them from self-control, respect, and cooperation just because they are hungry and you want them to eat and be happy.

Remember, keep your perspective and keep your cool. Watch your *overs*, set standards, shop wisely for groceries, hold the line—even though your child protests—and keep your good humor. Now, what's for dinner?

The Sweet Spot

An imbalance of family power (IFP) is not just a stage. Left unchecked, a child's inflated power can yield devastating effects—particularly if it continues into adolescence. Life can become a living nightmare for these children and for those who love them. The epidemic of IFP that is sweeping the nation is seriously compromising the long-term development of our children and causing them to suffer, while robbing our families of peace and security in each other's love.

Many times, parents of children aged ten and under have told me that they feel as if they are prisoners of their children's demanding, unruly, or anxious behavior. While their description aptly captures their experience, I can assure you these parents' sense of being held hostage doesn't hold a candle to the anger, fear, and despair they will face when their child becomes a teenager with monster power whom they can't reach and who is spiraling downward.

Raising children effectively is a pleasure, yet I always hear people talk about what hard work it is. It is true, there will be long days and long nights throughout the years, but overall, it doesn't have to be that hard. It makes me think of an analogy used in tennis: People can try to hit the ball by swinging with all their might, really going at it—wrenching their back and shoulders in the process and usually not even hitting a good shot, despite all their effort and exertion. Playing the game like this is frustrating, exhausting, and no fun. But when you learn to hit the ball in the center of the racket with a nice, smooth swing, the ball really responds, and all of a sudden, without nearly as much effort, you are placing winning shots. The feel of the game changes dramatically, you feel coordinated, you aren't working nearly as hard, your back doesn't hurt, the time flies by, and you are loving the game. This is called hitting the ball in the sweet spot.

You can find the same groove in parenting when you establish a rhythm of leading with your children that is effective, reliable, and respectful. Get in this sweet spot with them and you will see what I mean. You won't be working nearly as hard, your children will flourish, and you will reap the joy of having them in your life. Your kids will never say, "Stupid, stupid mommy!" "You're not the boss of me," or "I want to run away." Instead, they will be happy to work with you, cooperate as a matter of course, and love to please you. When you are least expecting it, your child will hug you, thank you, and tell you what a great mom or dad you are. This is parenting in the sweet spot.

Your children's new capacity for self-control, their respectful demeanor, and their cooperative spirit will shape the course of your family life together now and hold your children in good stead for the rest of their lives. The joys of self-control, respect, and cooperation are the best gifts you can give your children.

While children suffering from IFP will never be able to tell you what is wrong or ask you directly for more effective leadership, they certainly know when you are getting it right. There is no happier child than the one who is freed from the burden of too much power and who is able to rely on the competent authority and leadership of his effective parents.

Our children need us.

You know what to do.

Commit. Be deliberate. Be confident.

Don't stop until you find the sweet spot.

Go forward, together with your children, lovingly, in harmony, and with joy. Not side by side . . . but with you in the lead.

Bibliography

Borba, Michele. *Don't Give Me That Attitude! 24 Rude, Selfish, Insensitive Things Kids Do and How to Stop Them.* San Francisco: Jossey-Bass, Wiley Imprint, 2004.

Brazelton, T. Berry, and Joshua D. Sparrow. *Touchpoints 3 to 6. Your Child's Emotional and Behavioral Development.* Cambridge, MA: Da Capo Press (Perseus Publishing), 2002.

Briggs, Dorthy Corkille. *Your Child's Self-Esteem. Step-by-Step Guidelines for Raising Responsible, Happy Children.* New York: Broadway Books, 2001.

Chandler, Cristine, with Laura McGrath. *4 Weeks to a Better-Behaved Child: Breakthrough Discipline Techniques That Really Work.* New York: McGraw-Hill, 2004.

Cline, Foster, and Jim Fay. *Parenting with Love & Logic: Teaching Children Responsibility.* Colorado Springs: Pinon Press, 1990.

Dobson, James C. *The Strong-Willed Child.* Wheaton, IL: Tyndale House Publishers, Inc., 1978.

Dobson, James C. *The New Dare to Discipline.* Wheaton, IL: Tyndale House Publishers, Inc., 1992.

Faber, Adele, and Elaine Mazlish, *How to Talk So Kids Will Listen & Listen So Kids Will Talk.* New York: Avon Books, 1980.

Faber, Adele, and Elaine Mazlish, with Lisa Nyberg and Rosalyn Anstine Templeton. *How To Talk So Kids Can Learn.* New York: A Fireside Book, Simon & Schuster, Inc., 1995.

Federici, Ronald S. *Help for the Hopeless Child: A Guide for Families.* Alexandria, VA: Federici and Associates, 2003.

Ferber, Richard. *Solve Your Child's Sleep Problems.* New York: A Fireside Book, Simon & Schuster, Inc., 1986.

Fraiberg, Selma H. *The Magic Years: Understanding and Handling the Problems of Early Childhood.* New York: A Fireside Book, Simon & Schuster, Inc., 1996.

Frost, Jo. *Supernanny: How to Get the Best from Your Children.* New York: Hyperion, 2005.

Ginott, Haim G. *Between Parent and Child*, revised and updated by Dr. Alice Ginott and Dr. H. Wallace Goddard. New York: Three Rivers Press, 2003.

Gordon, Thomas. *Parent Effectiveness Training: The Proven Program for Raising Responsible Children*, revised edition. New York: Three Rivers Press, 2000.

Greene, Ross W. *The Explosive Child. A New Approach for Understanding and Parenting Easily Frustrated "Chronically Inflexible" Children*. New York: HarperCollins, 1998.

Hart, Betsy. *It Takes a Parent. How the Culture of Pushover Parenting Is Hurting Our Kids and What to Do about It*. New York: G.P. Putnam's Sons, 2005.

Hendrix, Harville, and Helen LaKelly Hunt. *Giving the Love that Heals: A Guide for Parents*. New York: Atria Books, 1997.

Kelly, Jeffrey A. *Solving Your Child's Behavior Problems: An Everyday Guide for Parents*. New York: Little Brown and Co., 1983.

Kennedy, Rod Wallace. *The Encouraging Parent. How To Stop Yelling at Your Kids and Start Teaching Them Confidence, Self-Discipline and Joy*. New York: Three Rivers Press, 2001.

Hogg, Tracy, and Melinda Blau. *Secrets of the Baby Whisperer. How to Calm, Connect, and Communicate with Your Baby*. New York: Ballantine Books, 2001.

Kohn, Alfie. *Unconditional Parenting: Moving from Rewards and Punishments to Love and Reason*. New York: Atria Books, 2005.

Leach, Penelope. *Your Growing Child: From Babyhood through Adolescence*. New York: Alfred A. Knopf, 2001.

Levy, Ray, Bill O'Hanlon, with Tyler Norris Goode. *Try and Make Me! Simple Strategies That Turn Off the Tantrums and Create Cooperation*. New York: Rodale, 2001.

Maslin, Bonnie. *Picking Your Battles: Winning Strategies for Raising Well-Behaved Kids*. New York: St. Martin's Press, 2004.

McGraw, Phil. *Family First: Your Step-by-Step Plan for Creating a Phenomenal Family*. New York: Free Press, 2004.

Murphy, Tim, and Loriann Hoff Oberlin. *The Angry Child. Regaining Control When Your Child Is Out of Control*. New York: Three Rivers Press, 2001.

Nelsen, Jane. *Positive Discipline*, revised edition. New York: Ballantine Books, 1996.

Nelsen, Jane H. *Positive Time-Out: And Over 50 Ways to Avoid Power Struggles in the Home and the Classroom*. New York: Three Rivers Press, 1999.

Novick, Kerry Kelly, and Jack Novick. *Working with Parents Makes Therapy Work*. Lanham, MD: Jason Aronson, 2005.

Peairs, Lillian and Richard H. Peairs. *What Every Child Needs.* New York: Harper and Row Publishers, 1974.

Phelan, Thomas W. *1-2-3 Magic: Effective Discipline for Children 2-12. Third Edition.* Glen Ellyn, IL: Parentmagic, Inc., 2003.

Riley, Douglas A. *The Defiant Child: A Parent's Guide to Oppositional Defiant Disorder.* Dallas: Taylor Publishing Company, 1997.

Rosemond, John. *New Parent Power.* Kansas City: Andrews McMeel Publishing, 2001.

Samalin, Nancy, with Catherine Whitney. *Loving Without Spoiling and 100 Other Timeless Tips for Raising Terrific Kids.* New York: Contemporary Books, 2003.

Sears, William, and Martha Sears. *The Discipline Book. How to Have a Better Behaved Child from Birth to Age Ten.* New York: Little Brown and Company, 1995.

Seligman, Martin E. P., with Karen Reivich, Lisa Jaycox, and Jane Gillham. *The Optimistic Child: A Proven Program to Safeguard Children against Depression and Build Lifelong Resilience.* New York: Harper Perennial of HarperCollins, 1996.

Siegel, Daniel, and Mary Hartzell. *Parenting from the Inside Out: How a Deeper Self-Understanding Can Help You Raise Children Who Thrive.* New York: Jeremy P. Tarcher/Penguin, 2004.

Spock, Benjamin. *Dr. Spock's Baby and Child Care, 8th Edition*, updated and revised by Robert Needleman. New York: Pocket Books, 2004.

Turecki, Stanley, with Leslie Tonner. *The Difficult Child.* New York: Pocket Books, 1994.

Warner, Judith. *Perfect Madness: Motherhood in the Age of Anxiety.* New York: Riverhead Books, 2005.

White, Burton L. *The New First Three Years of Life,* revised. New York: A Fireside Book, Simon & Schuster, 1995.

Ziegler, Dave. *Achieving Success with Impossible Children. How to Win the Battle of Wills.* Phoenix, AZ: Acacia Publishing Co., 2005.

Ziegler, Dave. *Raising Children Who Refuse to Be Raised: Parenting Skills and Therapy Interventions for the Most Difficult Children.* Phoenix, AZ: Acacia Publishing, Inc., 2000.

Acknowledgments

It is time for the thank-you's—which means the book is actually done! The process of writing a book is one you can never really understand or appreciate until you have experienced it. At times it is deeply gratifying and energizing; at other times it is challenging and completely draining. The fact that we have gotten through it and have a final result we are pleased with and proud of is in large measure a reflection of the many wonderful, talented, and encouraging people we have had in our corner along the way. We thank you all, from our hearts. In this limited format, however, we can only give specific tribute to the core group that brought us to the finish line.

First—and they are indeed first—is the formidable team of women we were so fortunate to have assembled, who served as the primary architects, brokers, shapers, and sellers of this work. Michelle McKenna was the first professional to have a hand in the project. She was brave to sign on in the early stages when our ideas and writing were raw and rambling. She quite literally gave the book structure and a strong spine, and we remain very grateful to her for both. Jennifer Richards, from Over The River Public Relations Firm, has been from the beginning a constant wellspring of advice, referrals, and enthusiasm. She, in fact, guided us to the two most important people any book can have—our literary agent and our proposal editor.

To Joelle Delbourgo, our agent, we extend our deepest respect and gratitude. Joelle is a force—talented, tenacious, and confident. She believed in us and in the ideas in this book, and when times were tough, she proved tougher. Thank you, Joelle, for your confidence, your advocacy, and your friendship.

How many hours went into this book, I would shudder to count. But there was one person who really lightened the burden and liberated me from the constraints of trying to make every idea come out just right—our editor from BookCrafters, Elizabeth Zack. She was reliably enthusiastic, prompt, and spot-on in all the work she did for us. We extend a huge thank-you to Elizabeth, and we look forward to working with her on projects yet to come. The manuscript was also improved upon by the concentrated efforts of Elaine Goldberg, who signed onto the project for a brief stint just before we sold the book and extended us the benefits of her experienced and skilled red pen.

Joelle Delbourgo sold our manuscript to Sterling Publishing in December 2006. It was this deal that brought the last woman to our powerhouse team, book editor Jennifer Williams. We know how lucky we are to have met with such a sharp, skilled, and gracious person. Jennifer took our work and, rather miraculously, kept it the same yet made it infinitely better. She is a true craftsman, and we admire her skill. Thank you, Jennifer.

I would like to thank the many, many colleagues who helped hone the ideas of this book. In the past ten years in particular, the work and teachings of Dr. Habib Davanloo, who pioneered the theory and practice of Intensive Short-Term Dynamic Psychotherapy, have centrally informed my work and practice.

As the manuscript went through successive drafts, we have been the fortunate beneficiaries of insightful and constructive input of several colleagues who were willing to read portions of the work. Both critical and supportive, their comments made this a better book. Specific thanks to Marilyn Ritholz, Thomas Linscheid, Jack Lagos, Ruth McKnight, Ginny Cusack, Marsha Stencel, and Dave Ziegler. I also want to thank Christopher Barbrack for the always incisive and clear counsel he offers whenever I need it.

Now to our friends and family—a large, wonderful, and entertaining bunch, a powerhouse group in and of themselves. We are so fortunate to share our love and our lives with so many smart, interesting, giving people. All of you— parents, spouses, children, brothers and sisters, friends—have given of yourselves in important and meaningful ways as we toiled on this project. You are part of the pages of this book, just as you are part of our hearts.

I want to extend a special tribute to my loving and steadfast husband, Tim Byrne. He is quite simply the best, in every way. He supported me, encouraged me, and challenged me at all the right times through this process. He is the best sounding-board and has an uncanny knack for knowing what I am really trying to say and then saying it better. For you there are no adequate thanks.

To my children, Matthew and Anna—well, you guys take my breath away. You're both incredible, and I have so enjoyed and appreciated your enthusiasm for this project. You really get this stuff, and on numerous occasions helped sharpen descriptions of scenarios that transpire between parents and children. Way more computer savvy than I will ever be, you were patient (most of the time) with my questions and pleas for help when I got stuck in word processing. Also, thanks for your good humor over all the missed Sunday dinners as Jan and I plowed through the manuscript. I am grateful for your many contributions to this venture, but most of all, I am grateful every day that you are mine.

Jan's family members have left their imprint on this book as well. One of the most fortuitous and indispensable contributions made to our project was that of

Jan's husband, John Burton. A small-scale publisher himself, we had access to his experience, know-how, and computer/printer equipment—the likes of which fledgling and naive authors can usually only dream of. We most certainly could not have written this book without his help and that of his assistant, Florence Blum, whom we adopted as our own. Everything we didn't know how to do, they did. In the technical department, there is one more person who requires a special thank-you. Rebecca Burton was our personal helpline for computer problems large and small. She is a terrific troubleshooter, teacher, and problem solver, and she has our heartfelt gratitude. Mr. Scott Burton—you also loom large in the final product of this book. You offered your razor-sharp editing prowess at a most critical juncture and literally elevated the project to a whole new level. You're amazing, and we thank you. And I am indebted to Johnny Burton for leading the recovery efforts when fate landed your mother in the hospital in the middle of chapter five!

With sadness, I remember and honor my father, who died on August 24, 2007, just as this book was entering the final editing phase. He was among my biggest fans, and in large measure I owe to his example my interest in people and my intellectual curiosity. From my heart, Dad, this book is for you. Also to my mother, a living example of maternal devotion, who gave each of her children the opportunities and confidence to find their voice and follow their ambitions. This book, Mom, is also for you.

I also want to thank the many, many families with whom I have worked over the years. The parents, children, and I have quite literally been a team in this work, and the ideas and strategies have all been road-tested by them. In fact, it is primarily their enthusiasm and testimony to how valuable it is to go beyond time-out that compelled me to write this book. You are all in these pages, and in my heart as well.

Finally, this book is a product of collaboration in the best sense of the word. While the book is written in my voice—the voice of the child clinician—the engine behind this book is really a "we." Jan and I have enjoyed the rare gift of a collegiality and friendship these past fifteen years that has enriched both our personal and professional lives and selves. Jan started out as my clinical supervisor and has remained so ever since. With over thirty-five years of experience, she is a gifted, insightful, and ever-curious clinician. We shared a private practice for about ten years, during which time the ideas and techniques in this book were incubating. An unlikely pairing, as many years separate us, but there has always been a connection, a synergy, a momentum, and a clarity that is generated by our conversations and work together. *Beyond Time-Out* is a proud testament to this amazing friendship.

Index